Warman's
Carnival Glass
Identification and Price Guide

Ellen T. Schroy

©2004 KP Books

Published by

kp books
An imprint of F+W Publications, Inc.

700 East State Street • Iola, WI 54990-0001
715-445-2214 • 888-457-2873

Our toll-free number to place an order or obtain
a free catalog is (800) 258-0929.

Library of Congress Catalog Number: 2004093863
ISBN: 0-87349-816-X

Designed by Kay Sanders
Edited by Kris Manty

Cover photo: Northwood's Grape and Cable midsize punch bowl and base, amethyst/purple,
$1,000-$2,000. The punch bowl rests on the base. Together they count as two pieces when part of a
set including cups. (Courtesy George and Dorothy Pientka)

Printed in the United States of America

Acknowledgments

Writing this new addition to the *Warman's* line of price guides has been an enjoyable education in yet another area of American glassware production. By reading the old texts and the new texts, a feel for the hard work of the pioneers became very apparent. I remembered personal conversations years ago with Marion Hartung, a pioneer in the glass-researching field, who was eager to impart her wisdom about this beautiful glassware. She stressed how important it was that we consider these pieces as parts of sets, not just water pitchers or tumblers, but water sets. She impressed me with how important knowing the base color is to carnival glass. I am fortunate to have known this great lady as well as those who are currently carrying the research forward today.

We appreciate the efforts of auctioneers who regularly catalog and sell the iridescent rainbow of carnival glass all cross the country. They eagerly shared catalogs and photographs with me. A special thank you goes to longtime carnival glass experts Tom and Sharon Mordini, Freeport, IL, for their invaluable pricing assistance, and to Kris Remmen of Remmen Auction & Appraisal Service, Portland, OR, for his pricing help and photographs.

Several private collectors also shared their love of carnival glass by lending treasured pieces as well as photographs. Jackie and Randy Poucher, who live in the Tampa Bay area in Florida, graciously invited us into their home, allowing us to photograph one of the finest carnival glass collections in the world. Also deserving of our appreciation are Dick and Sherry Betker, Franklin, WI, and George and Dorothy Pientka, Stevens Point, WI. Without their help and guidance this project would not have been possible. Other private collectors include Susan K. Bargar, Delaware, OH; Miriam Fischer, New York, NY; Susan Howell, Carrollton, TX; Kasi Kirby, Houston, TX; S. Louis Rouse, Niota, TN; Jennifer Smith, Baltimore, OH; Kathryn Smith, San Bernardino, CA; Lynn Tice, Pickens, SC; and Cheryl Webber, Tacoma, WA. A special thank you to photographer Paul Goodwin for his excellent work. To all of the collectors and auctioneers who helped us, we say thanks. You are as wonderful as the glass you treasure.

Strawberry Scroll, Fenton, water pitcher and six tumblers, marigold, $2,500.

Contents

Introduction

Warman's Carnival Glass Price Guide is a price guide devoted to the magical glass that collectors fondly call mass-produced iridescent glassware.

Carnival glass has an interesting history and to many collectors, the majesty of these techniques continue today, allowing them to add more and more examples to their collecting hobby. During the early production years of carnival glass, production was world wide, just as it is today.

For the purposes of information gathering, we've chosen to concentrate on the original major American manufacturers for the first edition of *Warman's Carnival Glass Price Guide.*

The term "carnival glass" has evolved through the years as glass collectors have responded to the idea that much of this beautiful glassware was made as give-away glass at local carnivals and fairs. However, more of it was made and sold through the same channels as pattern glass and Depression glass. Some patterns were indeed giveaways, and others were used as advertising premiums, souvenirs, etc. Whatever the origin, the term "carnival glass" today encompasses glassware that is usually pattern molded and treated with metallic salts, creating that unique coloration that is so desirable to collectors.

Early names for iridescent glassware, which early 20th Century consumers believed to have all come from foreign manufacturers, include Pompeian Iridescent, Venetian Art, and Mexican Aurora. Another popular early name was "Nancy Glass" as some patterns were believed to have come from the Daum, Nancy glassmaking area in France. This was at a time when the artistic cameo glass was enjoying great success.

While the iridescent glassware being made by such European glassmakers as Loetz influenced the American market place, it was Louis Tiffany's Favrile glass that really caught the eye of glass consumers of the early 1900s.

It seems an easy leap to transform Tiffany's shimmering glassware to something that could be mass produced, allowing what we call carnival glass today to become "poor man's Tiffany." However, this seemingly easy leap really took years of experimentation by several of the major glasshouses to develop techniques and formulas that gave the desired results.

To better understand carnival glass, it's necessary to understand some of the basic elements of glass making. Up until the time Deming Jarvis invented and patented glass-making equipment, most glassware was made by blowing hot molten glass into molds or fashioning a piece entirely by hand.

Glassware of this period tended to be very expensive and until Jarvis and his associates got the fledging industry running in New England, most glassware was imported to America. However, the industrial advances made using natural materials found in America soon changed that. Quantities of natural materials such as silica, salts, wood, and gas led to the development of glass manufacturers in New England, and after transportation improvements led Americans West, soon another area of glass manufacturing sprang up in the western Pennsylvania region, as well as the Ohio River region.

By using and improving on the techniques developed by Jarvis, molten glass could be taken and put into molds that were pressed into shapes and designs. These designs evolved to reflect the themes that were popular at the time, such as florals, patterns that reflected nature, and fanciful designs.

Most of the early glassware production created clear glassware, but some colors were introduced by combining various chemicals into the molten glass. This pressed glass was commonly called "pattern glass" as it became the norm for American consumers to use in their households and commercial enterprises.

Carnival glass is iridized glassware that is created by pressing hot molten glass into molds, just as pattern glass had evolved. Some forms are hand finished, while others are completely formed by molds. After the glassware was made, an iridized coating is added to give the luminescent look we associate with carnival glass today. It was the glass gatherer's skill that allowed him to carefully fill a mold with just the right amount of molten glass. He quickly cut it off with shears, allowing it to gently drop into the mold. A plunger was then usually pressed into the mold and the resulting pressure squeezed the molten mixture to fill the entire mold. After the pressing process was completed, a tool called a "snap" was attached to the collar base, known as the "marie." Any necessary hand finishing would take place at this point. If necessary, the piece was re-heated gently so that the metallic coatings would adhere properly.

Molds used to make carnival glass are very similar to those used to make pattern glass and later Depression glass. Some molds were hinged in two to four places to allow for easy removal of the piece. Many patterns had a limited number of molds, such as a bowl and tumbler.

During the production process, a bowl could become a plate, a tumbler could become a hat, and a bonbon could become a calling card tray, by simple maneuvers of the molds and hand-finishing techniques. Making molds for the glass industry was often the responsibility of the designers at individual glass houses, but also to specialty companies, such as the Hipkins Novelty Mould Shop in Martin's Ferry, Ohio. Because making molds was so expensive, it should be no surprise that early glassware manufacturers got as much use out of these molds as they could.

Early pattern glass molds were wood and some carnival glass pattern wooden molds are known to exist, but by the time carnival glassware production got into high gear, the molds were constructed of durable metals, such as iron. Because these molds were longer lasting, greater quantities of any particular pattern could be produced. And, if and when a glasshouse failed, the molds could be sold as a valuable asset to another glassmaker. This explains how some patterns traveled from maker to maker. Imperial Glass bought Heisey Glass molds after it closed in 1958.

In 1960, Imperial added molds from Cambridge Glass to its inventory. Often the second- or third-generation owner would use the molds to create new colors just as glassmakers are doing today with old molds.

To achieve the marvelous iridescent colors that carnival glass collectors seek, a process was developed where a liquid solution of metallic salts was put onto the still hot glass form after it was unmolded. As the liquid evaporated, a fine metallic surface was left which refracts light into wonderful colors. The name given to the iridescent spray by early glassmakers was "dope." Mixing the chemicals for this metallic mixture usually took place in a separate building at the glass factory, referred to as a "dope house."

After the glass was doped, it was sent to annealing lehrs to cool. After the glassware cooled, it was inspected for defects and then often packed in large shipping barrels, filled with straw, and then transported to eager consumers.

Many of the forms created by carnival glass manufacturers were accessories to the china American housewives so loved. Sets to serve berries, numerous types of bowls, water sets, as well as groupings known as table sets, which included covered butter dishes, creamers, covered sugars, and spooners, were sold with the idea that they would make accent pieces on sideboards and dining room tables.

Some pieces were more decorative in nature and meant to help display one's wealth by having it as a centerpiece. By the early 1900s, consumers could find carnival glassware at such popular stores including F. W. Woolworth or McCrory's. To capitalize on the popular fancy for these colored wares, some other industries bought large quantities of carnival glass and turned them into "packers." This term reflects the practice where baking powder, mustard, or other household products were packed into a special piece of glass that could take on another life after the original product was used.

Lee Manufacturing Co. used iridized carnival glass as premiums for its baking powder and other products, causing some early carnival glass to be known by the generic term "baking powder glass."

Every glasshouse had its own special metallic salts recipe. By experimentation, they discovered that metallic salts applied to very hot glassware turned in a matte or satin-like finish, known as *satin*. Applying the iridescent materials to slightly cooler glassware created bright shiny surfaces. These shiny finishes are referred to as *radium* when they have a mirror-like quality. Shades of blue and purple that seem to have an electric quality to their iridescent finish are known as *electric*. Because the pieces were shaped before being iridized, minute breaks in the iridescent surface can occur.

Some manufacturers took this into account when creating interesting designs. Patterns created with three-dimensional characteristics, such as Heavy Grape, took advantage of the fact that the iridized covering would be more colorful on the background than on the plump grapes, making them stand out by contrast. Pieces could be sprayed on both the inside and outsides, while forms such as creamers, pitchers, and tumblers were sprayed only on the outside. Because the "snap" was adhered over the marie, this area is left unsprayed. By observing the color of the marie, collectors know what color the base glass was.

When the glass form was re-heated, some design aspects, often edges, whitened, creating an opalescent quality and colors such as aqua opalescent or peach opalescent. If a piece received a further acid treatment, an icy or frosted effect was created, resulting in some of the pastels, such as ice blue, ice green, and white. Whenever the glassware was reheated, the chances of damage increased, causing the manufacturer to endure more cost in the way of time for the artisan and also in the length of time it took from the first gather of glass to the end product.

Just as it is today, "time is money" so pieces created in pastels or opalescent colors were more scarce, their production was limited, and usually their values are higher than ordinary carnival colors.

Today's manufacturing methods are different in that pieces can be sprayed on both sides, eliminating the un-sprayed marie. This can be used as a clue in determining the age of some carnival glass patterns, as well as observing the colors, finding an embossed trademark, etc. Today carnival glass is being made by the great American glasshouse, Fenton Glass. Visitors to the Fenton facilities in Williamstown, WV, can watch as actual pieces of glassware are created right in front of their eyes. Companies in India, Europe, and Egypt are creating other contemporary carnival glass pieces at the present time.

How well these pieces will be embraced by the glass collectors remains to be seen. Classic carnival glass production began in the early 1900s and continued about twenty years, but no one really documented or researched production until the first collecting wave struck in 1960. Today's collectors are much better informed, allowing them to carefully track the new carnival glassware patterns, makers, etc.

Glass researcher Marion T. Hartung was a pioneer in the glass-researching field when she started her project of documenting the myriad carnival glass patterns. By 1967, she had published several books on the topic. Her first series of seven books, published in 1960, included line drawings of the patterns, along with descriptive notes on the patterns and makers.

The hobby of collecting antiques in Hartung's day was vastly different than it is today; many of the glasshouses had been destroyed by fires or through bad economics. Since she didn't have the marvelous reference books collectors treasure today, she created them. She researched with original materials and examined as many pieces of iridescent glass as she could, and was responsible for naming many of the patterns that only had factory numbers or codes.

Her book, *Carnival Glass In Color, A Collector's Reference Book,* was the first to include color photographs of this beautiful iridized glassware. In this book, Hartung carefully discusses the times and fashions that influenced Americans in the early 1900s, noting that fashions were changing rapidly from 1900-1920, the prime time for carnival-glass production. When collectors think about how the styles of carnival glass patterns range from simple to complex geometrics to detailed naturalistic patterns, they can see how the changes in fashion influenced glass designs. Other advancements that took place during this time period also affected life, allowing more consumers to participate in the free marketplace and seek out their favorite styles and colors.

It is important to remember that carnival glasswares were sold in department stores as well as mass merchants, such as F. W. Woolworth, rather than through the general store often associated with a young America. Glassware by this time was mass-produced and sold in large quantities by such enterprising companies as Butler Brothers. When the economics of the country soured in the 1920s, those interested in purchasing iridized glassware were not spared.

Many of the leftover inventories of glasshouses that hoped to sell this mass-produced glassware found their way to wholesalers who in turn sold the wares to those who offered the glittering glass as prizes at carnivals, fairs, circuses, etc. Possibly because this was the last venue people associated the iridized glassware with, it became known as "carnival glass," rather than the exotic names such as Parisian Art, Vineland, Regal, Art Iridescent, Etruscan, or Aurora that the original salesmen of iridized glass probably preferred.

Carnival glass collecting as a hobby is one of the largest areas of the current antique glass marketplace. Part of the reason why is the excellent references today's collectors have in books such as Hartung's, as well as later researchers such as Rose Presznick, David Doty, Carl O. Burns, Bill Edwards, Mike Carwvile, Glen and Steve Thistlewood, and others. Add to this the idea that carnival glass collectors love to gather and swap information through club networks, newsletters, and meetings. These gatherings, whether in a small local group or a large convention, allow for the free exchange of information, as well as educational venues and associated auctions. Organizations such as the American Carnival Glass Association and the International Carnival Glass Association are the largest. Active associations can be found all across America and Canada. The United Kingdom has its own version known as the Carnival Glass Society, Ltd., and collectors Down Under can meet at the Australian Carnival Enthusiasts Association, Inc.

Carnival glass collecting has also gotten a real boost in the formation of two on-line Web sites devoted to carnival glass. Known as www. cga, this for-fee Web site offers collectors a daily Web-ring, opportunities for on-line chats, plus links to carnival glass related sites, auctions, and educational articles. The on-line world of contemporary carnival glass is represented by Contemporary Carnival Glass Web site, www. carnivalglass.net. Another excellent on-line resource is the Web site of David Doty, www.ddoty. com. Doty includes identification, values, and information about reproductions in this easy-to-use site. (Please see P. 256 for more information about collectors' clubs and Web sites.)

Collectors of carnival glass will not be surprised to see price ranges in this book. However, price ranges do offer a departure from the typical *Warman's* format. Why? Because the colors of the iridescent finish on a piece of carnival glass can vary from piece to piece and as such, so does the desirability of each piece change. Some carnival glass collectors seek a particular pattern; others specialize in patterns from one particular manufacturer. Other collectors look for particular colors, while others may choose only to collect a specific form. Add to this that the brilliant colors used for the basis of carnival glass can vary from what each set of eyes perceive and one can see how many variables come into play when evaluating the desirability of any given piece. Sometimes the ranges are vast, representing patterns or forms that offer many differences; other times the ranges are closer, usually reflecting forms that are sold more readily, so more data could be analyzed and numbers calculated. Where only a few pieces are available for the database or prices seem extraordinary high, the term "rare" is used along with a dollar figure. Collectors should assume that lesser priced items might exist for any of the prices listed herein, but also that higher prices may have been averaged into the range formulas. Collectors should always pay what their heart tells them is a fair price, using any price guide as a *guide* and not an absolute.

You will, however, also notice we have a single price for a piece. This single value represents a price realized in auction for that piece, or the price that piece garnered in a private transaction. At all times, we have taken great care in seeking out the finest pricing sources.

While appearing on the Good Neighbor Show with Kathy Keene and Mike Diamond, WHBY Radio, Appleton, WI, Dec. 1, 2003, a dear lady called in to inquire about the value of her Stag and Holly bowl. She told me it was orange and all kinds of pretty colors, and had little feet. She said she frequently looks for this pattern while browsing through antique shops, but rarely finds it. The best part of chatting with her was that she remembered her mother telling her that her father had spent 75 cents for that bowl and she remembers being quite put out at him at the time, telling him, "You could have bought a whole dress length's worth of cloth with that same 75 cents." We agreed a dress would probably have been long gone, but the bowl is still here to delight her.

It is stories that like that which make carnival glass collecting the wonderful hobby that it is today.

Company Histories

Much of vintage American carnival glassware was created in the Ohio valley, in the glasshouse-rich areas of Pennsylvania, Ohio, and West Virginia.

The abundance of natural materials, good transportation, and skilled craftsmen that created the early American pattern glass manufacturing companies allowed many of them to add carnival glass to their production lines. Brief company histories of the major carnival glass manufacturers follow:

Cambridge Glass Company (Cambridge)

Cambridge Glass was a rather minor player in the carnival glass marketplace. Founded in 1901 as a new factory in Cambridge, Ohio, it focused on producing fine crystal tablewares. What carnival glass it did produce was imitation cut-glass patterns.

Colors used by Cambridge include marigold, as well as few others.

Forms found in carnival glass by Cambridge include tablewares and vases, some with its trademark "Near-Cut."

Fenton Persian Medallion blue bowl, candy-ribbon edge, **$85**.

Fenton Art Glass Company (Fenton)

Frank Leslie Fenton and his brothers, John W. Fenton and Charles H. Fenton, founded this truly American glassmaker, in 1905 in Martins Ferry. Frank grew up around glasshouses, and started working at a glasshouse in Indiana, PA, upon graduating from high school. Within a year, he was foreman at this factory.

Three years later, he moved to Jefferson Glass, Steubenville, Ohio, and later to Bastow Glass, Couldersport, PA. After Bastow Glass burned down, he went to work with Harry Northwood,

Wheeling, WV. By 1905, he decided his future would be better if he and his brothers went into the glass business for himself. Early production was of blanks, which the brothers soon learned to decorate themselves. They moved to a larger factory in Williamstown, WV. Today the Fenton family still makes quality glassware in Williamstown.

By 1907, Fenton was experimenting with iridescent glass, developing patterns and the metallic salt formulas that it became so famous for. Production of carnival glass continued at Fenton until the early 1930s. In 1970, Fenton began to re-issue carnival glass, creating new colors and forms as well as using traditional patterns.

Colors developed by Fenton are numerous. The company developed red and Celeste blue in the 1920s. A translucent pale blue, known as Persian blue, is also one of its more distinctive colors, as is a light yellow-green color known as vaseline. Fenton also produced delicate opalescent colors, including amethyst opalescent and red opalescent. Because the Fenton brothers learned how to decorate their own blanks, they also promoted the addition of enamel decoration to some of their carnival glass patterns.

Forms made by Fenton are numerous. What distinguishes Fenton from other glassmakers is its attention to detail and hand finishing processes. Edges are found scalloped, fluted, tightly crimped, frilled, or pinched into a candy ribbon edge, also referred to as 3-in-1 edge.

Northwood ice blue Grape and Cable dresser tray, **$655**.

Northwood Glass Company (Northwood)

Englishman Harry Northwood founded the Northwood Glass Company. Like Frank L. Fenton, he, too, was from a glass-making family. His family was well known for making beautiful cameo glass in the Stourbridge area. Also located in that area was the glass-making facility of Thomas

Webb, who created "Bronze" and Iris" glass, both iridescent lines. By the time he immigrated to America in 1881, he was influenced by these glassmakers. He became a glass etcher for Hobbs Brockunier Glass Company, Wheeling, WV. He moved to La Belle Glass Works, Bridgeport, Ohio, then to Phoenix Glass Co. in Pennsylvania, and back to La Belle. In November of 1887, Northwood and other investors bought the old Union Flint Glass factory in Martin's Ferry, Ohio, and renamed it "Northwood Glass Company." By 1892, the factory was moved to Ellwood City, PA, but it didn't thrive at this location. In 1895, Northwood created the new Northwood Glass Company of Indiana, PA, by moving into the former factory of Indiana Glass Company. In 1899, this factory was sold to the new glass conglomerate, National Glass Company. Northwood returned to England as its sales representative. He must have missed the American glassmakers as he returned and purchased the old Hobbs Brockunier factory in Wheeling and started the Harry Northwood and Company factory, which continued until 1925. It was at this factory, he developed his glass formulas for carnival glass, naming it "Golden Iris" in 1908. Northwood was one of the pioneers of the glass manufacturers who marked his wares. Marks range from a full script signature to a simple underscored capital N in a circle. However, not all Northwood glassware is marked.

Colors that Northwood created were many. Collectors prefer its pastels, such as ice blue, ice green, and white. It is also known for several stunning blue shades. The one color that Northwood did not develop was red.

Forms of Northwood patterns ranged from typical table sets, bowls, and water sets to whimsical novelties, such as a pattern known as Corn, which realistically depicts an ear of corn.

Millersburg green Zig-Zag ice-cream shaped bowl with radium iridescence, **$125**.

Millersburg Glass Company (Millersburg)

John W. Fenton started the Millersburg Glass Company in September of 1908. Perhaps it was the factory's more obscure location or the lack of business experience by John Fenton, but the company failed by 1911. The factory was bought by Samuel Fair and John Fenton, and renamed the Radium Glass Company, but it lasted only a year.

Colors produced by Millersburg are amethyst, green, and marigold. Shades such as blue and vaseline were added on rare occasions. The company is well known for its bright radium finishes.

Forms produced at Millersburg are mostly bowls and vases. Pattern designers at Millersburg often took one theme and developed several patterns from it. Millersburg often used one pattern for the interior and a different pattern for the exterior.

Dugan white Double Stem Rose dome-footed bowl with 3-in-1 edge and super iridescence, **$60**.

Dugan Glass Company (Dugan)

The history of the Dugan Glass Company is closely related to Harry Northwood. Cousin Thomas Dugan came from the same region in England and grew up around the same glass houses as Harry Northwood. He immigrated to America in 1881. The cousins worked together at Hobbs Brockunier, Wheeling, WV, and also at Northwood Glass Co., Martin's Ferry, Ohio. Thomas Dugan became plant manager at the Northwood Glass Co., in Indiana, PA, in 1895. By 1904, Dugan and his partner W. G. Minnemayer bought the former Northwood factory from the now defunct National Glass conglomerate and opened as the Dugan Glass Company. Dugan brother Alfred joined the company and stayed until the company became the

Diamond Glass Company in 1913. At this time, Thomas Dugan moved to the Cambridge Glass Company, later Duncan and Miller and finally Hocking, Lancaster. Alfred left Diamond Glass, too, but later returned.

Understanding how the Northwood and Dugan families were linked helps collectors to understand the linkage of these three companies. Their productions were similar; molds were swapped, re-tooled, etc.

Colors attributed to Dugan and Diamond include amethyst, marigold, peach opalescent, and white. The company developed deep amethyst shades, some almost black.

Forms made by both Dugan and Diamond mirrored what other glass companies were producing. The significant contribution by Dugan and later Diamond were feet – either ball or spatula shapes. They are also known for deeply crimped edges.

Diamond Glass Company (Diamond)

This company was started as the Dugan brothers departed the carnival glass-making scene in 1913. However, Alfred Dugan returned and became general manager until his death in 1928. After a disastrous fire in June of 1931, the factory closed.

Imperial Ripple vase, 12" with 3-3/8" base, electric purple and electric highlights, **$100.**

Imperial Glass Company (Imperial)

Edward Muhleman and a syndicate founded the Imperial Glass Company at Bellaire, Ohio, in 1901, with production beginning in 1904. It started with pressed glass tableware patterns, as well as lighting fixtures.

The company's marketing strategy included selling to important retailers of its day, such as F. W. Woolworth and McCrory and Kresge, getting glassware into the hands of American housewives. Imperial also became a major exporter of glassware, including its brilliant carnival patterns. During the Depression, it filed for bankruptcy in 1931, but was able to continue on. By 1962, it was again producing carnival glass patterns. By April 1985, the factory was closed and the molds sold.

Colors made by Imperial include typical carnival colors such as marigold. It added interesting shades of green, known as helios, a pale ginger ale shade known as clambroth, and a brownish smoke shade.

Forms created by Imperial tend to be functional, such as berry sets and table sets. Patterns vary from wonderful imitation cut glass patterns to detailed florals and naturalistic designs.

US Glass Palm Beach tri-corner bowl, honey amber, **$125.**

United States Glass Company (US Glass)

In 1891, a consortium of 15 American glass manufacturers joined together as the United States Glass Company. This company was successful in continuing pattern glass production, as well as developing new glass lines. By 1911, it had begun limited production of carnival glass lines, often using existing pattern glass tableware molds. By the time a tornado destroyed the last of its glass factories in Glassport in 1963, it was no longer producing glassware.

Colors associated with US Glass are marigold, white, and a rich honey amber.

Forms tend to be table sets and functional forms.

Westmoreland Corinth teal jack-in-the-pulpit vase, **$50**.

Westmoreland Glass Company
(Westmoreland)

Started as the Westmoreland Speciality Company, Grapeville, PA, in 1889, this company originally made novelties, and glass packing containers, such as candy containers. Researchers have identified its patterns being advertised by Butler Brothers as early as 1908. Carnival glass production continued into the 1920s. In the 1970s, Westmoreland, too, begin to re-issue carnival glass patterns and novelties. However, this ceased in February of 1996 when the factory burned.

Colors originally used by Westmoreland were typical carnival colors, such as blue and marigold.

Forms include tablewares and functional forms, containers, etc.

Time Line:

1889	Westmoreland Specialty Glass Company is founded in Grapeville, PA
1901	Cambridge Glass is founded in Cambridge, OH
1904	Dugan Glass Company forms
1904	Glass production begins at Imperial Glass
1905	Fenton Glass Company founded in Martins Ferry
1907	Documentation exists showing Fenton experimenting with metallic salts to create iridescent colors
1908, Spring	Harry Northwood develops Golden Iris
1908, Sept.	John W. Fenton founds Millersburg Glass Company
1908, Sept.	Butler Brothers first advertise a "Golden Sunset Iridescent Assortment" of glassware. This assortment was made by Fenton and included its Beaded Star, Diamond Point Columns, and Waterlily and Cattails patterns
1910	Butler Brothers advertises Westmoreland patterns such as Scales, Louisa, and Smooth Rays as an "Antique Iridescent Novelty Assortment"
1911	Imperial advertises its Imperial Grape line in Amber Flame, Dragon Blue, Helios, and Azure
1911	Butler Brothers advertise Millersburg patterns such as Rose columns, Peacock at Urn, Dolphin, and Cherries
1911	Millersburg Glass Company files for bankruptcy
1911	Former Millersburg factory buys and renames Radium Glass Company
1911	US Glass starts production of carnival glass
1912	Radium Glass Company goes out of business
1912	Butler Brothers advertises US Glass patterns including Palm Beach and Cosmos & Cane
1913	Dugan Glass Company closes
1913	Diamond Glass Company forms
1915	Imperial advertises patterns such as Lustre Rose, Imperial Grape, Pansy, Double Dutch, Ripple, and Windmill
1915	Diamond advertises patterns such as Stork and Rushes, Vining Twigs, Beaded Basket, Maple Leaf, Persian Garden, Leaf Rays, and Windflower
1920s	Fenton introduces red and celeste blue
1920s, late	Westmoreland discontinues carnival glass production
1925	Harry Northwood and Company goes out of business
1930s	Fenton switches its focus from carnival glass to other glasswares
1931	Diamond Glass Company closes
1950s	Imperial buys out Cambridge Glass
1962	Imperial begins to re-make carnival glass
1963	US Glass closes
1970	Fenton re-issues carnival glass
1970s	Westmoreland re-issues carnival glass
1985	Imperial Glass closes
1996	Westmoreland closes

Colors of Carnival Glass

Think of "color, color, color" just as realtors go about shouting "location, location, location." Color is certainly what carnival glass is all about. There are two types of colors that carnival glass collectors need to know. The first is the base color. To determine the base color of carnival glass, you need to find the marie (non-iridized base). The next step is to hold the piece up to check the color. Having a strong light source is crucial to determining the base color. Knowing the base color will help you determine the value of your carnival glass. While still holding the piece near that strong light source, examine the iridescent coloration to determine the color of that as well as the base color. Knowing the pattern is the third most important element in determining value.

Carnival glass collectors now recognize more than 60 colors of glassware. It is important to remember that every glass manufacturer had its own recipes for batch colors and also secret combinations of the metallic salts that created the iridescent effect. Add to that the thought that every one of us perceives color slightly differently, and you can easily see how variations exist and that no two pieces of carnival glass are the same. Embracing these variations helps collectors to find the treasured pieces of carnival glass and enjoy them for years.

Listed here are brief explanations of the most often seen colors and examples to illustrate them.

Amber and honey amber

Amber is a yellow to brown tinted base glass, which usually shows off multicolored iridescence well. Honey amber is a brownish-marigold iridescence on a clear base. This color is usually restricted to US Glass pieces.

Amber, Ripple, Imperial, vase, 11-1/2" x 3", **$150-$250**.

Amber, Omnibus, US Glass, tumbler, 4-1/4", **$150-$250**.

Amberina

Amberina is a blend of red glass shading to a yellowish color. Putting selenium into the molten batch causes the red coloration. When the mixture is reheated, the colors blend into amberina. To determine amberina, look at the top of the piece for red shading to yellow at the base, or center.

Amberina, Double Scroll, Imperial, candlesticks, pair, **$600**.

Amethyst, Lavender/Purple

The terms amethyst, lavender, and purple were used inter-changeably for many years of carnival glass collecting. Today, collectors prefer to identify pieces as amethyst when the base color of a piece is a medium to light shade of purple; lavender pieces as the lightest shade of purple; and purple when they resemble deep purple grape juice.

Amethyst, Hobnail, Millersburg, tumbler, one rough hob, **$600**.

Amethyst, Holly, Fenton, flat plate, 9-1/2", **$700-$1,000**.

Lavender, Grape and Cable, Northwood, tumbler, 4",
$100-$150.

Aqua and aqua opalescent

Aqua carnival glass is a pretty shade of light blue with a hint of green. Some collectors call pieces "teal" when the blue is more predominate. Aqua opalescent is very popular with carnival glass collectors as it combines the vibrancy of aqua with the allure of milky white opalescence and marigold carnival iridescence. Northwood perfected the color and created most of the known aqua opalescent pieces. Butterscotch refers to the color created when marigold iridescence is found on an aqua opalescent base.

Purple, Greek Key, Northwood, tumbler, 4-1/4", **$125-$200**.

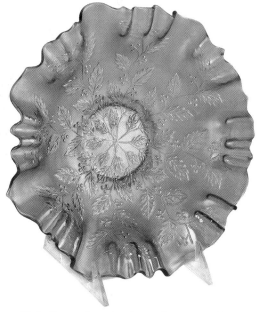

Aqua, Holly, Fenton, 3-in-1 bowl, 8-1/2", **$200-$350 (rare)**.

Purple, Heavy Grape, Imperial, chop plate, 11", **$400-$800**.

Aqua opalescent, Dandelion, Northwood, mug, 3-1/2",
$450-$600.

Aqua opalescent, Dragon and Lotus, Fenton, bowl, 9", **$2,200**.

Black amethyst

Black amethyst is such a dense color that it appears almost opaque. It is the name used to describe a very deep amethyst.

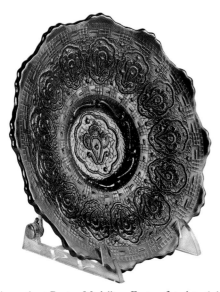

Black amethyst, Persian Medallion, Fenton, flat plate, 6-1/4", **$250-$400**.

Blues: blue, celeste, ice, Persian, powder, Renninger and sapphire

Generally when blue is used to describe the base color of a piece, it is cobalt blue, but there are many colors and variations, from pale blue to aqua and violet. Celeste blue is created when pastel iridescence is used over a blue base. Ice blue is a base color that is a very pale blue; Northwood introduced its ice blue in 1912. Persian blue is a light blue base with a pastel iridescent finish. Most pieces in this color exhibit a cloudy appearance. Powder blue is a medium blue opaque, often called slag glass by collectors. Renninger blue is created when a dark marigold iridescence is used over a dark blue to purple base, with some turquoise influence. The name Renninger blue was coined after so many examples of this shade of blue were found at Renninger's Flea Markets. Sapphire blue is created when marigold iridescence is used over a blue base.

Blue, Good Luck, Northwood, eight-ruffled bowl, 8-1/2", **$300-$550**.

Celeste blue, Lustre Rose, Imperial, tumbler, **$200**.

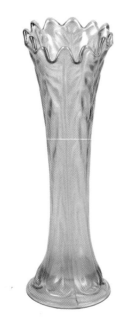

Ice blue, Leaf Columns, Northwood, vase, **$450.**

Powder blue opal, Peacocks on the Fence, Northwood, bowl, ruffle, **$7,000.**

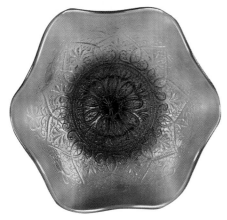

Renninger blue, Hearts and Flowers, Northwood, compote, 6", **$1,500-$2,000 (rare)**.

Sapphire, Leaf Columns, Northwood, squatty vase, 7", **$850-$1,000 (rare)**.

Clambroth

Clambroth is a color that is determined by the iridescence. The coloration is a light marigold over a slightly tinted base. Some collectors call pieces with a weak iridescence on a clear base clambroth. Imperial was responsible for most of the lightly tinted bases associated with this color. One of its most popular colors is known as "Ginger Ale" because of the close similarity to beverage color.

Greens: Green, emerald green, helios, ice green, lime green, lime green opalescent, olive green and russet green

As with many carnival colors, every manufacturer's recipe for green was slightly different. Fenton's green tends to be intense, while Millersburg is lighter. Emerald green carnival glass is a deep rich green; Both Imperial and Northwood made emerald green. Helios is Imperial's original name for its interesting shade of green that is found with a pale golden iridescence. Ice green is a pale green base color covered with a frosty-looking pastel iridescence; Northwood introduced its ice green in 1912. Lime green is a bright almost neon green; it can be found with marigold iridescence. Lime green opalescent is a lime green base with pastel iridescence. Olive green is a deep brownish green, usually found with a marigold iridescent finish. Russet green is an olive- to brown-toned green.

Ice green, Oriental Poppy, Northwood, water pitcher and one tumbler, **$6,800**.

Green, Peacocks, Northwood, bowl, pie-crust edge, 8-1/2", **$900-$1,400**.

Emerald green, Imperial Grape, Imperial, carafe, 9", **$2,000-$3,000**; outstanding condition, **$4,300 (rare)**.

Lime green, Ripple, Imperial, vase, 12" h x 2-1/2" b, **$150-$300 (rare)**.

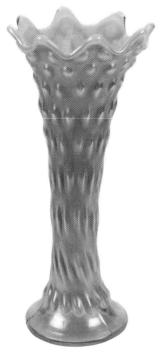

Lime green opalescent, Rustic, Fenton, vase, 9-1/4", **$1,250**.

Marigold, Corn, Northwood, vase, 6-1/2", plain base, **$900-$1,500 (scarce)**.

Horehound

Horehound is a smoky gray base color, usually with blue or green highlights. It can also be a brownish tone.

Marigold, marigold over milk glass, pastel marigold, and pumpkin marigold

The most predominate color in carnival glass is marigold. It is the only color that takes its coloration from the iridescent treatment because it is usually on a clear glass body. It is often a vibrant orange-toned hue reminiscent of marigold flowers that bloom in the garden. Marigold over milk glass is a combination that blends a bright marigold iridescence with a slightly translucent white milk glass base. Sometimes this is also called Moonstone.

Pastel marigold is marigold iridescence over a clear glass body, but the iridescent finish is reheated into a satin finish, creating a soft color, often more of a yellow tone than the brighter orange associated with marigold. Pumpkin marigold is a name commonly used by collectors to describe a deep dark marigold shade, more reminiscent of pumpkins rather than marigold blossoms.

Marigold, Diamond and Rib, Fenton, funeral vase, 21-1/2" plunger base, **$1,100**.

Marigold over milk glass, Holly, Fenton, bowl, 3-in-1, **$2,000**.

Peach opalescent

Peach opalescent is a color that varies with each piece as the opalescence was created by reheating. Bone ash is added to the glass to create this milky white effect as the piece cooled. Dugan perfected the process and made the greatest quantity of this color. In addition to the milky white opalescent areas, the pieces will usually have a marigold iridescence.

Peach opalescent, Fisherman's, Dugan, mug, 4", **$1,000-$1,200 (rare)**.

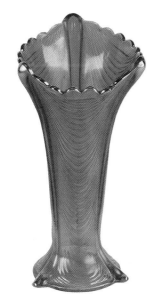

Pastel marigold, Rose Show, Northwood, plate, 9", **$1,200-$1,800**.

Pumpkin marigold, Drapery, Northwood, vase, 8", **$100-$200**.

Peach opalescent, Heavy Iris, Dugan, pitcher, tankard, **$2,000**.

Red

Red is one of the most sought after carnival base colors. The red coloration is caused by putting selenium into the molten batch. Fenton and Imperial both created strong reds.

Red, Holly, Fenton, bowl, 9", ruffled, **$1,200**.

Red, Lustre Rose, Imperial, bowl, footed, large, **$2,500**.

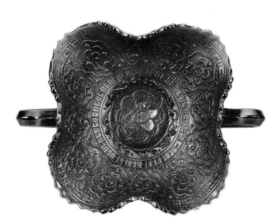

Red, Persian Medallion, Fenton, bon bon, two handles, **$700**.

Reverse amberina

Reverse amberina occurs when a piece shades from a red base to a yellow rim. The red coloration is caused by putting selenium into the molten batch. When the mixture is reheated, the colors blend into amberina.

Smoke

Smoke is a light gray base with iridescence that usually includes an iridescent cast of colors such as blue, green, amber, or brown. Both Imperial and Northwood made smoke-colored pieces.

Smoke, Poinsettia, Imperial, milk pitcher, 6", **$200-$300**.

Smoke, Fashion, Imperial, tumbler, **$150**.

Vaseline

The base color for vaseline is a light green-yellow. Because of uranium oxide added to create this color, it will glow if subjected to black light.

White, Drapery, Northwood, tumbler, **$3,100**.

Vaseline, Morning Glory, Imperial, miniature vase, 5", **$600-$800 (very rare)**.

White

White is another color that is found on a clear base. The coloration is derived from a pastel iridescent finish. Dugan, Fenton, Millersburg, and Northwood all made white forms, each one differing slightly in hue. Northwood introduced its icy white in 1912

White, Heavy Iris, Dugan, tumbler, 4" h, **$200-$300**.

Wisteria

Wisteria is a delicate light amethyst base color.

Glossary

Annealing lehr: the common name given to an annealing oven, where finished glass was placed to gradually cool down.

Ashtrays: ashtrays are rare in carnival glass.

Banana bowl, banana boat: this interesting shape is found usually on either a flat or collared base and is used to describe an oval bowl, usually with two opposing sides turned upward.

Banana shape compote, Folding Fan, 7", peach opal, **$150-$250**.

Basket: This term refers to a small bowl, usually with a handle or up-turned edge. The form could be used for candy, nuts, flowers, or as a decorative piece.

Basketweave: a design often found on the exterior of carnival glass patterns. The design consists of several rows of weaving, resembling a wicker basket.

Batch: the name given to the mixture of raw materials that are blended in a tank to make glass. The basic mixture consists of silica (sand), soda, lime, and sometimes cullet. Other ingredients are added to create colors.

Berry sets: these were a staple of carnival glass production. They consist of a large bowl to hold berries and six matching individual serving bowls. Generally they are flat, but some patterns are known with feet. Edges may be crimped, ruffled, or plain.

Bonbon, bon bon: Bonbons are small, round, or shaped forms designed to hold candy or to be used as decorative pieces. Bonbons always have two handles.

This Grape and Cable bon bon in aqua opal was made by Northwood, **$4,000.**

Bowls: bowls are made in a number of different styles and shapes and with different kinds of edges. An ice-cream shape bowl has an upturned rim and a slightly cupped shape. A bowl with a pie-crust edge refers to a bowl with an edge finished to resemble crimping found on the edge of pie. This simple technique was usually part of the mold, which did not require any further hand finishing. Bowl, ruffled: Another popular treatment to bowls was to ruffle the edges. Bowl, tricorn: This term refers to a three-sided bowl shape.

Breakfast set: a small-sized creamer and sugar.

Bud vase: a slender vase, designed to hold one blossom. They can be footed or flat, short or tall, but always have narrow necks.

Calling card trays: usually formed by adding a foot to a bonbon shape. Some have two sides turned inward and may have handles. The form was used to receive calling cards from visitors.

Candlesticks: these are a rare form in carnival glass.

Chop plates: chop plates are large, usually 10" or larger, very flat plates.

Collar base: a ring of glass on the bottom of a piece that raises it very slightly.

Compote: these are an interesting carnival glass form. They can be large or small, ruffled or plain, some have straight sides or flared rims.

Contemporary: contemporary carnival glass is glass that has been made using iridized metallic surfaces in the last decade or two.

Crimped: a term used to describe an edge treatment where it looks as though the glass was pinched in regular intervals. A special tool is usually used to create this uniform effect.

CRE: Abbreviation used for candy-ribbon edge, a deeply crimped edge that resembles the ruffled candy.

Cullet: broken pieces of glass that are recycled as they are remelted to make a batch.

Cup and saucer: these forms are rare in carnival glass.

Decanters: also known as wine decanters, wine bottles, or bottles with stoppers, these are a lesser-known form in carnival glass.

Dope: the name given to the iridescent spray by early glassmakers. The spray consisted of a liquid solution of metallic salts applied to the hot glass form.

Dope house: a place where the mixing of chemicals for the dope metallic mixture took place.

Dresser sets: what constitutes a dresser set varies from pattern to pattern, but generally includes cologne bottles, perfume bottles, powder jars, hat pin holders, pin trays, and a larger flat dresser tray, allowing a lady to include carnival glass and it's colors into her bedroom as well as her dining room.

Electric: term used to describe shades of blue and purple that seem to have a brilliant electric quality to their iridescent finish.

Epergne: refers to an elaborate centerpiece form, usually consisting of a lily-shaped vase and a bowl or plate on a pedestal base.

Fernery, ferner, fern dish: this name refers to a footed dish that is round, with straight vertical sides. Some ferneries were made with removable liners.

Footed, ftd: Many pieces of carnival glass were made with feet, usually short and rather stubby, but they allowed a piece to be elevated off slightly.

Fruit bowls: these are highly desirable forms of carnival glass. Often they are ruffled and found on separate bases.

Gather: the name given to the glassmaker who scooped up molten glass which he used to fill a patterned mold.

Gravy boat: a rare form in any glassware is a gravy boat.

Guest sets: rare forms in carnival glass. The term is derived from the fact that a tumbler is combined with a small water pitcher. Many guest sets were designed so that the tumbler would serve as a lid when inverted over the top of the matching pitcher.

Hand finishing: when additional crimping or shaping was required, it was sometimes done by the glassmaker by using hand tools. If necessary, the piece was re-heated gently so that the metallic coatings would adhere properly.

Hat: refers to a shape found in many carnival glass patterns. The top edge may be flared, sometimes with one or two sides turned up. They have flat bases.

Hatpin: Carnival glassmakers enjoyed making unusual forms, often referred to as whimsies. One type of whimsy is a hatpin.

Hatpin holder: a slender vase-like holder was designed to hold hatpins on a lady's dressing table.

Jack in the pulpit (JIP): this name refers to a hat, bowl, or vase that has one edge turned up and pointed, creating a collar form similar to the flower of the same name.

Lamp: Carnival glass manufacturers produced fluid lamps and later electrified lamps. Some married carnival glass elements to metal lamp parts such as brass and iron.

Ice cream sets: these sets were popular in carnival glass production. They consisted of a cupped shape bowl and six individual serving bowls, often footed.

Lemonade pitcher: this form is identified as a tall tankard pitcher and may be footed or have a collared base. When accompanied by tumblers or lemonade mugs, the forms become known as a "lemonade set."

Loving cup: this term is used to describe a stemmed vase with two or three handles.

Marie: a term given to the base of carnival glass, usually the base, where the glassmaker grips the glass during the iridizing process.

Married: carnival glass elements were sometimes incorporated into other forms using metal bases or stands. An example of this technique would be a bowl that is supported on a metal stem and base, creating an interesting compote form.

Milk pitcher: a pitcher, usually bulbous, that is larger than a creamer but smaller than a water pitcher.

Mold: this term refers to the metal or wooden form used to shape glass into specific patterns. Molds could be one piece or hinged to allow easier access to the finished piece.

Mugs: mugs are straight-sided drinking vessels with a handle. Many were used with punch bowls or designed as children's feeding vessels.

Nappy: a candy dish or small bowl form with one handle.

Nut bowl: a small round bowl, sometimes footed, with a fluted or smooth upper edge that rises straight up.

Orange bowl: this form is a large round, footed bowl, with a large opening that easily accommodates the display of oranges.

Pie-crust edge (PCE): this term is used to describe an edge that has a crimped edge on a bowl or plate that resembles the kind of crimps made in a pie crust. When Northwood used this edge, it was part of the mold, requiring no further shaping.

Pickle dish: a small oval dish, usually flat with slightly curved up or ruffled sides.

Picture frame: picture frames in vintage glassware production are extremely rare. Researchers have questioned whether this design was intended as a picture frame as there is no way to secure a photo or hang the heavy piece. Few 8" square examples exist, some do have the circular device in the center removed and the edges neatly trimmed.

Pin tray: several carnival glass manufacturers made interesting small trays which were used to hold hair pins on a lady's dressing table.

Plate, hand grip: the term hand grip is used to describe a plate that has one side turned down.

Plates: plates are generally made by using a bowl mold and flattening the form. One rule that carnival glass collectors adhere to is that a bowl must be flat enough so there is a space of two inches between the table and the base of the form. Plate edges may be plain or crimped.

Punch bowl: punch bowls are a highly desirable form in carnival glass collecting. Most are two pieces, with a separate base. Sometimes the bases were designed so they could be used as open compotes when not supporting a punch bowl. Punch bowls range in size from small to quite large.

Punch bowl set: these sets consist of a punch bowl, base, and six or more cups.

Punch cups: these are found in a variety of styles.

Radium: a term used to describe a mirror-like shiny surface, created when iridescent materials were applied to slightly cooler glassware.

Re-issue: one of the names used to describe carnival glass that has been made using original molds, sometimes by the original company, but after 1960, not during primary production years.

Reproductions: these mean carnival glass that has been made in colors or forms other than those that were created by the original glass manufacturer.

Ribbed back: many forms have ribbed backs with vertical ribbing that usually radiates from the center.

Rose bowls: these small bowls are identified by their cupped-in tops, often with additional crimping. They are usually round forms with an upper edge that is turned in toward the center or deeply ruffled.

Ruffled: this term refers to when edges are slightly undulating.

Satin: the name given to a matte finish. It was created by applying metallic salts to very hot glassware.

Snap: the name of a glass-making tool that was attached to the marie to release the piece from it's mold.

Spatula feet: these are small curved shapes, resembling spatulas, which flare out to act as feet.

Sweet pea vase: this term is used to describe a short vase with a wide mouth, usually found 10" to 12" h, but occasionally found from 16" to 18" h.

Swung vase: this term is used when a vase is made using some molding processes. As it is being hand finished, the glass blower actually swings the hot molten glass to lengthen the vase.

Table set: a covered butter dish, a creamer and sugar bowl, and spooner make up a table set.

Tankard pitcher: this term is used to describe a slender straight-sided cylinder-shaped water pitcher. This form usually has an applied handle.

Toothpick holder: this term is used to describe a small container that was designed to hold toothpicks on a table. Several patterns in carnival glass include this form.

3-in-1: this term refers to a deep ruffle edge that has a repeated effect with three ridges and a space.

Tumbler: tumblers are a common form in carnival glass.

Vase: vases are one of the most popular forms in carnival glass. They can be pressed into molds and then finished either totally by machine or with hand finishing. (Also see swung vase.)

Water pitcher: carnival glass water pitchers were made in several styles. One form is known as bulbous because the base is usually quite round. Tops may be ruffled, crimped, or plain with a pinched pouring spout. Handles can be applied or mold pressed.

Water sets: water sets, consisting of a water pitcher and tumblers, are one of the most popular forms of vintage carnival glass. The pitchers may be either bulbous or tankard styles. The number of matching tumblers can vary, with the most desirable being six matching tumblers.

Wine set: wine sets contain a stoppered wine decanter and serving glasses, usually stemmed wine glasses, cordial glasses, or small-sized tumblers.

Acanthus

Made by Imperial.

Colors known: aqua, blue, clambroth, emerald green, green, helios, marigold, purple, and smoke.

Forms: bowls and chop plates.

Identifying characteristics: Design consists of swirling acanthus leaves. Carnival glass clubs have used this pattern for souvenirs with Fenton using original Imperial molds to make these limited-edition novelties. This pattern was first advertised in 1911.

Also known as: Imperial's #465; Parrot Tulip Swirl.

Reproductions: Fenton made a celeste blue bowl as a souvenir for the International Carnival Glass Association's Dallas, 1995, convention.

Acanthus, Imperial, bowl, purple, electric iridescence, $150.

Acorn

Made by Fenton.

Colors known: amber opalescent, amethyst, aqua, blue, green, ice blue, lime green, marigold, marigold over milk glass, peach opalescent, powder blue, red, and vaseline.

Forms: bowls; rarely found in plates.

Identifying characteristics: Look for clusters of two raised acorns among swirling leaves. Made from 1915 to 1925.

Also known as: Fenton's #835; Grape Leaves and Acorns.

Acorn, Fenton, bowl, 6-1/2", dark red, ruffled, $400.

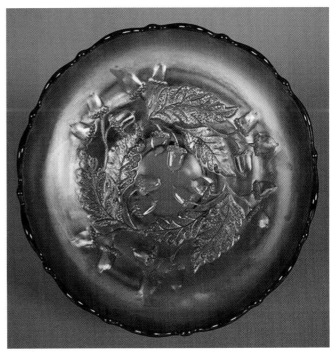

Acorn, Fenton, bowl, ice-cream shape, dark aqua, $20.

Acorn

Made by Millersburg.

Colors known: amethyst, green, marigold, and vaseline.

Forms: compotes.

Identifying characteristics: Pattern identified by large oak leaves that meet in the center and extend to outer edge with acorns interspersed between the leaves.

Acorn, maybe U.S Glass or possibly Millersburg, vase, vaseline, only one known in this color, $11,000.

Acorn, maybe U.S. Glass or possibly Millersburg, vase, green, one of two known, $9,000.

Acorn Burrs

Made by Northwood.

Colors known: amethyst, blue, green, ice blue, ice green, marigold, pastel, purple, and white.

Forms: bowls, punch sets, table sets, and water sets.

Identifying characteristics: This very three-dimensional pattern shows detailed leaves and large chestnut-type acorns. Production began in 1911.

Also known as: Acorn Burrs and Bark.

Acorn Burrs, Northwood, punch cup, 2-1/2", $150-$250 (rare).

Acorn Burrs, Northwood, punch bowl base, five cups, ice blue, $1,150.

Acorn Burrs, Northwood, punch bowl base, six cups, ice green, very few known, **$23,000**.

Acorn Burrs, Northwood, punch bowl base, six cups, white, **$6,500**.

Advertising

Several manufacturers made interesting plates and bowls that were used as promotional give-away pieces by advertisers. Today these advertising pieces command high prices.

Colors known: amethyst, blue, green, and marigold.

Forms: bonbons, bowls, hats, mugs, and plates.

Identifying characteristics: Names of advertisers are the predominate characteristic. Many advertisers chose popular patterns of the day to add their names to, such as Heart & Vine or Grape & Cable. Many of these premiums were made in limited quantities.

Advertising plate, Northwood, Fern Brand Chocolates, 6", amethyst, $1,300-$1,800.

Advertising plate, Fenton, "Eat Paradise Sodas," 6", amethyst, $500-$800.

Advertising plate, Northwood, Dreibus Parfait Sweets, 6", amethyst, $900-$1,300.

Advertising card tray, Fenton, Utah Liquors, 6", amethyst, $800-$1,000.

Apple Blossom Twigs

Made by Dugan.

Colors known: amethyst, blue, lavender, lavender slag, marigold, peach opalescent, purple, and white.

Forms: banana boats, bowls, and plates.

Identifying characteristics: This pattern features four branches with leaves that frame a central flower. Plates can have a serrated edge or smooth edge. The pattern was first made in 1912.

Apple Blossom Twigs, Dugan, 3-in-1 bowl, 9", 10 ruffles, purple, $200 to $300; outstanding condition, $800.

Apple Blossom Twigs, Dugan, I.C.S. bowl, 8-1/2", purple, $200 to $300.

April Showers

Made by Fenton.

Colors known: amethyst, amethyst opalescent, blue, green, marigold, red, vaseline, and white.

Forms: vases.

Identifying characteristics: This pattern looks as though there are three-dimensional raindrops sliding down the exterior walls. Because these vases are made using the "swung" method, heights range from 5 to 15 inches and variations exist in the scallops at the top. The bases are plain. The pattern was first made in 1911.

Also known as: Fenton #412.

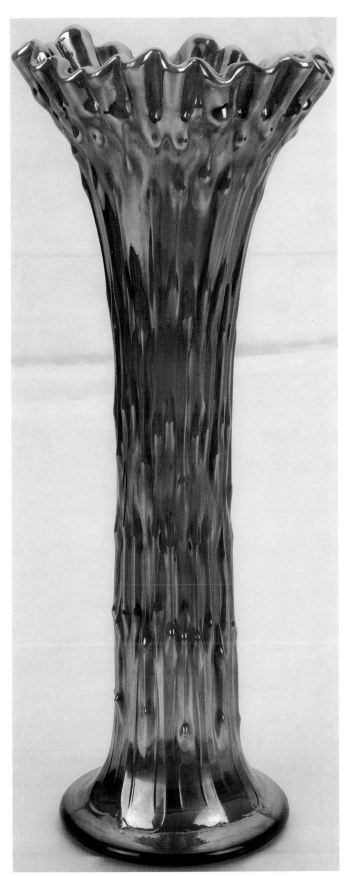

April Showers, Fenton, vase, 11-1/4", amethyst opal, $1,450.

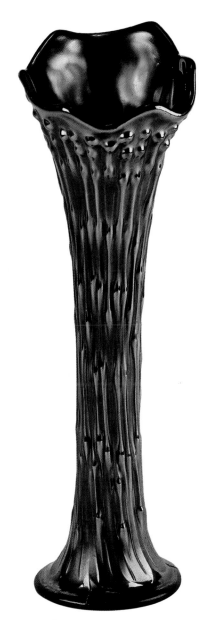

April Showers, Fenton, vase, 12", black amethyst, $80 to $150.

Beaded Bullseye

Made by Imperial.

Colors known: amber, cobalt blue, green, helios, lime green, marigold, purple, smoke, and teal.

Forms: vases.

Identifying characteristics: The pattern consists of large circles edged by beads, further separated by fine ribbing. The base is a 20-point star. Production began in 1912.

Also known as: Beaded Medallion and Teardrop.

Beaded Bulleye, Imperial, vase, 8 1/2", amber, $300-$400 (scarce).

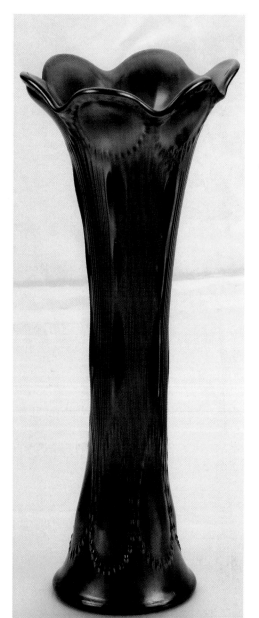

Beaded Bullseye, Fenton,
vase, 12", purple, $100.

Beaded Bullseye, Imperial,
vase, 10", marigold, $60-$100.

Beaded Bullseye, Imperial,
squat vase, 7", purple, $250-$350 (scarce).

Beaded Shell

Made by Dugan-Diamond.

Colors known: amethyst, blue, green, marigold, pastel opalescent, purple, red, and white.

Forms: bowls, mugs, table sets, water sets, and whimsies.

Identifying characteristics: This pattern with a naturalistic-looking shell motif was first made as pattern glass. Also found in custard and opalescent glass.

Also known as: New York; Shell.

Reproductions.

Beaded Shell, Dugan, water pitcher and six tumblers, marigold, $1,400.

Beaded Spears

Made by Jain.

Colors known: amethyst, blue, and marigold.

Forms: water sets.

Identifying characteristics: Tumblers are known in several different sizes and may be flared or straight at the top. Jain Glass Works, located in Firozabad, India.

Beaded Spears, foreign Jain, water pitcher and five tumblers (one shown), marigold, $1,000.

Beaded Spears, foreign Jain, tumbler, one of three known, cracked, teal, $75.

Big Basketweave

Made by Dugan-Diamond.

Colors known: amethyst, blue, celeste blue, horehound, ice blue, marigold, peach opalescent, purple, and white.

Forms: baskets, bowls, and vases.

Identifying characteristics: The pattern is found on the exterior of the forms as they resemble woven wicker items. Produced 1911-1913.

Also known as: Wicker Weave.

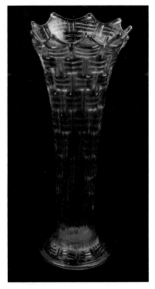

Big Basketweave, Dugan, vase, 11-1/4", ice blue, $600.

Big Basketweave, Dugan, vase, 9-1/2", horehound, $350.

Big Basketweave, Dugan, vase, 10", white, $500.

Big Fish

Made by Millersburg.

Colors known: amethyst, green, marigold, and vaseline.

Forms: bowls.

Identifying characteristics: A large center trout graces this pattern and is further enhanced by water lilies. The pattern was introduced in 1911.

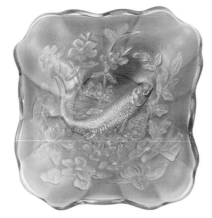

Big Fish, Millersburg, bowl, square, marigold, $900.

Big Fish, Millersburg, rosebowl, 6" w, 3" d, purple, only one known.

Birds and Cherries

Made by Fenton.

Colors known: amethyst, blue, green, marigold, pastel marigold, vaseline, and white.

Forms: bonbons, bowls, card trays, compotes, and plates.

Identifying characteristics: The pattern features birds on cherry tree branches, complete with blossoms, leaves, and cherries. The pattern was introduced in 1911.

Also known as: Fenton's #1075.

Bird and Cherries, Fenton, bowl, candy-ribbon edge, blue, $750.

Blackberry

Made by Fenton.

Colors known: amethyst, blue, green, marigold, purple, and white.

Forms: compotes and plates.

Identifying characteristics: This pattern featuring blackberries and leaves. The miniature compotes are found in several styles, including ruffled and tricorn. Production was from 1911 to 1913.

Blackberry, Fenton, ruffled bowl, green, $75.

Blackberry Block

Made by Fenton.

Colors known: amethyst, blue, green, marigold, and white.

Forms: water sets.

Identifying characteristics: This is an all-over squares pattern with vining berries and leaves. The tankard-shaped water pitcher has a scalloped rim and applied handle.

Blackberry Block, water pitcher, one tumbler, green, $4,000.

Blackberry Block, Fenton, ruffled-top tankard, 11" h, blue, $1,500-$1,800.

Blackberry Open Edge

Made by Fenton.

Colors known: amethyst, blue, celeste blue, green, marigold, powder blue, red, and white.

Forms: baskets, bowls, and whimsies.

Identifying characteristics: This blackberry pattern is often found with a basket-weave exterior. The pattern was introduced in 1911.

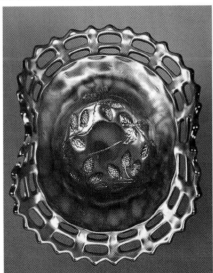

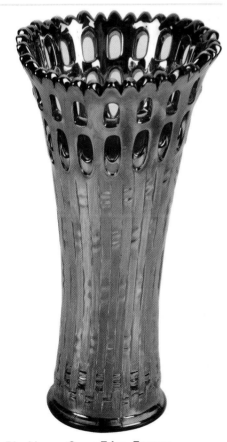

Blackberry Open Edge, Fenton, basket, 7", red, two sides up, $250.

Blackberry Open Edge, Fenton, two-row vase, 7", whimsy, blue, $2,000.

Blackberry Spray

Made by Fenton. 1908.

Colors known: amber, amberina, amethyst, aqua, aqua opalescent, blue, green, lime green, marigold, red, reverse amberina opalescent, vaseline, and white.

Forms: hats.

Identifying characteristics: This blackberry pattern features sprays of berries that encircle the interior edge. The exteriors are plain. The pattern was introduced in 1911.
Also known as: Fenton's #1216.

Blackberry Spray, Fenton, hat, ruffle, red opal, $650.

Blackberry Spray, Fenton, hat, jack-in-the-pulpit, sapphire opal, $1,700.

Blackberry Wreath

Made by Millersburg.

Colors known: amethyst, blue, clambroth, green, marigold, and vaseline.

Forms: bowls.

Identifying characteristics: This pattern features a plump berry in the center with three leaves. The wreath like border includes more berries, leaves, and tendrils. The pattern was introduced in 1911.

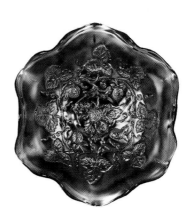

Blackberry Wreath, Millersburg, large bowl, ruffled, purple, $40.

Blackberry Wreath, Fenton, spitton, whimsey, marigold, $700.

Blossomtime

Made by Northwood.

Colors known: amethyst, green, marigold, and purple.

Forms: compotes.

Identifying characteristics: A circle of flowers and leaves are the major design element of this pattern. Some pieces also feature a Wildflower pattern exterior.

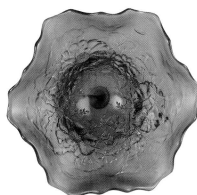

Blossomtime, Northwood, compote (top view), 5", marigold, $175-$300.

Blossomtime, Northwood, compote (top view), 5", green, $550-$750 (scarce).

Blossomtime, Northwood, compote, 5", green, $400-$700.

Blueberry

Made by Fenton.

Colors known: blue, marigold, and white.

Forms: water sets.

Identifying characteristics: This pattern has life-like blueberries. The tops of the water pitchers are scalloped and flared out, with handles always applied. Production began in 1912.

Also known as: #1562.

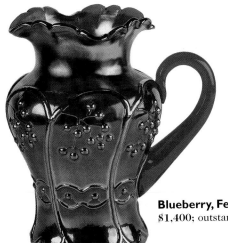

Blueberry, Fenton, ruffled-top tankard, 10" h, blue, $1,000-$1,400; outstanding condition, $4,500.

Blueberry, Fenton, water pitcher and three tumblers, two tumblers from icga, white, $1,450.

Bouquet

Made by Fenton.

Colors known: blue and marigold.

Forms: water sets.

Identifying characteristics: As the name implies, this design features flowers, but also incorporates a cable. The water pitchers have crimped tops and applied handles. The pattern was introduced in 1913.

Also known as: Spring Flowers.

Bouquet, Fenton, water pitcher, six tumblers, marigold, **$265**.

Broken Arches

Made by Imperial.

Colors known: marigold and purple.

Forms: punch sets.

Identifying characteristics: The name correctly describes this intricate pattern. The arches are broken in a keystone-type arrangement. The pattern was first advertised in 1911.

Also known as: Imperial's Snap-14.

Broken Arches, Imperial, punch bowl and base, 13" d, purple, $1,000-$1,300; outstanding condition, $2,000.

Broken Arches, Imperial, ruffled punch bowl and base, 13" d, purple, $1,500-$2,000 (very rare).

Broken Arches, Imperial, punch cup, 2-1/4" h, purple, $40-$70.

Bullseye and Beads

Made by Fenton.

Colors known: amber, blue, and marigold.

Forms: vases.

Identifying characteristics: This pattern features rows of stretched bull's eyes. Beads are found under the scalloped rim and at the base.

Bushel Basket

Novelty pattern made by Northwood.

Colors known: amethyst, amethyst slag, aqua opalescent, blue, green, ice blue, ice green, lavender, marigold, purple, sapphire blue, smoke, and white.

Forms: only two basket forms known – with either a round or octagon-shaped base.

Identifying characteristics: As the name implies, this pattern looks like a woven wicker basket, complete with two handles and small feet. Handles are commonly ribbed, but variations with smooth handles and more flare to the top exist. The pattern was made from 1910 to 1921.

Bushel Basket, Northwood, pastel marigold, $50.

Bushel Basket, Northwood, eight-sided, amethyst, $50.

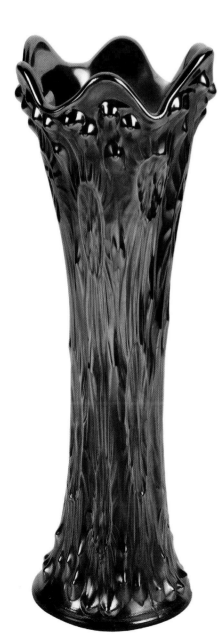

Bullseye and Beads, Fenton, vase, 11-1/4" h, blue, $350.

Bushel Basket, Northwood, round, purple, $70.

Butterfly

Made by Northwood.

Colors known: amethyst, blue, green, horehound, ice blue, marigold, purple, and smoke.

Forms: bonbons.

Identifying characteristics: Look for a single center butterfly in this pattern that looks like it will fly right over the rays that border it. This pattern was produced from 1910 to 1913.

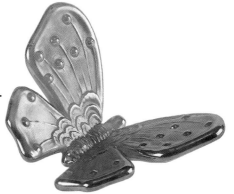

Butterfly, Feton, ornament, 3", marigold, $1,200-$1,500.

Butterfly, U.S. Glass, tumbler, one of four known, green, $10,000.

Butterfly and Berry

Made by Fenton.

Colors known: amethyst, blue, green, marigold, red, and white.

Forms: bowls, hatpin holders, table set, vases, water sets, and whimsies.

Identifying characteristics: This pattern is found in a paneled form with alternating butterflies and leaves in one panel, blackberries and leaves in other panels. This popular pattern was also used as an exterior pattern on Fenton bowls in the Hearts & Trees, Fantail, and Panther patterns. The pattern was produced from 1911 to 1926.

Also known as: Butterfly and Grape.

Reproductions: The large bowl has been reproduced in purple and white. Tumblers have been reproduced in amethyst.

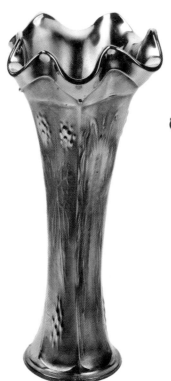

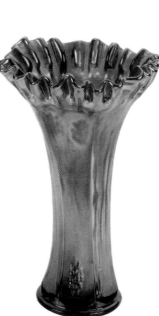

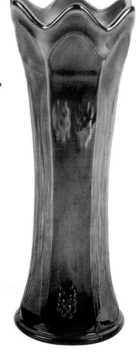

Butterfly and Berry, Fenton, vase, 8-1/2", red, flake, $525.

Butterfly and Berry, Fenton, vase, 7", candy-ribbon edge, blue, $100.

Butterfly and Berry, Fenton, vase, 7", amethyst, $150.

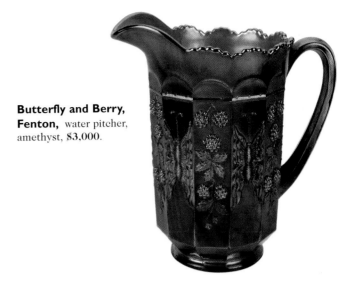

**Butterfly and Berry,
Fenton,** water pitcher,
amethyst, $3,000.

Butterfly and Berry, Fenton, fernery, turned in, amethyst,
$1,000.

Butterfly and Fern

Made by Fenton.

Colors known: amethyst, blue, green, and marigold.

Forms: water sets.

Identifying characteristics: The central motif is a
butterfly with leaves. Water pitcher tops are crimped,
and handles are applied.

Also known as: Fenton's #910; Butterfly and Plume.

Butterfly and Fern, Fenton,
water pitcher, six tumblers, amethyst,
$1,050.

Butterfly and Tulip

Made by Dugan.

Colors: amethyst, marigold, peach
opalescent, and purple.

Forms: bowls.

Identifying characteristics: A large
central butterfly appears ready to fly to the
well-designed tulips and leaves that extend
to the edges of this design. Feather Scroll
is commonly used as the exterior pattern.
This pattern was introduced in 1910.

Butterfly and Tulip, Dugan,
bowl, purple, open blister on foot, $2,100.

Butterfly and Tulip, Dugan, square-
ruffled bowl, footed, 11", purple, $2,000-
$3,500.

Captive Rose

Made by Fenton.

Colors known: amethyst, blue, green, and marigold.

Forms: bonbons, bowls, calling card trays, compotes, and plates.

Identifying characteristics: This detailed pattern has a lacy embroidered motif. Look for the rose in the center as well as the garland of roses. Production began in 1910.

Also known as: Battenburg Lace #2B.

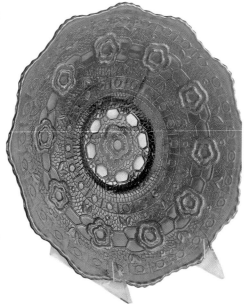

Captive Rose, Fenton, flat plate, 9", green, $900-$1,500; in outstanding condition, $4,500.

Captive Rose, Fenton, flat plate, 9", blue, $400-$700.

Chatelaine

Made by Imperial.

Colors known: purple.

Forms: water sets.

Identifying characteristics: This pattern is a very detailed design with fans, hobstars, and volutes. A clear example is shown in a 1909 Imperial catalog. The first carnival example was advertised in a 1913 *Butlers Brothers Wholesale* catalog.

Chatelaine, Imperial, tumbler, 4-1/4", purple, $200-$350 (rare).

Chatelaine, Imperial, water pitcher, 8-1/2", purple, $2,400-$3,000 (rare).

Checkerboard

Made by Westmoreland.

Colors known: amethyst and marigold.

Forms: goblets, punch cups and water sets.

Identifying characteristics: This pattern consists of raised blocks, criss-cross diagonals, and fans.

Also known as: Old Quilt.

Reproductions: Water pitchers and tumblers have been reproduced by L. G. Wright using old molds. Westmoreland also reissued the water set in honey, lime green, and ice blue.

Checkerboard, Westmoreland, water pitcher and six tumblers, amethyst, $4,100.

Cherries

Made by Dugan-Diamond.

Colors known: amethyst, electric blue, marigold, peach opalescent, and purple.

Forms: banana boat, bowls, and plates.

Identifying characteristics: This pattern features clusters of stemmed cherries on leaves and branches. It was made from 1909 until 1914.

Also known as: Cherry.

Reproductions: A round bowl has been made.

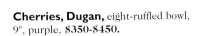

Cherries, Dugan, eight-ruffled bowl, 9", purple, $350-$450.

Cherries, Dugan, ruffled plate, candy-ribbon edge, 6-1/2", purple, $200-$350.

Cherries, Dugan, ruffled plate, candy-ribbon edge, 9", purple, $200-$350.

Carnival Glass **Warman's**
43

Cherry Chain

Made by Fenton.

Colors known: amethyst, blue, clambroth, electric blue, marigold, red, vaseline, and white.

Forms: bowls and plates.

Identifying characteristics: This cherry pattern features clusters of three plump cherries within a circle, surrounded by foliage and other elements. Another cluster of cherries is in the center. The Orange Tree pattern was used as the exterior design for this busy pattern. A pattern known as Cherry Chain Variant has clusters with five cherries each.

Reproductions: Fenton reissued this pattern in a number of shapes, such as the round bowl, ruffled bowl, chop plates, and rose bowls.

Cherry Chain, bowl, 3-in-1 edge, large, green, $200.

Cherry Chain, Fenton, chop plate, 10-3/4", marigold dark electric, $1,400.

Cherry Chain, Fenton, bon bon, red, large, $5,000.

Chrysanthemum

Made by Fenton.

Colors known: amethyst, blue, green, lime green, marigold, red, vaseline, and white.

Forms: bowls.

Identifying characteristics: This pattern features large full-blossomed chrysanthemum leaves, and windmills. Production began in 1914.

Also known as: Chrysanthemum and Windmills.

Chrysanthemum, Fenton, bowl, large, footed, electric blue, $250.

Circle Scroll

Made by Dugan.

Colors known: amethyst and marigold.

Forms: bowls, hats, table sets, vases, and water sets.

Identifying characteristics: The design motif includes a swirling vine within a circle. This pattern was also made in opalescent glass.

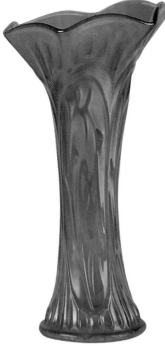

Circle Scroll, Dugan, vase, 7-1/2" h, marigold, $100-$200 (scarce).

Circle Scroll, Dugan, vase, 7-1/4" h, purple, $200-$400; outstanding condition, $750.

Circle Scroll, Dugan, water pitcher and six tumblers, SSCGA, marigold, $1,100.

Colonial Lady

Made by Imperial.

Colors known: marigold and purple.

Forms: vases.

Identifying characteristics: This pattern is a series of panels with a very distinctive rib between each.

Colonial Lady, Imperial, vase, purple, 6", $1,400.

Colonial Lady, Imperial, vase, 5-1/2", purple, $600-$1,000; outstanding condition, $2,300.

Colonial Lady, Imperial, vase, marigold, rare and beautiful, $525.

Concave Flute

Made by Westmoreland.

Colors known: amethyst, marigold, marigold with moonstone, and teal.

Forms: banana dish, rose bowls, and vases.

Identifying characteristics: This paneled pattern consists of nine flutes that radiate from a sharp arch.

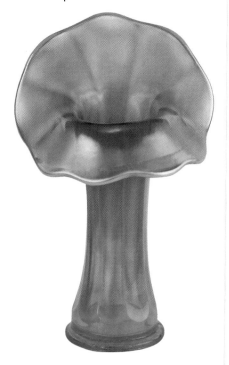

Concave Flute, Westmoreland, jack-in-the-pulpit vase, 9-1/2", blue opal, $350-$500.

Concord

Made by Fenton.

Colors known: amethyst, blue, green, marigold, and pumpkin marigold.

Forms: bowls and plates.

Identifying characteristics: This pattern features clusters of grapes, vines, and leaves, while the whole background resembles a net.

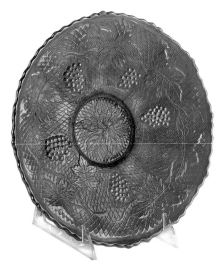

Concord, Fenton, flat plate, 9", purple, $2,000-$3,000.

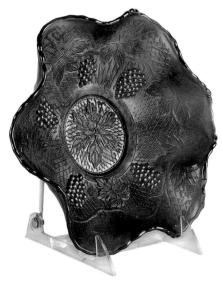

Concord, Fenton, six-ruffled bowl, 8-1/2", emerald green, $300-$500; **outstanding condition,** $850.

Concord, Fenton, blue ruffled bowl, pretty piece, has some loss of iridescence on grapes, $75.

Constellation

Made by Dugan.

Colors known: amethyst, lavender, marigold, peach opalescent, and white.

Forms: compotes.

Identifying characteristics: This pattern features a large center star with bubble dots and rays stretching towards the rim. The exterior is S-Repeat pattern.

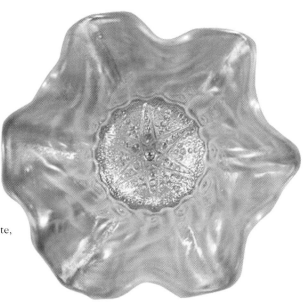

Constellation, Dugan, compote, white, $45.

Coral

Made by Fenton.

Colors known: blue, green, ice green, and marigold.

Forms: bowls, plates.

Identifying characteristics: This interesting pattern is one of only a few that has two bands. Abstract nautical motifs complete the design.

Coral, Fenton, plate, marigold, $1,100.

Corinth

Made by Westmoreland.

Colors known: amber, amethyst, marigold, marigold on milk glass, olive green, peach opalescent, teal, and white.

Forms: banana boats, bowls, and vases.

Identifying characteristics: This pattern features 12 heavy ribs. Vases have plain bases. Produced from 1904 to 1910. Dugan-Diamond made a similar pattern, which is valued the same.

Also known as: Westmoreland's #252.

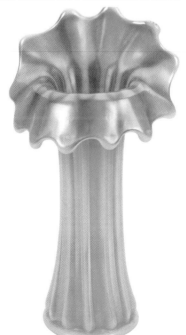

Corinth, Dugan, jack-in-the-pulpit vase, 10", peach opal, $150.

Corinth, Dugan, jack-in-the-pulpit vase, 8-3/4", blue opal, $175.

Corinth, Westmoreland, jack-in-the-pulpit vase, 9-1/2", blue opal, $300-$400.

Corn

Made by Northwood.

Colors known: amethyst, aqua opalescent, blue, green, ice blue, ice green, lime green, marigold, purple, teal, and white.

Forms: vases.

Identifying characteristics: This pattern looks like its name implies, an ear of corn, with the husk forming the base.

Corn, Northwood, vase, 6-1/2", stalk base, ice green, $400-$700.

Corn, Northwood, vase, 6-1/2", stalk base, aqua, $2,200-$3,000 (rare).

Corn, Northwood, vase, 6-1/2", stalk base, green, $700-$1,100.

Cosmos and Cane

Made by US Glass.

Colors known: amethyst, honey amber, marigold, and white.

Forms: baskets, berry sets, chop plates, compotes, rose bowls, spittoons, table sets, trays, and water sets.

Identifying characteristics: As the name implies, there is a panel of cane design and pretty cosmos flowers on this pattern. Produced from 1914 until 1917.

Also known as: Diamond Point and Daisy.

Cosmos and Cane, U.S. Glass, square bowl, honey amber, $70.

Cosmos and Cane, U.S. Glass, water pitcher and six tumblers, white, $4,500.

Curved Star

Attributed to U.S. Glass, Brockwitz of Germany, Karhula-Iittala, Finland.

Colors known: blue and marigold.

Forms: bowls, chalices, cheese dishes, compotes, epergnes, flower holders, fruit bowls, and table sets.

Identifying characteristics: This imitation cut-glass pattern features an elongated six-point star in each of the curved panels. The pattern has been documented in the 1938 catalog of Karnula-Iittala.

Also known as: Cathedral.

Curved Star, Brockwitz, small bowl, 4-1/2" w x 1-1/2" h, blue, **$80-$150**.

Curved Star Brockwitz,
cylinder vase, 7-1/2", blue, **$350-$500**.

Curved Star, Brockwitz,
cylinder vase, 7-1/2", marigold, **$350-$500**.

Dahlia

Made by Dugan.

Colors known: amethyst, marigold, and purple.

Forms: berry sets, table sets, and water sets.

Identifying characteristics: The intricate dahlia flower is raised in this pattern. Production began in 1912.

Reproductions: L. G. Wright created reproduction water pitchers in 1977 using original Westmoreland molds in amethyst and white. Tumblers have also been reproduced, possibly by Mosser, but are easier to identify, as they do not include the many-rayed star in the base.

Dahlia, Dugan, water pitcher and six tumblers, marigold, $1,750.

Daisy and Drape

Made by Northwood.

Colors known: amethyst, aqua, aqua opalescent, blue, green, ice blue, ice marigold, and white.

Forms: vases.

Identifying characteristics: This pattern features a drape like body with a ring of daisies around the top. Production began in 1912.

Also known as: Daisy Band and Drape.

Daisy and Drape, Northwood, vase, aqua opal, belonged to the owner's grandmother, $500.

Daisy and Drape, Northwood, vase, turned in, ice green, $4,000.

Daisy and Plume

Made by Northwood and also Dugan.

Colors known: amethyst, aqua, blue, green, horehound, marigold, peach opalescent, purple, and white.

Forms: bowls, candy dishes, compotes, and rose bowls.

Identifying characteristics: A large plume separates the stippled fields that hold a single daisy blossom in this pattern. Production was from 1909 until 1912.

Daisy and Plume, Northwood, rose bowl, footed, one of three known, possibly only butterscotch. Feet dam, aqua opal, **$7,000**.

Daisy Wreath

Made by Westmoreland.

Colors known: amethyst, aqua opal, blue opal, marigold, marigold on milk glass, and peach opalescent.

Forms: bowls, plates, and vases.

Identifying characteristics: This pattern features a central daisy surrounded by a wreath border. Production began in 1910.

Also known as: Daisy Bowl.

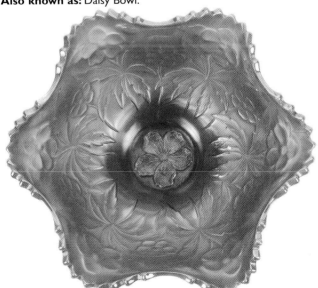

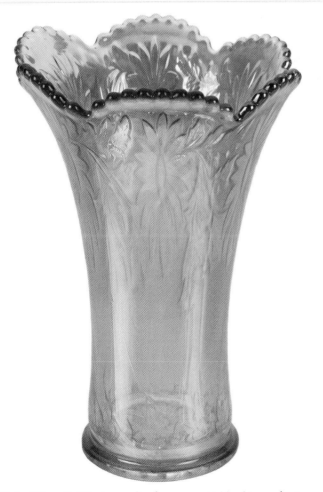

Daisy Wreath, Westmoreland, bowl, marigold over moonstone, $200.

Daisy Wreath, Westmoreland, vase, marigold, whimsey from bowl, 5", **$2,100**.

Dandelion

Made by Northwood.

Colors known: amethyst, aqua opalescent, blue, blue opalescent, green, ice blue, ice green, marigold, purple, and white.

Forms: mugs, vases, and water sets.

Identifying characteristics: This pattern features a large multi-petaled flower blossom and leaves. Mugs in this pattern are available with a Knights Templer decoration.

Dandelion, Northwood, water pitcher and six tumblers, marigold, $1,700.

Dandelion, Northwood, tankard, 14", purple, $600-$1,000; outstanding condition, $2,200.

Dandelion, Northwood, mug, 3-1/2", aqua opal, $450-$600.

Dandelion, Northwood, tumbler, 4-1/4", purple, $50-$150.

Dandelion, Northwood, tumbler, smoky lavender streaks, $425.

Diamond and Rib

Made by Fenton.

Colors known: amethyst, blue, green, marigold, and white.

Forms: jardinières and vases.

Identifying characteristics: This pattern features elongated ovals with ribbing in each one. Production began in 1911.

Also known as: Fenton's #504; Melon and Fan.

Reproductions: Fenton has re-issued vases, but most are marked.

Diamond and Rib, Fenton, jardinière vase, amethyst, damage, $1,500.

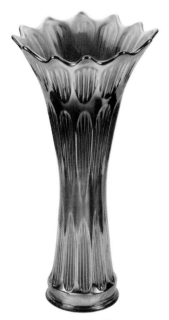

Diamond and Rib, Fenton, funeral vase, 19", 9" mouth, green, $1,200.

Diamond and Rib, Fenton, funeral vase, blue, $4,000.

Diamond and Rib, Fenton, jardinière, 6-1/2", marigold, $1,500-$1,800.

Diamond and Rib, Fenton, funeral vase, 21-1/2" plunger base, marigold, $1,100.

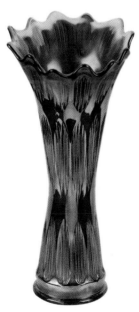

Diamond and Rib, Fenton, funeral vase, 18", 5-1/4", amethyst, $2,200.

Diamond and Rib, Fenton, vase, pinched in, green, whimsy, $1,350.

Diamond Lace

Made by Imperial.

Colors known: green, marigold, and purple.

Forms: berry sets, rose bowls, and water sets.

Identifying characteristics: This imitation cut-glass pattern was first made in crystal. It features hobstars, files, fans, etc. Production began in 1909.

Also known as: Imperial's #434-1/2.

Reproductions.

Diamond Lace, Imperial, tumbler, 4-1/4", purple, $50-$80.

Diamond Lace, Imperial, water pitcher, 8-1/2", purple, $325-$525.

Diamond Points

Made by Northwood.

Colors known: amethyst, aqua opalescent, blue, green, horehound, ice blue, ice green, marigold, sapphire blue, and white.

Forms: baskets, rose bowls, and vases.

Identifying characteristics: This pattern features squares set on the diagonal, each filled with further criss-cross diamond elements. Production was between 1912 and 1916.

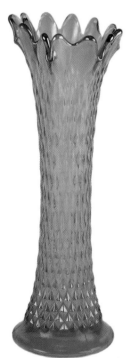

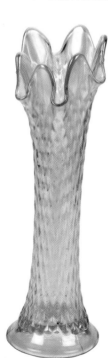

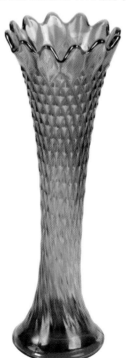

Diamond Point, Northwood, vase, 10-1/2", sapphire, $700-$1,100 (rare).

Diamond Point, Northwood, vase, 12", ice blue, $450.

Diamond Point, Northwood, vase, 11-1/2", teal blue, $1,150.

Diamond Point, Northwood, vase, 9-1/2", blue, $300-$400 (scarce).

Diamond Point, Northwood, vase, 10-1/2", aqua opal, pastel, $1,200.

Diamonds

Made by Millersburg.

Colors known: amethyst, aqua, green, and marigold.

Forms: punch bowls and water sets.

Identifying characteristics: This bold diamond pattern features a row of beading inside each diamond. An odd form was made in this pattern when a water pitcher form was created with a handle, but no pouring spout. Production was from 1910 to 1911.

Diamonds, Millersburg, water pitcher and six tumblers (one shown), green, $850.

Diamonds, Millersburg, water pitcher and four tumblers (one shown), amethyst, $850.

Diamonds, Millersburg, tumbler, 4", amethyst, $70-$110.

Dogwood Sprays

Made by Dugan.

Colors known: amethyst, blue, blue opalescent, marigold, peach opalescent, and purple.

Forms: bowls and compotes.

Identifying characteristics: Two large floral sprays, leaves and tendrils are the basis of this pattern. The center is a single four-petaled blossom with five leaves. Production was between 1910 and 1912.

Dogwood Sprays, Dugan, tri-corner bowl, 9", purple, $150-$300.

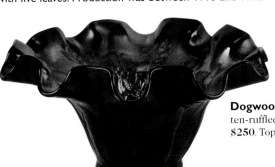

Dogwood Sprays, Dugan, ten-ruffled deep compote, 7-1/2", purple, $150-$250. Top view of compote is shown at right.

Double Star

Made by Cambridge.

Colors known: amethyst, green, and marigold.

Forms: bowls, water sets, and whimsies.

Identifying characteristics: This pattern features a large central buzz star over an interesting fan shape. Production began in 1913 and continued until 1915.

Also known as: Cambridge's #2699; Buzzstar; Hobstar and Torch.

Double Star, Cambridge, water pitcher and six tumblers (one shown), green, $1,400.

Double Star, Cambridge, water pitcher, amethyst, $850.

Dozen Roses

Attributed to Imperial.

Colors known: amethyst, green, marigold, and purple.

Forms: bowls.

Identifying characteristics: This pattern is the same on the interior as it is on the exterior—twelve shaped frames that each have a incised and raised rose blossom.

Dozen Roses, possibly Imperial, bowl, amethyst, $850.

Dragon and Lotus

Made by Fenton.

Colors known: amber, amethyst, aqua opalescent, blue, cobalt blue, dark blue, green, marigold, marigold on milk glass, peach opalescent, red, reverse amberina, and vaseline opalescent.

Forms: bowls and plates.

Identifying characteristics: This popular pattern shows ovals with a whimsical flying dragon alternating with rose type flowers. A busy inner band is found between the dragons and the lotus flowers in the center. Production started in 1915 and continued until 1920.

Dragon and Lotus, Fenton, bowl, 9", ruffled, aqua opal, $2,200.

Dragon and Lotus, Fenton, eight-ruffled bowl, 9", red, **$1,500-$2,500;** outstanding condition, **$5,000.**

Dragon and Lotus, Fenton, bowl, 8-1/2" ruffled collar, dark red, **$1,800.**

Dragon and Lotus, Fenton, bowl, ice cream shape, marigold over moonstone, $1,000.

Dragon and Strawberry

Made by Fenton.

Colors known: amethyst, blue, green, and marigold.

Forms: bowls.

Identifying characteristics: This pattern was a contemporary of Dragon and Lotus. It is less detailed than Dragon and Lotus, and shows plump berries in addition to the dragon. Made in 1915.

Also known as: Dragon and Berry.

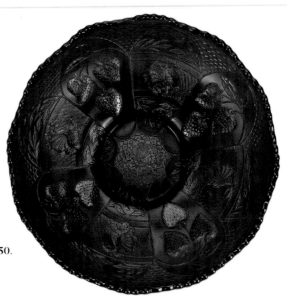

Dragon and Strawberry, Fenton, bowl, 8-3/4", blue, $650.

Drapery

Made by Northwood.

Colors known: amethyst, aqua opalescent, blue, electric blue, green, ice blue, ice green, lavender, lime green, marigold, purple, Renninger blue, and white.

Forms: candy dishes, rose bowls and vases.

Identifying characteristics: Think of heavy folded drapes with sturdy ribs when envisioning this popular pattern. Production began in 1914 and continued until 1916.

Also known as: Northwood's Drapery.

Reproductions: Fenton has made rose bowls in contemporary colors, which are generally marked.

Drapery, Northwood, vase, 7-1/4", ice blue, $200.

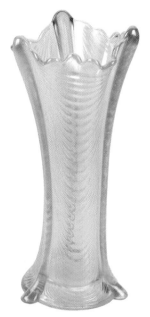

Drapery, Northwood, vase, 8", ice green, $250.

Drapery, Northwood, tumbler, white, $3,100.

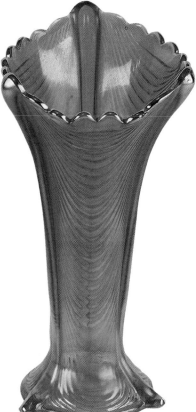

Drapery, Northwood, vase, 8", ice pumpkin marigold, $100-$200.

Drapery Variant

Attributed to Fenton and Northwood.

Colors known: blue, marigold, purple, and sapphire blue.

Forms: bowls, vases.

Identifying characteristics: The folds found in this variant are less defined than those of the original Drapery pattern.

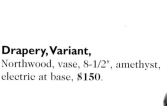

Drapery, Variant, Northwood, vase, 8-1/2", amethyst, electric at base, $150.

Embroidered Mums

Made by Northwood.

Colors known: amethyst, aqua opalescent, blue, electric blue, green, ice blue, ice green, lavender, lime green opalescent, marigold, peach opalescent, purple, sapphire blue, and white.

Forms: bonbons, bowls, and plates.

Identifying characteristics: This elegant pattern features a Greek key ring with interspersed chrysanthemums and leaves. An embroidered-type star flower is in the center. Production was from 1911 to 1912.

Also known as: Mums and Greek Key.

Embroidered Mums, Northwood, bowl, purple, very pretty electric highlights, $250.

Embroidered Mums, Northwood, bowl, 8-1/2", blue electric, $500.

Embroidered Mums, Northwood, eight-ruffled bowl, 8-1/2", blue, $550-$850.

Enameled patterns

Various manufacturers.

Colors known: amethyst, blue, green, marigold, purple, and white.

Forms: goblets, plates, vases, and water sets.

Identifying characteristics: Many patterns of carnival glass are found which have been further enhanced by enamel decoration. Some collectors specialize in these interesting patterns. Most are limited in forms and productions. This edition contains a sampling of what is available in the carnival glass market, but be aware more color patterns await those searching for these gems.

Enameled Grape, Northwood,
water pitcher and six tumblers, blue, $875.

Estate

Made by Westmoreland.

Colors known: aqua, aqua opalescent, marigold, and smoke.

Forms: mugs, perfumes, and pin dishes.

Identifying characteristics: This pattern features an almost Celtic-like band.

Also known as: Capital.

Estate, Dugan, vase, 6", purple, has open bubble on base, $25.

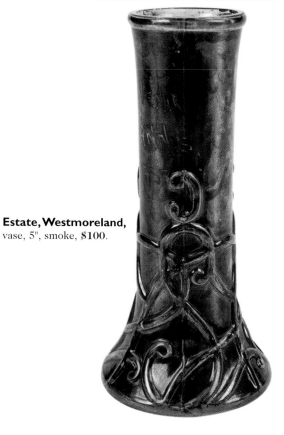

Estate, Westmoreland,
vase, 5", smoke, $100.

Fanciful

Made by Dugan.

Colors known: amethyst, blue, electric blue, electric purple, lavender, marigold, peach opalescent, purple, root beer, and white.

Forms: bowls and plates.

Identifying characteristics: A design that looks like quilted strawberries dance around an inner border with scrolls.

Also known as: Battenburg Lace #3C.

Fanciful, Dugan, low 10-ruffled bowl, 9", purple, $300-$600; outstanding condition, $1,300.

Fantail

Made by Fenton.

Colors known: blue, green, marigold, and white.

Forms: bowls and chop plates.

Identifying characteristics: This pattern is a whimsical depiction of six swirling peacock tails, which come together in the center. Butterfly & Berry is often used as the exterior pattern. Production began in 1911.

Also known as: Peacock Tail and Daisy.

Reproductions: 9" bowls with the Butterfly and Berry exterior are known in blue and red, complete with the original Fenton logo.

Fantail, Fenton, ice cream-shaped bowl, 9", blue, $250-$350.

Farmyard

Made by Dugan.

Colors known: green, peach opalescent, and purple.

Forms: bowls.

Identifying characteristics: This pattern is found on the interior of bowls and features a rooster and chickens. The exterior pattern used is Jeweled Heart.

Also known as: Busy Chickens.

Reproductions: Reproductions of bowls and chop plates are known in contemporary colors.

Farmyard, Dugan, bowl, ruffled, purple, $5,500.

Fashion

Made by Imperial.

Colors known: clambroth, emerald green, helios, horehound, marigold, purple, and smoke.

Forms: bowls, breakfast sets, compotes, punch cups, rose bowls, and water sets.

Identifying characteristics: Fashion is one of Imperial's imitation cut-glass patterns. It's not quite as detailed as most, but includes a hobstar and zippered band, as well as fans and diamonds. Production began in 1910.

Also known as: Imperial's #402-1/2

Reproductions: This pattern never was made in a toothpick holder, but those creating reproductions made one, often found in blue, purple, or red.

Fashion, Imperial, tumbler, smoke, $150.

Fashion, Imperial, tumbler, 4-1/4", purple, $300-$500; outstanding condition, $800 (rare).

Fashion, Imperial, rose bowl, 6-1/2" wide, purple, $1,200-$1,600; outstanding condition, $2,400.

Fashion, Imperial, pitcher, 8-1/2", purple, $900-$1,500; outstanding condition, $2,500 (rare).

Fashion, Imperial, compote, smoke, $900.

Feather and Heart

Made by Millersburg.

Colors known: amethyst, green, and marigold.

Forms: water sets and whimsies.

Identifying characteristics: This pattern features well-defined feathers over arcs containing hobstars, diamonds, and fans. Produced from 1910 until 1912.

Also known as: Heart Band and Herringbone.

Feather and Heart, Millersburg, water pitcher and six tumblers, dark marigold, **$875**.

Feathered Serpent

Made by Fenton.

Colors known: amethyst, blue, green, and marigold.

Forms: bowls.

Identifying characteristics: This pattern is a series of feathered swirls with four swirled feathers in the center. Production began in 1910.

Also known as: Feathered Scroll.

Feathered Serpent, Fenton, lady's spittoon, 3-3/4" w, 2-1/4" h, green, **$7,500**.

Feathered Serpent, Fenton, bowl, candy-ribbon edge, amethyst, **$150**.

Fentonia

Made by Fenton.

Colors known: blue and marigold.

Forms: berry sets, table sets, and water sets.

Identifying characteristic: Fentonia is one of Fenton's all-over patterns of diamonds filled with scales and embroidery stitches.

Also known as: Diamond and Cable.

Fentonia, Fenton, water pitcher and two tumblers (one shown), blue, **$875**.

Field Flower

Made by Imperial.

Colors known: amber, aqua, clambroth, cobalt blue, helios, marigold, olive, purple, red, smoke, and violet.

Forms: milk pitchers and water sets.

Identifying characteristics: The design is a flower framed by two strands of wheat, all on a stippled background, double arches border the stippling and serve as panels. Production began in 1912.

Field Flower, Fenton, water pitcher and six tumblers, marigold, $450.

Field Flower, Imperial, tumbler, 4", purple, $90-$150.

Field Flower, Imperial, water pitcher, 9", purple, $400-$700; outstanding condition, $1,200.

Field Thistle

Made by U.S. Glass.

Colors known: green, ice blue, and marigold.

Forms: berry sets, breakfast sets, compotes, plates, table sets, and water sets.

Identifying characteristics: A motif of thistles and open-petaled flowers swirl from a flower center.

Field Thistle, Jenkins, vase, light marigold, $325.

File

Made by Imperial.

Colors known: marigold and purple.

Forms: bowls, compotes, table sets, and water pitchers.

Identifying characteristics: As the name implies, this pattern looks like a series of two rows small files standing upright.

Also known as: Imperial's #256.

File, Imperial, ruffled bowl, electric purple, $55.

File, Imperial, water pitcher and six tumblers, marigold, $600.

Fine Rib

Made by Fenton.

Colors known: amberina, amethyst, aqua, aqua opalescent, blue, celeste blue, green, lime green opalescent, marigold, marigold over milk glass, peach opalescent, powder blue, red, sapphire blue, teal, smoke, and vaseline.

Forms: bowls, vases, and plates.

Identifying characteristics: This pattern is divided into six sections, each having six ribs when the base is large. Smaller bases have five ribs. Base diameters of the standard size vases range from 2-1/4 inches to 2-3/4 inches, with the large standard size vase having a diameter of 3 inches. Heights of vases range from 8 inches to 17 inches. Look for a banded top edge on Fenton's Fine Rib vases, which helps distinguish it from the plain top edge on Northwood's Fine Rib. Production began in 1911.

Also known as: Fenton's #1126.

Fine Rib, Fenton, vase, red opal, $600.

Fine Rib, Fenton, vase, 9-1/2", red with red streaks, $450.

Fine Rib, Fenton, vase, 10", red, $300-$500.

Fine Rib

Made by Northwood.

Colors known: amethyst/purple, blue, green, ice blue, ice green, marigold, sapphire, and white.

Forms: vases.

Identifying characteristics: This finely ribbed pattern has ribs that are of equal size. The top edge is plain. The base should measure 3-1/2" d. Some are marked with the Northwood trademark "N."

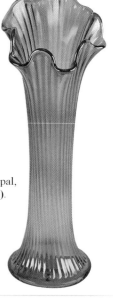

Fine Rib, Northwood,
standard vase, 11", aqua opal,
$1,200-$1,900 (very rare).

Fisherman's Mug

Made by Dugan/Diamond.

Colors known: amethyst, blue, custard, horehound, lavender, marigold, and peach opalescent.

Forms: mug.

Identifying characteristics: This mug must have been designed with a fisherman in mind as it shows a fish, water lilies, and cattails. The design is found only on one side, the other side is blank. Butler Brothers included this pattern in its 1911 catalog. Production continued from 1911 until 1914.

Also known as: Cattails and Fish.

Reproductions by L. G. Wright.

Fisherman's, Dugan,
mug, 4", purple, $100-$250.

Fisherman's, Dugan,
mug, 4", amethyst, $100-$250.

Fisherman's, Dugan, mug, 4", marigold,
$200-$300; outstanding condition, $600.

Fisherman's, Dugan, mug, 4", peach opal,
$1,000-$1,200 (rare).

Fisherman's, Dugan,
mug, 4", blue, $1,000-$1,200 (rare).

Fish Scale and Beads

Made by Dugan.

Colors known: amber, amethyst/purple, aqua, marigold, pastels, peach opalescent, and white.

Forms: bowls and plates.

Identifying characteristics: This pattern was named Fishscale and Beads by carnival researcher Marion T. Hartung. It does look like fish scales with its honeycomb design on the interior, while a garland of beads is on the exterior.

Also known as: Honeycomb Collar; Honeycomb Variant.

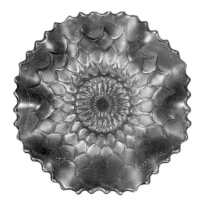

Fishscales and Beads, Dugan, bowl, marigold, $55.

Fishscales and Beads, Dugan, small plate, 6", purple, $200-$300; outstanding condition, $600.

Fleur De Lis

Made by Millersburg.

Colors known: amethyst, green, marigold, and vaseline.

Forms: bowls.

Identifying characteristics: This detailed pattern has a more formal look about it with numerous fleur-de-lis shapes. It is often found with a Hobstar & Feather or Country Kitchen exterior. Production began in 1910.

Fleur De Lis, Millersburg, ruffled radium bowl, green, has minor buffing on edge, $70.

Fleur De Lis, Millersburg, square pedestal base, 8" w, 4-1/2" h, vaseline, $5,000.

Floral and Grape

Made by Dugan.

Floral and Grape Variant

Made by Fenton.

Colors known: amethyst/purple, blue, horehound, marigold, and purple.

Forms: water sets, whimsies.

Identifying characteristics: The designs used by both Fenton and Dugan are remarkably similar. Water pitchers produced by Dugan have ribs in the bands that lean to the left, while the Fenton pitchers have the same element leaning to the right. A raised cable on either side of the ribs distinguishes a tumbler as Dugan rather than Fenton, whose tumblers do not have a cable at all. Production was from 1910 to 1911.

Also known as: Floral and Grapevine.

Floral and Grape Variant, Fenton, tankard, candy-ribbon edge, 9-1/2" h, blue, $300-$500; outstanding condition, $900.

Floral and Grape Variant, Fenton, tumbler, 4" h, blue, $60-$120.

Floral and Grape, Fenton, pitcher, white, has internal fracture in handle, $75.

Floral and Grape, Dugan, ruffled-top pitcher, 8-1/2" h, purple, $250-$400.

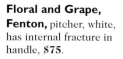

Floral and Optic

Made by Imperial.

Colors known: clambroth, marigold, marigold on milk glass, purple, red, smoke, teal, and white.

Forms: bowls, cake plates, and rose bowls.

Identifying characteristics: This common paneled pattern features a border band with fines, flowers, and leaves. Production began in 1914.

Floral and Optic, Imperial, bowl, footed, red, $150.

Floral and Optic, Imperial, rose bowl, footed, marigold over milk glass, $250.

Flowers and Frames

Made by Dugan.

Colors known: peach opalescent and purple.

Forms: bowls.

Identifying characteristics: This pattern has six loops that form frames which each contain one stemmed flower with leaves. Fleur-de-lis shapes protrude from each of the Vs formed by the loops. Production began in 1910.

Flowers & Frames, Dugan, tri-corner bowl, 9", purple, $400-$600; outstanding condition, $900.

Flowers & Frames, Dugan, 10-ruffled bowl, 9", purple, $300-$450.

Fluffy Peacock

Made by Fenton.

Colors known: amethyst, cobalt blue, green, and marigold.

Forms: water sets.

Identifying characteristics: One of the peacock patterns, Fenton used a rather stylized peacock for this design with a large feather being used as a divider between panels.

Fluffy Peacock, Fenton, water pitcher and six tumblers, amethyst, $1,050.

Flute

Made by Imperial.

Colors known: aqua, blue, clambroth, emerald green, helios, lime green, marigold, purple, red, smoke, and vaseline.

Forms: berry sets, bowls, breakfast sets, cruets, cups, punch sets, table sets, toothpicks, vases, and water sets.

Identifying characteristics: Imperial used a simple side paneled loop to create this popular pattern. Production began in 1909.

Also known as: Imperial's #700.

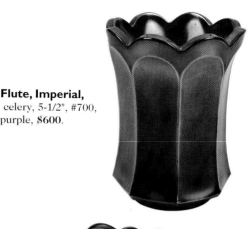

Flute, Imperial, celery, 5-1/2", #700, purple, $600.

Flute, Imperial, vase, squatty, smokey blue, damage, $150.

Flute, Imperial, water pitcher and six tumblers (one shown), #700, purple, $1,650.

Flute, Imperial, toothpick holder, 2-1/4", green, $60-$90.

Flute, Imperial, toothpick holder, 2-1/4", purple, $70-$90.

Flute, Imperial, toothpick holder, 2-1/4", blue, $700-$1,000 (rare).

Flute, Imperial, sugar bowl, 3-1/4" h, purple, $80-$100.

Flute

Made by Northwood.

Colors known: amethyst, aqua opalescent, blue, green, marigold, sapphire blue, vaseline, white.

Forms: berry sets, breakfast sets, nut cups, plates, salts, sherbets, table sets, vases, water sets.

Identifying characteristics: Northwood used twelve wide panels as their flutes.

Also known as: Northwood's #21.

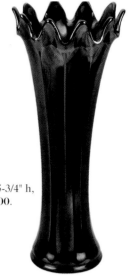

Flute, Northwood, funeral vase, mid-size, 15-3/4" h, 4-3/4" base, purple, $1,200.

Flute and Cane

Made by Imperial.

Colors known: marigold.

Forms: bowls, compotes, milk pitchers, stemware, and water sets.

Identifying characteristics: This pattern has narrower flutes which top a band of cane pattern. Production began in 1909.

Also known as: Cane.

Flute and Cane, Imperial, milk pitcher, small, marigold, $150.

Flute and Cane, Imperial, tumbler, marigold, $450.

Formal

Made by Dugan.

Colors known: black amethyst, marigold, and purple.

Forms: hatpin holders and vases.

Identifying characteristics: This pattern features vertical rows of mirrored dots separated by a band of random threading.

Formal, Dugan, jack-in-the-pulpit vase, 7", black amethyst, $600-$900; outstanding condition, $1,300.

Four Flowers

Made by Dugan, Diamond, and possibly Riihimaki.

Colors known: amethyst, green, marigold, peach opalescent, powder blue, and smoke.

Forms: bowls and plates.

Identifying characteristics: Four Flowers is a bold pattern with four open flowers alternating with a pointed oval. The design forms a striking geometric design.

Also known as: Posy and Pods; Pods and Posies; Stippled Posy and Pods.

Four Flowers, Dugan, eight-ruffled bowl, 10", purple, $300-$500; outstanding condition, $1,700.

Four Flowers Variant

Attributed to Dugan and Eda Glassworks, Sweden.

Colors known: Dugan: amber, amethyst/purple, black amethyst, green, marigold, peach opalescent, teal, vaseline; Eda: lavender, and teal.

Forms: bowls and plates.

Identifying characteristics: This variation shows pointed ovals that are a little broader, allowing room for a flower bud in each. The alternating flowers are also less full blossomed.

Four Pillars

Made by Northwood, Dugan, Diamond.

Colors known: amber, amethyst, aqua opalescent, green, ice blue, ice green, lime green, marigold, olive green, peach opalescent, and white.

Forms: vases.

Identifying characteristics: This pattern features sturdy looking ribs with graceful ribs between each corner. Forms with advertising on the base are known. Some pieces are marked with the Diamond D mark.

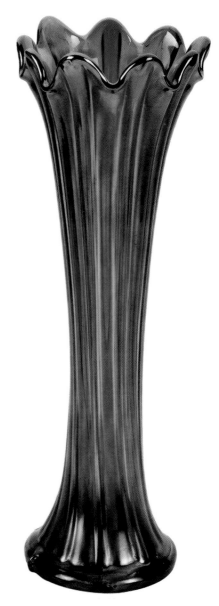

Four Pillar, Northwood, vase, 9-1/2", blue, damaged feet, $200.

Four Seventy Four

Made by Imperial.

Colors known: aqua, cobalt blue, emerald green, helios, lavender, lime green, marigold, olive green, purple, red, teal, and violet.

Forms: bowls, compotes, punch bowls, stemware, vases, and water sets.

Identifying characteristics: This pattern features an open cut-type flower with petals, stem, leaves with bands of cane like elements. This pattern was popular in crystal, as well as carnival glass. Production began in 1911.

Also known as: Imperial's #474; Mayflower.

Reproductions: New colors and forms were made in the 1960s-70s as compotes, covered boxes, mugs, salt and pepper shakers, sugar shakers, vases, and water sets.

Four Seventy Four, Imperial, vase, 10", marigold.

Four Seventy Four, Imperial, punch bowl base and six cups, marigold, **$100**.

Four Seventy Four, Imperial, water pitcher and six tumblers, marigold, **$575**.

Frolicking Bears

Made by U.S. Glass.

Colors known: gunmetal luster over olive green.

Forms: water sets.

Identifying characteristics: This oddity has bears enjoying their natural habitat, with mountains in the background, and grapes on a grapevine twist around the top. Even the handle has a twig-like quality to its design. This is an extremely rare pattern.

Also known as: Bears Tumbler.

Reproductions: The International Carnival Glass Association commissioned this pattern in several new forms to be used as its convention souvenirs. These are becoming quite collectible, too.

Frolicking Bears, U.S. Glass, water pitcher and one tumbler, green, one of three known, **$42,000**.

Fruits and Flowers

Made by Northwood.

Colors known: amethyst/purple, amethyst opalescent, aqua opalescent, blue, electric blue, green, ice blue, ice blue opalescent, ice green, lavender, marigold, Renninger blue, sapphire blue, teal, violet, and white.

Forms: berry sets, bonbons, and plates.

Identifying characteristics: This pattern features realistic cherries, apples, and pears, plus flower blossoms. The centers are plain. Backgrounds can be plain or stippled. Production began in 1911.

Reproductions: Bonbons were made by Fenton in purple in the 1970s. L. G. Wright made 14" chop plates and bowls. The chop plates include a fake Northwood "N" logo.

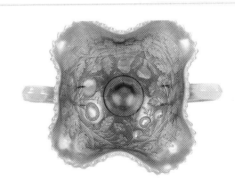

Fruits and Flowers, Northwood, bon bon, two handles, aqua opal, **$450**.

Garden Path
Garden Path Variant

Made by Dugan.

Colors known: amethyst/purple, marigold, peach opalescent, and white.

Forms: bowls, chop plates, and rose bowls.

Identifying characteristics: These two patterns are very similar. Garden Path features a busy field of hearts, fleur-de-lis, and arches. Garden Path Variant has an additional six winged hearts. Values for each pattern are the same.

Garden Path Variant, Dugan, bowl, 9-1/2", ice-cream shape, purple, $1,100-$1,400.

Garden Path Variant, Dugan, chop plate, 11", purple, $3,000-$6,000; outstanding condition (scarce), $13,500.

Garden Path Variant, Dugan, small plate, 7", purple, $900-$1,200 (rare).

Gay Nineties

Made by Millersburg.

Colors known: amethyst, green, and marigold.

Forms: water sets.

Identifying characteristics: This is a rare pattern that features stripes of leaf veining alternating with a smooth ray that has a stippled petal at the base.

Gay Nineties, Millersburg, water pitcher and one tumbler, green. Only one perfect known, second known pitcher, second known tumbler, $24,000.

God and Home

Made by Dugan, later by Diamond.

Colors known: cobalt blue.

Forms: water sets.

Identifying characteristics: The pattern features a laurel wreath and shield, a rising sun with long rays. One side is lettered "In God We Trust," the other side reads "God Bless Our Home." Production began in 1912.

Also known as: Constitution.

Reproductions: Reproductions have been by L. G. Wright in amethyst, cobalt blue, green, ice green, and red. They contain the Westmoreland "W" in circle trademark. Ice blue production was made in 1976 for Levay.

God and Home, Diamond, water pitcher and six tumblers, blue. First set ever sold at auction, $2,250.

Good Luck

Made by Northwood.

Colors known: amethyst/purple, aqua, aqua opalescent, blue, green, horehound, ice blue, ice blue opalescent, ice green, lavender, lime green, marigold, peach opalescent, Renninger blue, sapphire blue, teal, and white.

Forms: bowls and plates.

Identifying characteristics: Look for the traditional good luck sign, a horseshoe and the words "Good Luck" in the center of this design. A riding crop crosses the center of the horseshoe while floral sprays dance around the rest of the design. Bowls and plates may have basket weave, ribbed, or stippled features, and values are fairly similar. Production began in 1911.

Reproductions: Ruffled bowls have been reproduced by Fenton in light amethyst and contain a modern Fenton logo. Ruffled bowls also are known in blue, green, and marigold, and they exhibit a harsh metallic iridescence.

Good Luck, Northwood, eight-ruffled bowl, 8-1/2", marigold, **$175-$300**; outstanding condition, **$950**.

Good Luck, Northwood, eight-ruffled bowl, 8-1/2", sapphire, **$1,600-$2,300**.

Good Luck, Northwood, eight-ruffled bowl, 8-1/2", ice blue, **$3,500-$4,500**.

Good Luck, Northwood, plate, 9", Electric blue, **$4,500-$5,500**; outstanding condition, **$8,000**.

Good Luck, Northwood, bowl, 8-1/2", ruffle/rib, ice blue, **$4,000**.

Good Luck, Northwood, bowl, blue, enameled; only one known, **$800**.

Good Luck, Northwood, bowl, ribbed exterior, ruffled, sapphire, **$2,100**.

Gothic Arches

Made by Imperial.

Colors known: marigold and smoke.

Forms: vases.

Identifying characteristics: This interesting pattern has large graceful arched loops that start at the flared top and gently flow to the round base.

Reproductions: Reproduction vases have been made by Imperial in ice blue and pale yellow.

Gothic Arches, Imperial, vase, 11", mouth 8", marigold, **$1,200.**

Gothic Arches, Imperial, vase, 11", mouth is 7-1/2", smoke, **$1,100.**

Grape and Cable

Made by Fenton.

Colors known: amberina, amethyst, blue, celeste blue, green, lime green, marigold, marigold over milk glass, moonstone, powder blue, red, vaseline, and violet blue.

Forms: bowls and plates.

Identifying characteristics: Fenton's Grape and Cable is bolder than the Northwood design. Expect to find large oval-shaped grapes and large leaves as well as the cable design. Orange bowls in this pattern sometimes are found with a Persian Medallion interior pattern. Production began in 1920 and continued until 1925. Scroll feet forms usually are Fenton, as are scalloped and fluted edges.

Also known as: Fenton Grape.

Reproductions: Ruffled bowls and spittoons, made from an original humidor mold, are known. Fenton produced a punch set in light amethyst and called in Paneled Grape. Noted carnival glass researcher Rose Presznick had Fenton make amethyst humidors in 1969. However, these are marked with Fenton's logo and information about Presznick's museum.

Grape and Cable, Fenton, bowl, 6", ice-cream shaped, red-slag, **$225.**

Grape and Cable

Made by Northwood.

Colors known: amethyst, aqua, aqua opalescent, black amethyst, blue, electric blue, emerald green, green, horehound, ice blue, ice green, lavender, lime green, marigold, pastels, peach opalescent, pearl (custard), purple, sapphire blue, smoke, teal, and white.

Forms: an extensive pattern, with more than 30 forms known.

Identifying characteristics: Grape and Cable represents the largest number of pieces of any carnival glass pattern. Look for delicate grapes, detailed leaves, and tendrils, along with a detailed cable running through each form. Both Northwood and Fenton made forms with spatula-shaped feet and collar bases. Bowls with piecrust edges are Northwood. Northwood began to produce this ever-popular pattern in 1910.

Reproductions: Reproductions include a butter dish made by Mosser in amber, cobalt blue, and ice blue. Fenton is making a variety of shapes and finishes using original Northwood molds for the descendents of the Northwood family. Hatpin holders have also been reproduced.

Grape and Cable, Northwood, fernery with crystal inset, amethyst, damage, $400.

Grape and Cable, Northwood, bowl, one point ground, pie-crust edge/rib, aqua opal pastel, $3,000.

Grape and Cable, Northwood, tumbler, 4", lavender, $100-$150.

Grape and Cable, Northwood, cologne, 9", purple, $250-$350.

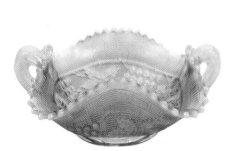

Grape and Cable, Northwood, bon bon, stippled, aqua opal, $4,000.

Grape and Cable, Northwood, hatpin holder, aqua opal, $20,000.

Grape and Cable, Northwood, hatpin holder, 7", green, $250-$400.

Grape and Cable, Northwood, hatpin holder, 7", purple, $250-$400.

Grape and Gothic Arches

Made by Northwood.

Colors known: blue, electric blue, marigold, pearl (custard), and smoke.

Forms: berry sets, table sets, vases, and water sets.

Identifying characteristics: Arches reminiscent of Grandmother's grape arbor form a border over the full grapes of this pattern. Also made in crystal, and crystal, with gold decoration. Pattern made from 1910 until 1916.

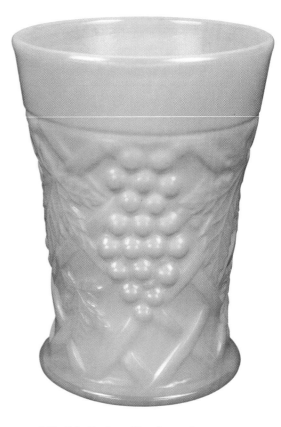

Grape and Gothic Arches, Northwood, tumbler, pearlized custard, $800.

Grape and Gothic Arches, Northwood, tumbler, 4", blue, $50-$125.

Grape and Gothic Arches, Northwood, water pitcher and two tumblers (one shown), emerald green, $4,250.

Grape Arbor

Made by Northwood.

Colors known: amethyst/purple, blue, ice blue, ice green, iridized custard, marigold, and white.

Forms: hats and water sets.

Identifying characteristics: This three-dimensional pattern features large life-like grapes and leaves, with a lattice design around the bases of the tumblers and water sets. Northwood also made this pattern in custard glass. Dugan made a similar pattern, which was less three-dimensional than Northwood's.

Grape Arbor, Northwood, water pitcher, electric blue, $14,000.

Grape Arbor, Northwood, tumbler, 4-1/4", electric blue, $400-$550.

Grape Arbor, Northwood, tumbler, 4-1/4", lavender, $150-$250.

Grape Arbor, Northwood, tankard, 11-1/2", purple, $600-$900.

Grape Arbor, Northwood, water pitcher and one tumbler, ice green, one of three known, $10,000.

Grape Delight

Made by Dugan/Diamond.

Colors known: amethyst, black amethyst, blue, electric purple, horehound, marigold, peach opalescent, and white.

Forms: nut bowls and rose bowls.

Identifying characteristics: This pattern features round, plump grapes and full, well-defined leaves.

Reproductions: Highly reproduced, some with a fake Northwood mark. Reproductions are known in amethyst, blue, ice blue, ice green, and white.

Grape Delight, Dugan,
rose bowl, footed, electric purple, $80.

Grape Leaves

Made by Northwood.

Colors known: amber, amethyst, black amethyst, blue, ice blue, green, lavender, and marigold.

Forms: bowls.

Identifying characteristics: This grape pattern features a cluster of four grape stems and leaves and four bunches of grapes that cluster in the center and radiate toward the edges. The exterior pattern often found with this pattern is Blossom and Palm. Production was from 1900 until 1912.

Also known as: Wild Grapes.

Grape Leaves, Northwood,
ruffled bowl, lavender, $50.

Grape Leaves, Northwood,
ruffled bowl, marigold, $10.

Grapevine Lattice

Made by Dugan/Diamond.

Colors known: amethyst, marigold, and white.

Forms: bowls, hats, plates, and water sets.

Identifying characteristics: This pattern features detailed criss-crossed twigs. It is similar to Apple Blossom and Twigs, but has no flowers. Production began in 1912 and continued into the 1920s.

Also known as: Grapevine Diamonds.

Reproductions: L. G. Wright has made reproduction water sets.

Grapevine and Lattice, Dugan, ruffled bowl, 7", white, $30.

Grapevine Lattice, Dugan,
water pitcher and two tumblers, white, $1,000.

Grapevine Lattice, Dugan,
plate, 7-1/2", flat, purple, $250-$400.

Greek Key

Made by Northwood.

Colors known: amethyst/purple, blue, green, ice green, and marigold.

Forms: bowls, plates, and water sets.

Identifying characteristics: A band of a traditional Greek Key design flows through this pattern. This pattern began production in 1909 and found such favor with buyers that it was expanded to other forms in 1911 and production continued until 1913.

Greek Key, Northwood,
tankard, 11-1/2", purple, $700-$1,100.

Greek Key, Northwood,
tumbler, 4-1/4", green, $100-$150.

Greek Key, Northwood,
tumbler, 4 1/4" purple, $125-$200.

Greek Key, Northwood,
bowl, 9", pie-crust edge, electric blue, $700.

Greek Key, Northwood,
water pitcher and six tumblers, amethyst, $2,000.

Hanging Cherries

Made by Millersburg.

Colors known: amethyst, blue, green, and marigold.

Forms: bowls, chop plates, compotes, table sets, and water sets.

Identifying characteristics: Clusters of hanging cherries dominate this popular pattern.

Also known as: Millersburg Cherries.

Reproductions: Fenton made a very similar pattern in 1974. Production was limited to amethyst creamer and sugars.

Hattie

Made by Imperial.

Colors known: amber, clambroth, helios, marigold, purple, and smoke.

Forms: bowls, chop plates, and rose bowls.

Identifying characteristics: This detailed pattern features arched lines and floral elements and is the only carnival glass pattern used on both the interior and exterior. Production began in 1911.

Also known as: Imperial's #496; Busy Lizzie.

Reproductions: Reproduction bowls are known in green, pink, smoke, and white. This bowls are all marked with the IG trademark.

Hanging Cherries, Millersburg,
water pitcher and six tumblers, green pitcher is damaged, $3,200.

Hattie, Imperial, chop plate, 10", purple, $1,600-$2,000.

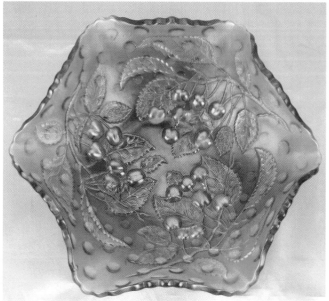

Hanging Cherries, Millersburg,
bowl, ruffled, marigold, Hobnail exterior, $1,400.

Hearts and Flowers

Made by Northwood.

Colors known: amethyst, aqua opalescent, blue, blue opalescent, clambroth, electric blue, green, ice blue, ice green, lavender, marigold, pearl (custard), purple, and white.

Forms: bowls, compotes, and plates.

Identifying characteristics: This intricate pattern features a circular band of heart shapes. Production began in 1912.

Also known as: Battenburg Lace #1.

Reproductions: Domed 11" ruffled bowls are known in amberina, amethyst, and red and usually have the Fenton logo.

Hearts and Flowers, Northwood, compote, 6", marigold, $150-$300.

Hearts and Flowers, Northwood, bowl, 8", ruffle/rib, ice blue, $400.

Hearts and Flowers, Northwood, compote (top view), 6", purple, $400-$700.

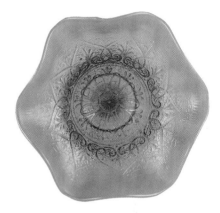

Hearts and Flowers, Northwood, compote (top view), 6", aqua opal, $600-$1,000.

Hearts and Flowers, Northwood, compote, 6", Renninger blue, $1,500-$2,000.

Hearts and Flowers, Northwood, compote, 6", electric blue, $400-$600; outstanding condition, $900.

Hearts and Flowers, Northwood, compote, 6", green, $1,500-$2,000 (scarce).

Heavy Grape

Made by Imperial.

Colors known: amber, purple, aqua, cobalt blue, helios, ice green, light blue with marigold overlay, marigold, olive green, purple, smoke, and white.

Forms: bowls, chop plates, nappy, plates, and punch sets.

Identifying characteristics: This member of the carnival grape pattern family is enhanced by a diamond-quilted effect around the edge and a simple fluted back. Production began in 1910.

Also known as: Imperial's #700; Imperial's Heavy Grape.

Reproductions: Fenton has reproduced this pattern using original Imperial molds, but included the Fenton logo. The 7-1/2" w ruffled bowl was made in aqua opalescent as a convention souvenir for the Southern California Carnival Glass Club in 1996.

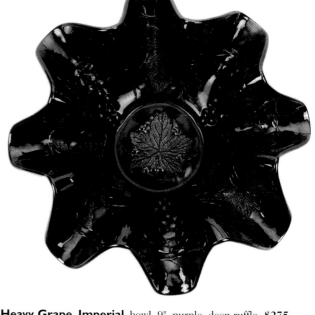

Heavy Grape, Imperial, bowl, 9", purple, deep ruffle, **$275**.

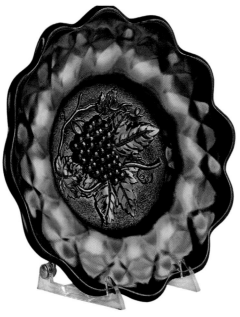

Heavy Grape, Imperial, plate, 8", purple, **$100-$200**.

Heavy Grape, Imperial, chop plate, 11", purple, **$400-$800**.

Heavy Grape, Imperial, deep round bowl, 6-1/2", blue, **$600-$1,000 (rare)**.

Heavy Iris

Made by Dugan.

Colors known: amber, amethyst, ice blue, horehound, lavender, marigold, pastel marigold, peach opalescent, purple, and white.

Forms: water sets.

Identifying characteristics: This pattern was very sculpted, giving it a realistic three-dimensional quality.

Also known as: Iris.

Reproductions: L. G. Wright reproduced this pattern in 1978. Reproductions can be identified because they have a plain band around the top between the pattern and the ruffled top. Tumblers have been made in aqua opalescent, cobalt blue, and vaseline opalescent.

Heavy Iris, Dugan, tumbler, 4" h, white, $200-$300.

Heavy Iris, Dugan, tumbler, 4" h, purple, $75-$150; outstanding condition, $400.

Heavy Iris, Dugan, tumbler, purple, $150.

Heavy Iris, Dugan, water pitcher, tankard, peach opal, $2,000.

Heavy Iris, Dugan, water pitcher and one tumbler, white, tankard, $1,600.

Heron

Made by Dugan.

Colors known: amethyst, black amethyst, marigold, and purple.

Forms: mugs.

Identifying characteristics: A lonely heron, facing to the left, stands among cattails and rushes. A companion pattern is Dugan's Stork and Rushes, which has four birds.

Heron, Dugan, mug, 4", black amethyst, $250-$350.

Hobnail

Made by Millersburg.

Colors known: amethyst, blue, green, marigold, and purple.

Forms: spittoons, rose bowls, table sets, vases, and water sets.

Identifying characteristics: As the name implies, this design features pointy hobnails arranged in alternating rows. Most pieces of this interesting pattern have a brilliant radium finish. Production began in 1910 and continued until 1912.

Also known as: Stippled Dots.

Hobnail, Millersburg,
spittoon, 5" d, amethyst, $800-$1,000.

Hobnail, Millersburg,
water pitcher, blue, $4,100.

Hobnail, Millersburg,
one of four known,
tumbler, green, $2,700.

Hobnail, Millersburg,
tumbler, marigold, $1,550.

Hobnail, Millersburg,
tumbler, blue, $1,800.

Hobstar

Made by Imperial.

Colors known: emerald green, helios, marigold, purple.

Forms: bowls, bride's baskets, covered jars, pickle castors, punch sets, table sets.

Identifying characteristics: This typically geometric pattern from Imperial features a large hobstar surrounded by circle arches of diamond borders, fans, and other typical imitation cut-glass elements. Carnival production began in 1912, production of crystal began before that time.

Also known as: Imperial's #282.

Reproductions: Green cracker jars, complete with the IG logo, are known. Punch sets were also reissued by Imperial.

Hobstar, Imperial, creamer, purple, $100-$180.

Hobstar, Imperial, covered butter dish, purple, $200-$300.

Hobstar and Feather

Made by Millersburg.

Colors: amethyst, clear, frosted, green, marigold, and white.

Forms: bowls, compotes, punch sets, rose bowls, table sets, water sets, and whimsies.

Identifying characteristics: large feathered leafed stems dominate this large-scale pattern with large hobstars filling the space between each leaf. Production began in 1910.

Also known as: Intaglio Mazie.

Reproductions: Reproduced tumblers are reported.

Hobstar and Feather, Millersburg, punch bowl base and eight cups, master, marigold, $2,750.

Hobstar Flower

Made by Imperial.

Colors known: emerald green, helios, lavender, marigold, purple, and smoke.

Forms: compotes.

Identifying characteristics: This geometric pattern features a large hobstar along with the popular imitation cut glass motifs that Imperial designers so often used. Production began in 1909.

Also known as: Imperial's #302 and #302-1/2.

Hobstar Flower, Imperial, compote, 5" h, purple, $100-$200.

Holly

Made by Fenton.

Colors known: amethyst, aqua opalescent, blue, blue opalescent, celeste blue, green, lime green, lime green opalescent, marigold, marigold on milk glass, moonstone, powder blue, red, vaseline, and white.

Forms: bowls, compotes, goblets, hat, plates, rose bowls, and vases.

Identifying characteristics: Fenton's popular Holly pattern features sprigs of holly berries and leaves that converge in the center and radiate to the edges of the pattern. Production began in 1911.

Also known as: Carnival Holly.

Reproductions: Ruffled bowls have been reproduced in aqua opalescent and amethyst.

Holly, Fenton,
flat plate, 9-1/2", marigold, $200-$300.

Holly, Fenton,
flat plate, 9-1/2", blue, $300-$500.

Holly, Fenton,
flat plate, 9-1/2", green, $700-$900.

Holly, Fenton,
flat plate, 9-1/2", amethyst, $700-$1,000.

Holly, Fenton, bowl, 9", ruffled, red, $1,200.

Holly, Fenton,
bowl, 3-in-1 edge, marigold over milk glass, $2,000.

Holly, Fenton, rose bowl, blue, $275.

Holly and Berry

Made by Dugan.

Colors known: black amethyst, blue, marigold, peach opalescent, and purple.

Forms: bowls and nappies.

Identifying characteristics: This holly pattern features springs of holly and large berries that surround the center motif of more leaves and berries. Production began in 1909 and continued until 1912.

Holly & Berry, Dugan,
six-ruffled bowl, 7-1/2", purple, $100-$200.

Holly & Berry, Dugan,
seven-ruffled nappy, 7", purple, $100-$200.

Holly & Berry, Dugan,
tri-corner nappy, 7", purple, $100-$200.

Holly Sprig

Made by Millersburg.

Colors known: amethyst, clambroth, green, lavender, marigold, and vaseline.

Forms: bonbons, bowls, calling card trays, and nappies

Identifying characteristics: Millersburg's Holly Sprig has a wreath of holly leaves and small berries, with four leaves that point to the blank center. This interior pattern is often paired Near Cut Wreath of Flute on the exterior. Production began in 1910.

Also known as: Holly; Holly Spray; Millersburg Holly.

Holly Sprig, Millersburg,
bowl, purple with radium iridescence, $100.

Homestead

Made by Imperial.

Colors known: amber, cobalt blue, electric purple, emerald green, forest green, helios, marigold, purple, smoke, and white.

Forms: chop plates, with some marked "Nu-Art."

Identifying characteristics: Original chop plates have a ribbed back and smooth base. Production began in 1911.

Also known as: Imperial's #525; Nu-Art Homestead; and Nu-Art Currier and Ives.

Reproductions: Imperial reissued this chop plate in ice blue, marigold, pink, smoke, and white. Reproduction chop plates have a plain back and stippled base. Another reproduction by Summit Art Glass Company is known in vaseline.

Homestead, Imperial,
chop plate, electric purple, signed NuArt, $3,200.

Homestead, Imperial,
chop plate, pastel and radium marigold. First one seen with radium iridescence, signed Nuart, $450.

Imperial Grape

Made by Imperial.

Colors known: amber, aqua, clambroth, cobalt blue, emerald green, helios, horehound, lavender, light blue with marigold overlay, marigold, marigold over milk glass, olive green, purple, smoke, and violet.

Forms: bowls, compotes, cups and saucers, plates, water sets, and wine sets.

Identifying characteristics: This extensive pattern is found with lush round grapes attached to meandering grapevines, realistic leaves, plus an arched border trim. The molded handles are texture to resemble the bark found on grapevines. Production began in 1912.

Also known as: Imperial's #473; Grape.

Reproductions: Imperial reissued this pattern in the 1960s. Forms it issued include a small bowl, pedestal creamer and sugar, cruet, goblet, footed juice glasses, salt and pepper shakers, water carafe, wine set, and other forms. Colors of new Imperial forms include amber, aurora jewels, helios, marigold, smoke, and other colors. The Imperial molds have been sold to other glass companies, such as Wetzel Glass and Summit Art Glass. Colors produced by these companies include electric blue, iridized custard, red, vaseline, and possibly other colors.

Imperial Grape, Imperial,
wine decanter, 12", marigold, $70-$125.

Imperial Grape, Imperial,
punch bowl base with seven cups, electric purple, $1,700.

Imperial Grape, Imperial,
stemmed wine, 4", marigold, $20-$35.

Imperial Grape, Imperial, water pitcher, emerald green, $2,500.

Imperial Grape, Imperial, carafe, 9", emerald green, $2,000-$3,000; outstanding condition, $4,300 (rare).

Imperial Grape, Imperial, tumbler, 4", purple, $60-$100.

Imperial Grape, Imperial, water pitcher, 10-1/2", purple, $250-$400; outstanding condition, $800.

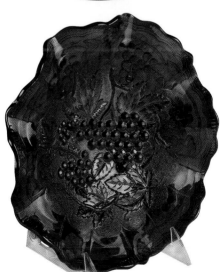

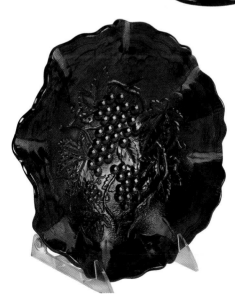

Imperial Grape, Imperial, low ruffled bowl, 9", purple, $200-$300.

Imperial Grape, Imperial, low ruffled bowl, 9", blue, $6,000 (very rare, only one known).

Imperial Grape, Imperial, flat plate, 6-1/2", purple, $250-$350.

Inverted Feather

Made by Cambridge.

Colors known: amethyst, green, and marigold.

Forms: compotes, cracker jars, milk pitchers, punch sets, stemware, table sets, and water sets.

Identifying characteristics: This geometric pattern includes a row of hobstars over upright feathers over another row of hobstars. Production began in 1915 and continued to 1917.

Also known as: Cambridge's #2651; Feather and Hobstar.

Inverted Feather,
cracker jar, green, **$175**.

Inverted Feather, Cambridge,
water pitcher and tankard, ACGA-Funk, marigold, **$8,100**.

Inverted Strawberry

Made by Cambridge.

Colors known: amethyst, blue, green, and marigold.

Forms: berry sets, candlesticks, celery vases, compotes, milk pitchers, powder jars, spittoons, table sets, and water sets.

Identifying characteristics: Cambridge made several exquisite intaglio patterns, including Inverted Strawberry and Inverted Thistle. The strawberries on this pattern are very detailed and are highlighted by strawberry blossoms and leaves. Many, but not all, pieces are marked with the trademark "Near Cut."

Reproductions: Both the tumblers and water pitchers have been reproduced. A miniature punch bowl has been created. The American Carnival Glass Association commissioned a pedestaled creamer in purple slag as its convention souvenir in 1996. Other table set forms and a spittoon were made for other ACGA conventions.

Inverted Strawberry,
water pitcher and tankard, green,
$2,800.

Inverted Thistle

Made by Cambridge.

Colors known: amethyst, blue, green, and marigold.

Forms: berry sets, chop plates, nut bowls, table sets, and water sets.

Identifying characteristics: Like Inverted Strawberry, this is an intaglio pattern with very detailed thistle blossoms and leaves.

Inverted Thistle, Cambridge,
water pitcher and six tumblers, amethyst, $1,500.

Jeweled Heart

Made by Dugan.

Colors known: amethyst, marigold, peach opalescent, and white.

Forms: bowls, plates, water sets, and whimsies.

Identifying characteristics: This pattern takes its name from the oval "jewel" included in the stylized heart that predominates the design. Carnival production began in 1910.

Also known as: Victor when found in opalescent glass.

Jeweled Heart, Dugan, water pitcher and six tumblers, pedestal, marigold, $1,600.

Kittens

Made by Fenton.

Colors known: amethyst, aqua, blue, green, marigold, pastel powder blue, teal, and topaz (vaseline).

Forms: banana boats, bowls, cups and saucers, plates, and vases.

Identifying characteristics: This pattern is one of the very few that was geared toward children and is often considered as children's toy dishes. The first ads for Fenton's Kittens appeared in 1918.

Also known as: Fenton's #299.

Kittens, Fenton, bowl, ruffled, peach opal, **$150**.

Kittens, Fenton, cup and saucer, marigold, **$200**.

Knotted Beads

Made by Fenton.

Colors known: amber, aqua, blue, marigold, red, and vaseline.

Forms: vases.

Identifying characteristics: This pattern can be identified by its four rows of six ovals, each filled with connected beading. Production began in 1915.

Also known as: Fenton's #509; Variegated Vase.

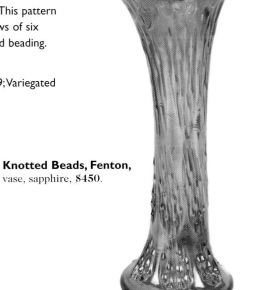

Knotted Beads, Fenton, vase, sapphire, **$450**.

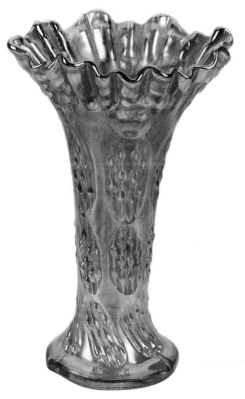

Knotted Beads, Fenton, vase, 7-1/2", candy-ribbon edge, high shelf, marigold, **$75**.

Lattice and Daisy

Made by Diamond.

Colors known: amethyst, blue, marigold, and white.

Forms: bowls, hats, and water sets.

Identifying characteristics: This elegant-looking pattern features bands of latticework along with delicate daisies and leaves. Production began in 1915 and continued until 1920.

Also known as: Daisy and Lattice Band.

Lattice and Daisy, Dugan,
water pitcher and six tumblers, tankard, marigold, **$175**.

Lattice and Grape

Made by Fenton.

Colors known: blue, marigold, and white.

Forms: water sets.

Identifying characteristics: This design has a zigzag dotted border over a cluster of grapes which are suspended over a lattice border, again with dots in the center of each diamond shaped block.

Also known as: Lattice and Grapevine.

Lattice and Grape, Fenton,
six tumblers, marigold, $60.

Lattice and Grape, Fenton,
tankard, marigold, **$100**.

Lattice and Points

Made by Dugan.

Colors known: amethyst, blue, marigold, peach opalescent, and white.

Forms: bowls and vases.

Identifying characteristics: This pattern has intersecting lines of lattice that form distinctive points. The center is a daisy.

Also known as: Vining Twigs.

Lattice and Points, Dugan,
eight-ruffled hat shape, 5-1/2", peach opal, **$75-$150**.

Lattice and Points, Dugan,
bowl, 7", low, eight ruffles, purple, **$50-$100**;
outstanding condition, **$300**.

Lattice and Points, Dugan,
vase, 8", purple, **$150-$250**.

Laurel Band

Maker unknown.

Colors known: marigold.

Forms: water sets.

Identifying characteristics: A delicate laurel-type flower highlights the band at the top of this ribbed pattern.

Laurel Band, unknown,
water pitcher and four tumblers,
pedestal, electric marigold,
$285.

Leaf and Beads

Made by Northwood.

Colors known: amethyst, aqua, aqua opalescent, blue, green, ice blue, ice green, lavender, marigold, peach opalescent, purple, Renninger blue, teal, and white.

Forms: bowls, candy dishes, nut bowls, plates, and rose bowls.

Identifying characteristics: Rows of vertical beads cascade toward the well defined leaves found at the base or center of this design. Northwood clearly used the same mold to create the rose bowl, and then widened it to create the candy dish and nut bowl forms. The interiors of the rose bowls can be plain, rayed, or have a sunflower design.

Also known as: Stippled Leaf and Beads.

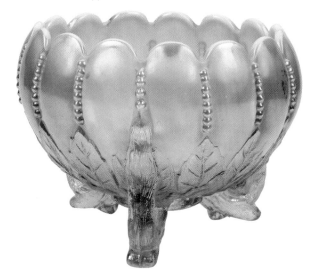

Leaf and Beads, Northwood,
rose bowl, aqua opal, $300.

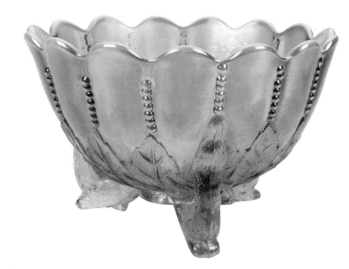

Leaf and Beads, Northwood,
nut bowl, footed, flared, aqua opal, $1,500.

Leaf Chain

Made by Fenton.

Colors known: amberina, amethyst, aqua, aqua opalescent, blue, celeste blue, clambroth, green, ice blue, ice green, lavender, marigold, red, teal, vaseline, and white.

Forms: bowls and plates.

Identifying characteristics: This busy pattern features a ring of open flowers surrounded by stars, scale background between each flower, and a looped edge. The center shows a ring of stars, scale, and an open flower. Production began in 1921.

Also known as: Leaf Medallion.

Leaf Chain, Fenton, flat plate, 9", blue, $700-$1,200; outstanding condition, $3,100.

Leaf Columns

Made by Northwood.

Colors known: amethyst, green, horehound, ice blue, ice green, marigold, purple, sapphire blue, teal, and white.

Forms: vases.

Identifying characteristics: This pattern features an upright form of leaves radiating off a center stem. The bases are a standard 3-1/2" d while the height can range from 6" to a slender 12".

Leaf Columns, Northwood, squatty vase, 6-1/2", green, **$250-$350**.

Leaf Columns, Northwood, squatty vase, 7", white, **$350-$600**.

Leaf Columns, Northwood, squatty vase, 7", purple, **$250-$350**.

Leaf Tiers

Made by Fenton.

Colors known: marigold.

Forms: berry sets, table sets, and water sets.

Identifying characteristics: This pattern features rows of detailed vertical leaves, which are staggered so they completely cover the forms.

Also known as: Stippled Leaf.

Leaf Tiers, Fenton, covered sugar and creamer, marigold, **$200**.

Leaf Tiers, Fenton, footed tumbler, marigold, one of the best, **$70**.

Leaf Tiers, Fenton, water pitcher, glued on foot, second one known in blue, **$1,150**.

Lined Lattice

Made by Dugan.

Colors known: amethyst, marigold, peach opalescent, purple, smoky lavender, and white.

Forms: vases.

Identifying characteristics: This is one of the most popular swung vase designs. The pattern includes a delicate lattice motif with each diamond the lattice creates filled in with lines. The sizes range from 5" to 15" h.

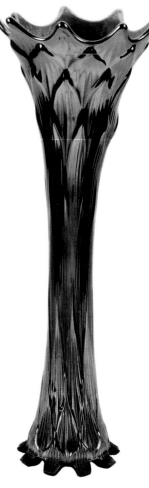

Lined Lattice, Dugan,
vase, 5-1/4", squatty, flared, peach opal,
$265.

Lined Lattice,
squatty vase, 5-1/2" h, purple, $250-$400
(scarce).

Lined Lattice, Dugan,
vase, 15", feet, amethyst, $100.

Little Fishes

Made by Fenton.

Colors known: amethyst, aqua, blue, green, and marigold.

Forms: bowls.

Identifying characteristics: A band of fish swim among decorative borders. Bases can be three ball-shaped feet or collar.

Also known as: Sea Lanes.

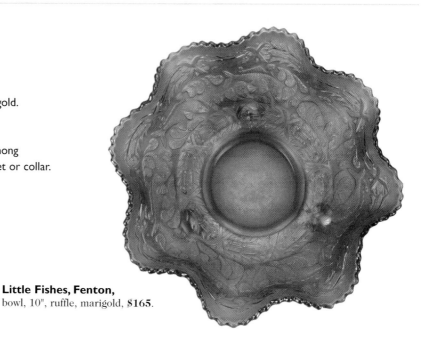

Little Fishes, Fenton,
bowl, 10", ruffle, marigold, $165.

Little Flowers

Made by Fenton.

Colors known: amberina, amethyst, aqua, blue, green, marigold, powder blue, red, and vaseline.

Forms: bowls and plates.

Identifying characteristics: Rows of large petal flowers with stems that extend to form arches are interspersed with smaller daisy-like flowers, completed by a wheel-type device center. Production began in 1910.

Also known as: Stippled Diamond and Flower.

Little Flowers, Fenton, bowl, 9-1/2", ruffle, red/amberina, $2,000.

Little Flowers, Fenton, bowl, 8", blue, $150.

Little Stars

Made by Millersburg.

Colors known: amethyst, blue, clambroth, green, marigold, and pastel marigold.

Forms: bowls and plates.

Identifying characteristics: This pattern has elongated loops each containing a stemmed flowers, small six-pointed stars alternate with the loops and stippled ground. Production began in 1910.

Also known as: Stippled Clematis.

Little Stars, Millersburg, ice-cream bowl, 9", rare size, marigold, $850.

Little Stars, Millersburg, bowl, 10", ruffle, blue, $550.

Loganberry

Made by Imperial.

Colors known: amber, emerald green, helios, marigold, purple, and smoke.

Forms: vases.

Identifying characteristics: This pattern was made only in baluster-shaped vases, using a life-like three-dimensional effect for the berries that cluster around the middle to the base. Production began in 1912.

Also known as: Imperial's #477.

Reproductions: Ruffled vases in green, ice green, and pink are known. Old vases have a plain or starred base, new ones have a stippled ground, often with the LIG or IG mark.

Loganberry, Imperial, vase, amber, $475.

Loganberry, Imperial, vase, 10", purple, $1,500-$2,800.

Long Thumbprint

Made by Fenton.

Colors known: amethyst, aqua, blue, green, marigold, and olive green.

Forms: vases.

Identifying characteristics: It is easy to see how this pattern probably got its name. Oval thumbprint-type devices vary in length as they descend to the base of these vase forms. Production was between 1911 and 1915.

Long Thumbprint, Dugan,
vase, 6-3/4", 5" mouth, amethyst, $100.

Long Thumbprint Variant,
Dugan, vase, whimsey 5-1/4", amethyst, $1,200.

Lotus and Grape

Made by Fenton.

Colors known: amethyst, aqua, blue, green, lime, marigold, Persian blue, purple, red, red slag, teal, and vaseline.

Forms: bonbons, bowls, and plates.

Identifying characteristics: This pattern shows alternating grape clusters and full blossomed lotus flowers and leaves, with two opposing lotus flowers in the center. Production of this pattern began in 1911 and continued until 1915.

Also known as: Ruffled Magnolia and Grape.

Lotus and Grape, Fenton,
ice-cream shaped bowl, Persian blue,
$575.

Lustre Rose

Made by Imperial.

Colors known: amber, amberina, aqua, clambroth, cobalt blue, emerald green, helios, lavender, light blue with marigold overlay, lime green, marigold, marigold on milk glass, purple, olive, red, smoke, teal, vaseline, and white.

Forms: berry sets, bowls, plates, table sets, vases, and water sets.

Identifying characteristics: Modern researchers have agreed that the patterns known as Lustre Rose and Open Rose are actually the same pattern. The pattern can be identified by the three-dimensional open rose and foliage that dominates each form. The backgrounds have a pebbly or stippled effect. This pattern was made from 1911 until 1914.

Also known as: Imperial's #489; Imperial Rose; Open Rose.

Reproductions: Bowls, plates, table sets, and water sets have been reproduced in amber, helios, meadow green, marigold, pink, purple, red, smoke, and white. These reproductions were made by Imperial and those who succeeded them. Imperial reproductions are marked with IG, LIG, or ALIG logos.

Lustre Rose, Imperial,
tumbler, celeste blue, $200.

Lustre Rose, Imperial,
water pitcher and six tumblers, electric purple, $2,200.

Lustre Rose, Imperial, fernery, 7-1/2", violet blue, $900-$1,200 (rare).

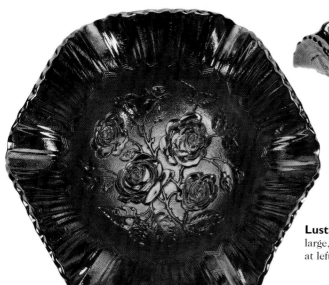

Lustre Rose, Imperial, bowl, red, footed, large, $2,500. A top view of the bowl is shown at left.

Lustre Rose, Imperial, tumbler, 5" mouth, whimsey, powder blue/marigold, $500.

Many Fruits

Made by Dugan.

Colors known: blue, green, marigold, purple, and white.

Forms: punch sets.

Identifying characteristics: The fruits found in this pattern are full and well defined, as are the leaves that compliment each fruit. Production began in 1911.

Also known as: Multi Fruits and Flowers.

Many Fruits, Dugan,
punch bowl base, base is ruffled, purple, $950.

Many Fruits, Dugan,
punch bowl base with five cups, white, ruffle, mold roughness, $1,800.

Many Stars

Made by Millersburg.

Colors known: amethyst, blue, green, and marigold.

Forms: bowls and chop plates.

Identifying characteristics: This pattern may remind collectors of starry nights with its rows of stippled stars and a bright stippled star center, which can be either a five-point or six-point star. Production began in 1910.

Many Stars, Millersburg, ruffled bowl, has radium iridescence, amethyst, **$450**.

Many Stars, Millersburg, bowl, ice-cream shape, green radium, **$375**.

Many Stars, Millersburg, bowl, 9", 3 in 1, amethyst, **$650**.

Maple Leaf

Made by Dugan/Diamond.

Colors known: amethyst, blue, green, marigold, and purple.

Forms: berry sets, table sets, and water sets.

Identifying characteristics: This exterior pattern shows a detailed maple leaf against a stippled veined background. Berry sets may have Peacock Tail as their interior pattern. Production began in 1912 and continued until 1928.

Reproductions: Westmoreland reproduced table sets and water sets for L. G. Wright. Reproduction toothpick holders and tumblers are also reported.

Maple Leaf, Dugan, spooner, pumpkin marigold, the best, $125.

Maple Leaf, Dugan, pitcher, has flake on rim, marigold, $25.

Maple Leaf, Dugan, water pitcher and one tumbler, blue, $550.

Mary Ann

Made by Dugan/Diamond.

Colors known: amethyst, lavender, marigold, pink, and purple.

Forms: loving cups and vases.

Identifying characteristics: This pattern with a well defined open flower and leaves was named for Fanny Mary Ann Dugan, sister of Thomas E. and Alfred Dugan. It can be found in crystal, satin glass, and also opalescent glass. Production began about 1915 and continued until 1918.

Also known as: Cordelia.

Reproductions.

Mary Ann, Dugan,
three-handled vase, amethyst, $800.

Memphis

Made by Northwood.

Colors known: amethyst, blue, ice blue, ice green, marigold, purple, and white.

Forms: berry sets, fruit bowls, and punch sets.

Identifying characteristics: Memphis is an ornate pattern with a checkerboard motif between the caned arcs and hobstar designs. This pattern is unique in that it comes with a stand that fits both the fruit bowl and the punch bowl. To determine which bowl is which, collectors need to study the collar base of the bowl: the punch bowl has a collar base that fits into the stand while the fruit bowl has a large octagonal collar that fits over the top of the stand.

Also known as: Northwood's #19.

Memphis, punch bowl base and six cups, green, $3,200.

Memphis, Northwood, punch bowl base with six cups, white, $4,000.

Memphis, Northwood, punch bowl base and six cups, electric marigold, $600.

Morning Glory

Made by Imperial.

Colors known: amber, clambroth, cobalt blue, emerald green, helios, lavender, light blue with marigold overlay, marigold, olive green, purple, red, smoke, and white.

Forms: pitchers, tumblers, and vases.

Identifying characteristics: As the name implies, the pattern reflects on the beauty of a morning glory with slight ribs that extend to the base. Vases range from 4" h to 22". The pattern was first advertised 1910 and continued until 1917.

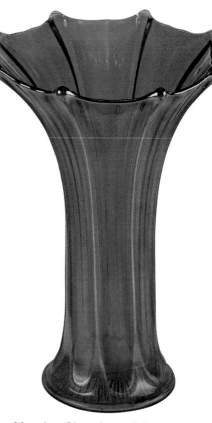

Morning Glory, Imperial,
vase 12-1/2", marigold, $200-$350.

Morning Glory, Imperial,
miniature vase, 3-1/2", marigold, shortest to be known, $150-$250.

Morning Glory, Imperial,
vase 12-1/2", purple, $500-$800.

Morning Glory, Imperial,
miniature vase, 4-3/4", smoke, $100-$180.

Morning Glory, Imperial,
miniature vase, 5", vaseline, $600-$800
(very rare).

Morning Glory, Imperial,
vase, 5", squatty, smoke, $165.

Morning Glory, Imperial,
funeral vase, 14-1/4", 8-1/2" mouth,
purple, $700.

Multi-Fruits and Flowers

Made by Millersburg.

Colors known: amethyst, green, and marigold.

Forms: compotes, punch sets, and water sets.

Identifying characteristics: Millersburg designers added as many fruits to this pattern as they could fit—cherries, peaches, pears, and grape clusters are surrounded by leaves and flowers.

Also known as: Multi-Fruits.

Multi Fruits and Flowers, water pitcher, green, $15,000.

Multi Fruits and Flowers, Millersburg,
tumbler, small chip, amethyst, $375.

Nautilus

Made by Dugan and also Northwood.

Colors known: marigold, peach opalescent, and purple.

Forms: table sets and vases.

Identifying characteristics: This pattern is modeled after a seashell and includes marine motifs on the base. The original molds were made for Northwood's custard glass production and later used by Dugan.

Also known as: Argonaut Shell when found in custard or opalescent glass.

Reproductions: Toothpick holders, never originally made by Dugan or Northwood, are now being made.

Nesting Swan

Made by Millersburg.

Colors known: amethyst, blue, green, and marigold.

Forms: bowls.

Identifying characteristics: A graceful swan dominates the center of this design, which is further enhanced by a bed of reeds, leaves, blossoms, and cattails. The exteriors are Diamond and Fan. Production began in 1911.

Nesting Swan, Millersburg,
bowl, green with satin iridescence, small
nick on rim, **$110.**

Nautilus, Dugan,
vase, 9-1/2" h, purple, **$300-$500.**

Nippon

Made by Northwood.

Colors known: amethyst, aqua, blue, green, ice blue, ice green, lime green, lime green opalescent, marigold, teal, and white.

Forms: bowls and plates.

Identifying characteristics: This design is based on graceful peacock feathers, each radiating from the center flower design. The pattern was first advertised in 1912.

Nippon, Northwood, ruffled bowl with
basket-weave exterior, purple with near-electric
iridescence, **$475.**

Octagon

Made by Imperial.

Colors known: amber, aqua, clambroth, helios, ice blue, light blue with marigold overlay, marigold, olive green, purple, smoke, teal, and white.

Forms: berry sets, nappies, stemware, toothpicks, table sets, water sets, and wine sets.

Identifying characteristics: Imperial designers included many cut-glass type motifs in this pattern which has a vertical feel to it with its upright bands of hobstars, buttons, and diamonds. Production began in 1911.

Also known as: Imperial's #505; Princess Lace.

Reproductions: Imperial has issued an 8" vase in red which contemporary carnival glass collectors call "Imperial Lace." Other shapes reissued include large bowls, butter dishes, small compotes, and toothpick holder. Reissues are found in blue or green.

Octagon, Imperial,
wine decanter, 10-1/2", purple, $1,300-$1,600 (rare).

Octagon, Imperial,
small-sized pitcher, 8", purple, $1,900-$2,300 (rare).

Octagon, Imperial,
stemmed wine, 4", purple, $100-$200; outstanding condition, $400 (rare).

Octagon, Imperial,
water pitcher, large, six tumblers, marigold, $450.

Ohio Star

Made by Millersburg.

Colors known: amethyst, clambroth, crystal, green, marigold, and white.

Forms: compotes, relishes, and vases.

Identifying characteristics: The design includes a circled six-pointed star over another and another with graceful caned arches between each vertical row. This pattern was first made by Millersburg in crystal in 1909.

Ohio Star, Millersburg,
vase, 10", green, $4,400.

Open Edge

Made by Fenton.

Colors known: amber, amberina, aqua, black amethyst, celeste blue, green, ice blue, ice green, lime green, marigold, olive green, powder blue, red, and white.

Forms: bowls, baskets, and hats.

Identifying characteristics: This pattern uses a design that resembles the weaving found in reeded baskets.

Also known as: Basketweave Open Edge; Open Edge Basketweave.

Reproductions: Fenton reissued this pattern in 1970-73 in amethyst and in marigold in 1976-77. The Canadian Carnival Collectors Association commissioned red baskets for its convention in 1990.

Open Edge, Fenton,
basket, amberina, $75.

Open Edge, Fenton,
basket, with "Miller's Furniture" advertising, marigold, $25.

Orange Tree

Made by Fenton.

Colors known: amber, amberina, amethyst, aqua, aqua opalescent, blue, chocolate, green, lime green, marigold, marigold on milk glass, peach opalescent, Persian blue, powder blue, red, vaseline, and white.

Forms: bowls, breakfast sets, hatpin holders, mugs, plates, punch bowls, shaving mugs, table sets, and water sets.

Identifying characteristics: This pattern is one of the most popular Fenton created. The number of items available is extensive as well as the colors available, making it easy to collect and enjoy. The motif is reflected in the name with well-designed orange trees, ripe with fruit. Production began in 1911.

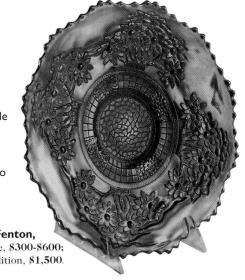

Orange Tree, Fenton, flat plate, 9", blue, $300-$600; outstanding condition, $1,500.

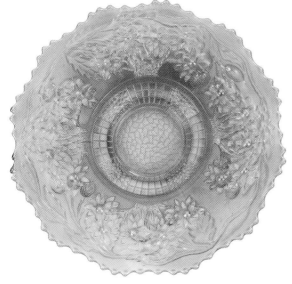

Orange Tree, Fenton, plate, 9-1/4", sawtooth, dark marigold, $350.

Orange Tree, Fenton, bowl, ice-cream edge, marigold over moonstone, $1,500.

Orange Tree Orchard, Fenton, water pitcher and six tumblers, blue, $750.

Oriental Poppy

Made by Northwood.

Colors known: blue, green, ice blue, ice green, lime green, marigold, purple, and white.

Forms: water sets.

Identifying characteristics: Northwood used a tankard-style pitcher to show off this design of an opened poppy flower and delicate foliage. Production began in 1911.

Oriental Poppy, Northwood,
tumbler, 4-1/4", blue, **$250-$400 (rare)**.

Oriental Poppy, Northwood,
tumbler, 4-1/4", purple, $50-$100;
outstanding condition, $250.

Oriental Poppy, Northwood,
tankard, 14", blue, **$7,000-$10,000 (rare)**.

Oriental Poppy, Northwood,
water pitcher and one tumbler, ice green, $6,800.

Oriental Poppy, Northwood,
water pitcher and four tumblers, ice blue, $2,500.

Palm Beach

Made by U.S. Glass.

Colors known: amethyst, honey amber, lime green, marigold, and white.

Forms: berry sets, bowls, plates, rose bowls, table sets, vases, and whimsies.

Identifying characteristics: This pattern started as a crystal pattern by the conglomerate known as U.S. Glass. It features clusters of rounded grapes and foliage on a vine that curves from the top to the base. Pieces in this pattern are often found with gold or silver trim. Some have additional amethyst flashing in the interior.

Palm Beach, U.S. Glass, whimsey rose bowl, smoke, $600.

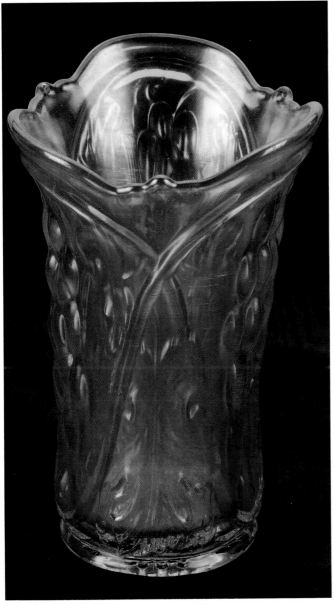

Palm Beach, U.S. Glass, vase, white, $250.

Palm Beach, U.S. Glass, vase, whimsey, 6-1/2" h, 3-1/2" base, marigold, $800.

Paneled Dandelion

Made by Fenton.

Colors known: amethyst, blue, green, and marigold.

Forms: water sets.

Identifying characteristics: Fenton used a tankard-style water pitcher to show off this whimsical pattern that reminds one of all those dandelion puffs that pop up every year and get blown off into the wind. Production began in 1910.

Pansy

Made by Imperial.

Colors known: amber, aqua, clambroth, cobalt blue, helios, ice blue, lavender, marigold, purple, and smoke.

Forms: bowls, breakfast sets, dresser trays, nappies, pickle dishes, and table sets.

Identifying characteristics: A cluster of spring pansies and leaves awaits the viewer of this pretty pattern. Production began in 1910.

Also known as: Imperial's #478.

Reproductions: Creamers, nappies, pickle dishes, and sugars have been reissued by Imperial.

Paneled Dandelion, Fenton, vase, blue; whimsey, no handle, made from a water pitcher, $16,000.

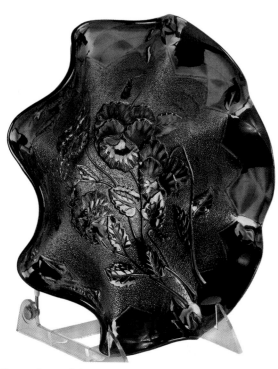

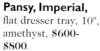

Pansy, Imperial, flat dresser tray, 10", amethyst, $600-$800.

Pansy, Imperial, nappy, 5-1/2", blue, $800-$1,100 (rare).

Pansy, Imperial, bowl, 9", eight ruffles, purple, $150-$250; outstanding condition, $500.

Panther

Made Fenton.

Colors known: amberina, amethyst, aqua, blue, clambroth, ginger ale, green, lavender, marigold, nile green, olive green, and red.

Forms: berry sets.

Identifying characteristics: This interior pattern features two large stalking panthers accented by scrolling foliage. The exterior pattern used is Butterfly and Berry. Production began in 1914.

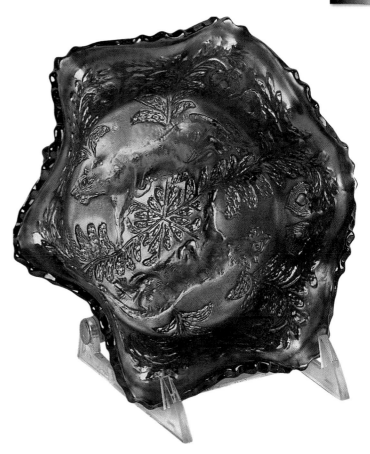

Panther, Fenton,
bowl, 6", six ruffles, footed, red, $800-$1,200.

Peach

Made by Northwood.

Colors known: blue, marigold, and white.

Forms: berry sets, table sets, and water sets.

Identifying characteristics: This pattern features rounded peaches and foliage, which appear to be hanging from the cable border. Production was during the years of 1911 to 1912.

Also known as: Northwood Peach.

Peach, Northwood,
water pitcher, powder blue slag, only one known, $1,000.

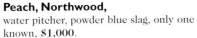

Peacock

Made by Millersburg.

Colors known: amethyst, blue, green, and marigold.

Forms: berry sets, bowls, plates, and rose bowls.

Identifying characteristics: This pattern features a large well-defined standing peacock with an urn in the background. It is identified by the lack of a bee and no beading on the urn. Production began in 1910.

Also known as: The Fluffy Bird.

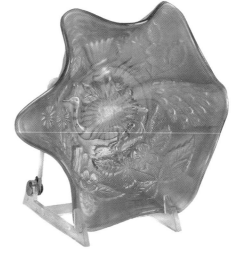

Peacock, Millersburg, sauce, 6", six ruffles, marigold, **$175-$300;** outstanding condition, **$700.**

Peacock, lamp, purple, **$675.**

Peacock, Millersburg, large berry bowl, 9-1/2", amethyst, **$400-$550.**

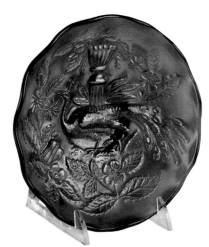

Peacock, Millersburg, sauce, 6", ice-cream shape, amethyst, **$100-$200.**

Peacock, Millersburg, sauce, 6", six ruffles, amethyst, **$150-$250.**

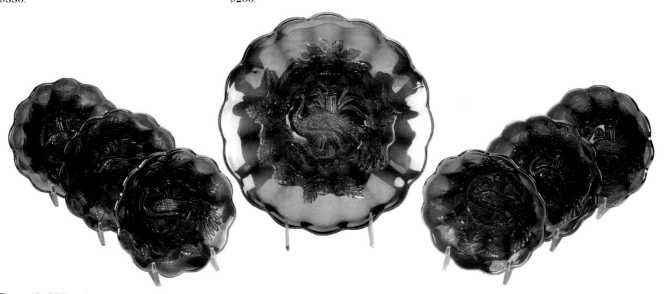

Peacock, Millersburg, master berry bowl, six small, variant, no bee, deep flared, amethyst, **$1,100.**

Peacock and Grape

Made by Fenton.

Colors known: amethyst, aqua, blue, green, lime green opalescent, marigold, peach opalescent, pumpkin marigold, and red.

Forms: bowls and plates.

Identifying characteristics: This pattern is similar to Peacock & Dahlia, but instead of a dahlia, there is a cluster of grapes and leaves. The top of the wedges have a flat border rather than a scallop. Production began in 1911.

Also known as: Fenton's #1646.

Peacock and Grape, Fenton, bowl, 9", ruffle, marigold over moonstone, $500.

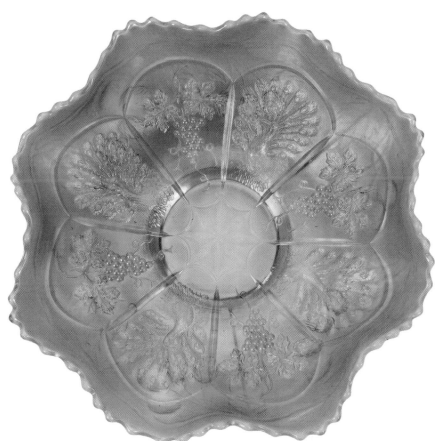

Peacock and Grape, Fenton, bowl, lime green opal, $600.

Peacock and Urn

Made by Fenton.

Colors known: amethyst, aqua, blue, green, marigold, marigold over milk glass, olive, Persian blue, purple, red, vaseline, and white.

Forms: bowls, compotes, and plates.

Identifying characteristics: This peacock pattern shows a detailed standing stiff-necked peacock with its tail extending through the floral wreath border. The background urn contains a bouquet of roses. Exterior pattern may be Bearded Berry. The sawtooth-edge treatment of this pattern is distinctive among the peacock patterns. Production began in 1915.

Peacock and Urn, Northwood, master bowl, 10", ice-cream shape, blue, $1,500-$2,500; outstanding condition, $7,200.

Peacock and Urn, Northwood, master bowl, 10", ice-cream shape, blue stipple, $1,500-$2,500; outstanding condition, $4,200.

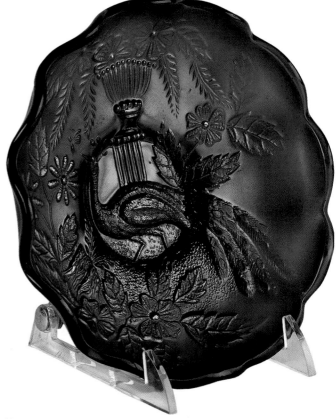

Peacock and Urn, Northwood, sauce, 5-1/2", ice-cream shape, blue, $150-$250.

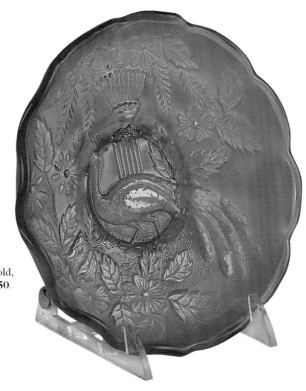

Peacock and Urn

Made by Millersburg.

Colors known: amethyst, blue, green, marigold, and olive green.

Forms: berry sets, bowls, compotes, and plates.

Identifying characteristics: Like Millersburg's Peacock pattern, this pattern shows a standing peacock with a flower-filled urn behind it. This time the peacock has caught a bee and holds it in its beak. Bases have a many-rayed star. Production was centered about the 1910 to 1911 period.

Peacock and Urn, Northwood,
sauce, 5-1/2", ice-cream shape, marigold,
$75-$125; outstanding condition, **$550**.

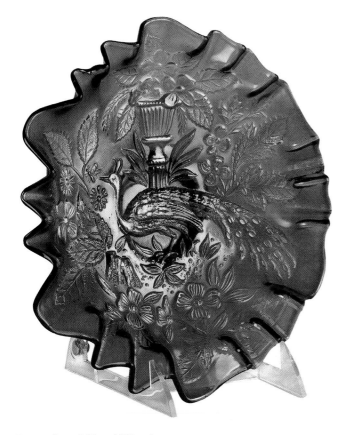

Peacock and Urn, Millersburg,
3-in-1 mystery bowl, 9", green, **$450-$600**.

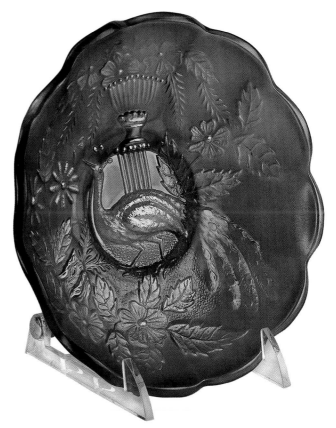

Peacock and Urn, Northwood,
sauce, 5-1/2", ice-cream shape, green, **$700-$900**.

Peacock and Urn

Made by Northwood.

Colors known: amethyst, aqua opalescent, blue, clambroth, green, honey amber, horehound, ice blue, ice green, lime green, marigold, pumpkin marigold, purple, Renninger blue, and white.

Forms: berry sets, ice cream sets, and chop plates.

Identifying characteristics: The Northwood version of the popular Peacock and Urn pattern has three rows of beading on the urn and more open area surrounding the central design. Bases are smooth. Production began in 1912 and continued until 1914.

Peacock and Urn, Northwood, sauce, 5-1/2", ice-cream shape, purple, $75-$125; outstanding condition, $400.

Peacock and Urn, Northwood, master ice cream, ice-cream edge, one small, electric blue, $2,500.

Peacock and Urn, Northwood, chop plate, three rows, three beads, flared, purple, $1,400.

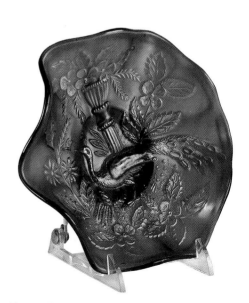

Peacock and Urn Variant

Made by Millersburg.

Colors known: amethyst.

Forms: sauce bowls.

Identifying characteristics: This variation of the peacock pattern has a strutting peacock with a bee in its beak, three rows of beads on the urn, and four rows of tail feathers.

Peacock and Urn Variant, Millersburg, sauce, six ruffles, 6", amethyst, $750-$1,000 (very rare).

Peacock at the Fountain

Made by Northwood.

Colors known: amethyst, aqua opalescent, blue, blue opalescent, iridized custard, green, horehound, ice blue, ice green, lavender, lime green, marigold, purple, Renninger blue, sapphire blue, smoke, and white.

Forms: berry sets, compotes, orange bowls, punch sets, table sets, and water sets.

Identifying characteristics: This peacock pattern includes a detailed peacock, as well as a detailed fountain. Production began in 1912.

Also known as: Northwood's #637.

Peacock at the Fountain, Northwood, punch bowl base with nine cups, set with four cups-Mordini 85, five cups-Morrow 8850, aqua opal, **$9,500**.

Peacock at the Fountain, Northwood, punch bowl base and six cups, blue, **$2,500**.

Peacock at the Fountain, Northwood, tumbler, 4", emerald green, **$300-$400 (rare)**.

Peacock at the Fountain, Northwood, orange bowl, aqua opal, **$15,000**.

Peacock at the Fountain, Northwood, berry sauce 5" d, blue, **$25-$50**; outstanding condition, **$150**.

Peacock at the Fountain, Northwood, tumbler, 4", blue, **$70-$90**; outstanding condition, **$200**.

Peacocks on the Fence

Made by Northwood.

Colors known: amethyst, aqua, aqua opalescent, blue, blue slag, electric blue, green, horehound, ice blue, ice blue opalescent, ice green, iridized custard, lavender, lime green opalescent, marigold, pastel, powder blue, purple, Renninger blue, sapphire blue, smoke, and white.

Forms: bowls and plates.

Identifying characteristics: This pattern shows two peacocks, the one of the left with a fully displayed tail, the other looking back over its shoulder. The exterior pattern can be either ribbed or basketweave. Backgrounds can be plain or stippled. Production was centered around the years of 1911 to 1912.

Reproductions: Reproduction bowls are known.

Also known as: Peacocks.

Peacock on the Fence, Northwood, plate, blue, unbelievable color, $1,100.

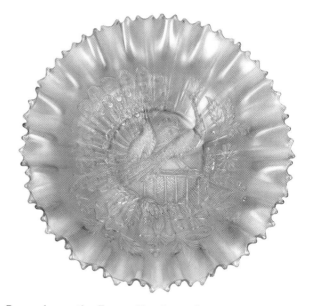

Peacocks on the Fence, Northwood, bowl, pie-crust edge, ribbed, ice blue, average iridescence, $2,000.

Peacocks on the Fence, Northwood, bowl, ruffle, Evans/Mordini, powder blue opal, $7,000.

Peacock on the Fence, Northwood, bowl, 8-1/2", ruffle/rib, marigold, pumpkin, $400.

Peacock Tail

Made by Fenton.

Colors known: amber, amethyst, blue, green, marigold, peach opalescent, and red.

Forms: bonbons, bowls, compotes, hats, and plates.

Identifying characteristics: This pattern features peacock feathers that radiate from the center. The pattern was first advertised in 1911.

Also known as: Fenton's #409; Flowering Almonds.

Peacock Tail, Fenton, spectacular plate, 9", marigold, has two very minute flakes on rim, **$2,200**.

Peacock Tail, Fenton, 3-in-1 edge bowl, 9-1/2", amethyst, **$70**.

Pearly Dots

Made by Westmoreland.

Colors known: amethyst, aqua, blue, blue opalescent, marigold, and peach opalescent.

Forms: bowls, compotes, and rose bowls.

Identifying characteristics: The Pearly Dots pattern features rows of dots. Production began in 1910.

Also known as: Coin Dot; Polka Dot.

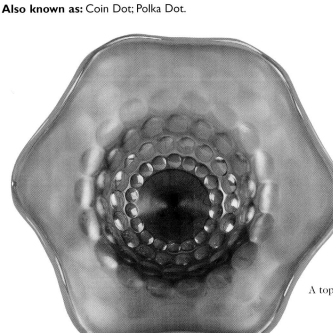

Pearly Dots, Westmoreland, compote, 4-1/2", blue opal, **$200-$350 (scarce)**.

A top view of the Pearly Dots compote.

Perfection

Made by Millersburg.

Colors known: amethyst, green, marigold, and purple.

Forms: water sets.

Identifying characteristics: This pattern has rows of beaded ovals over leaves.

Also known as: Beaded Jewel and Leaf.

Perfection, Millersburg, water pitcher and four tumblers, one tumbler damaged, marigold, **$8,250.**

Persian Garden

Made by Dugan/Diamond.

Colors known: amethyst, blue, green, lavender, marigold, peach opalescent, purple, and white.

Forms: berry sets, ice cream sets, and plates.

Identifying characteristics: This intricate pattern has a row of fleur-de-lis along the outward edge of the first scallop band, a row of flowers, another scallop band, more flowers, and a open flower center. Production centers around the 1910-1911 period.

Also known as: Fan and Arch.

Persian Garden, Dugan, small plate, 6-1/2", purple, **$500-$800;** outstanding condition, **$1,600.**

Persian Garden, Dugan, small plate, 7-1/2", blue, **$3,000-$4,000 (very rare).**

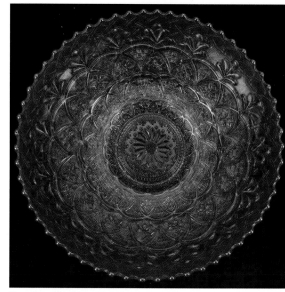

Persian Garden, Dugan, master ice cream, white, **$200.**

Persian Medallion

Made by Fenton.

Colors known: amber, amethyst, black amethyst, blue, green, lime green, marigold, red, reverse amberina, vaseline, and white.

Forms: bonbons, bowls, compotes, hair receivers, plates, and rose bowls.

Identifying characteristics: The central motif of this pattern reminds one of elements found in Middle Eastern rugs, along with scrolled borders, and stylized leaves in an outer border. Production began in 1911.

Reproductions: Fenton has issued baskets, bowls, compotes, goblets, plates, and stemmed rose bowls using original molds.

Persian Medallion, Fenton,
flat plate, 6-1/4", black amethyst, $250-$400.

Persian Medallion, Fenton,
sauce, six ruffles, 6", blue, $50-$80.

Persian Medallion, Fenton,
flat plate, 6-1/4", marigold, $50-$80.

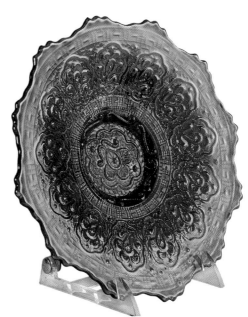

Persian Medallion, Fenton,
flat plate, 6-3/4", green, $400-$600; outstanding condition, $1,700.

Persian Medallion, Fenton,
tri-fold, 6-3/4", blue, **$150-$300 (scarce)**.

Persian Medallion, Fenton, flat plate, 9", blue, **$400-$700**;
outstanding condition (rare) **$1,500**.

Persian Medallion, Fenton,
flat plate, 6-3/4", blue, **$100-$250**.

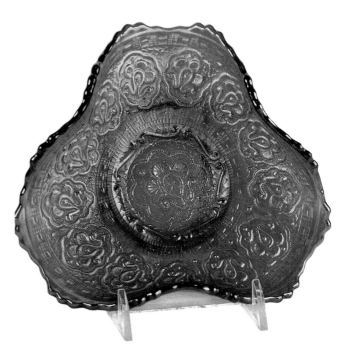

Persian Medallion, Fenton,
tri-fold, 6-3/4", amethyst, **$150-$300 (scarce)**.

Petal and Fan

Made by Dugan.

Colors known: amethyst, marigold, peach opalescent, purple, and white.

Forms: bowls and plates.

Identifying characteristics: The pattern is a series of alternating plain and stippled petals on a ribbed background with a fan device between each petal. Production was in 1911.

Petal and Fan, Dugan,
bowl, six ruffles, 10-1/2", purple, $400-$600; outstanding condition, $1,000.

Petal and Fan, Dugan,
plate, candy-ribbon edge, 6-1/2", purple, $400-$600.

Peter Rabbit

Made by Fenton.

Colors known: blue, green, and marigold.

Forms: bowls and plates.

Identifying characteristics: Fenton designers incorporated a fanciful border on both sides of the wreath that contains rabbits. This pattern was made in 1912.

Peter Rabbit, Fenton,
flat plate, 9", green, $4,000-$6,000.

Peter Rabbit,
plate, green, $5,500.

Pine Cone

Made by Fenton.

Colors known: amber, amethyst, blue, green, marigold, and white.

Forms: bowls and plates.

Identifying characteristics: Detailed pinecones swirl with exaggerated pine needles and swirls in this pattern.

Also known as: Pine Cone Wreath.

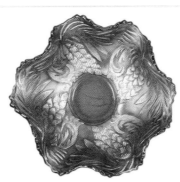

Pine Cone, Fenton,
ruffled bowl, 7", marigold, $20.

Plaid

Made by Fenton.

Colors known: amethyst, blue, celeste blue, green, lavender, marigold, purple, red, and teal.

Forms: bowls and plates.

Identifying characteristics: This pattern has a very modern look to it compared to traditional carnival glass patterns. It is a series of vertical and horizontal lines, creating a plaid design. Production began in 1925.

Also known as: Granny's Gingham.

Plaid, Fenton, plate, amethyst, $650.

Plaid, Fenton, bowl, 8-1/2", red, $2,500.

Plaid, Fenton, 3-in-1 bowl, blue, only one known, $1,100.

Plume Panels

Made by Fenton.

Colors known: amethyst, blue, green, marigold, olive green, red, sapphire blue, and vaseline.

Forms: vases.

Identifying characteristics: The design is named from the panels of plumes that rise from the base to the flared top. Production began in 1912.

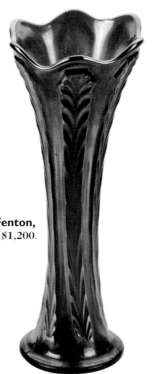

Plume Panels, Fenton, vase, 10-1/2", red, $1,200.

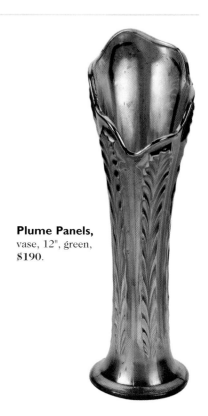

Plume Panels, vase, 12", green, $190.

Poinsettia

Made by Imperial.

Colors known: emerald green, helios, lavender, marigold, purple, and smoke.

Forms: milk pitchers.

Identifying characteristics: A well-defined poinsettia blossom with a detailed center is linked around the top of this pattern and hovers over the beaded leaf forms. This pattern was made from 1910 until 1914.

Poinsettia, Imperial, milk pitcher, 6", marigold, $100-$150.

Poinsettia, Imperial, milk pitcher, 6", green, $300-$500.

Poinsettia, Imperial, milk pitcher, 6", smoke, $200-$300.

Poinsettia, Imperial, milk pitcher, 6", purple, $1,500-$2,500; outstanding condition, $4,200.

Pony

Made by Diamond.

Colors known: amethyst, aqua, ice green, lavender, and marigold.

Forms: bowls and plates.

Identifying characteristics: The central motif of this pattern is a detailed pony's head profile. A band of Roman Key motif surrounds the central element. Production began in 1921 and continued until 1930.

Also known as: Pony Rosette.

Reproductions: Bowls have been reproduced from original molds by L. G. Wright in the 1980s.

Pony, Dugan,
bowl, ruffle, amethyst,
$150.

Pony, Dugan,
bowl, ruffle, ice green,
$800.

Pony, Dugan,
bowl, ruffle, marigold,
$100.

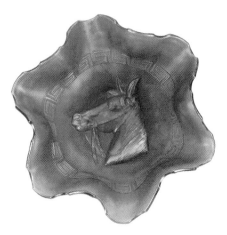

Poppy Show

Made by Imperial.

Colors known: amber, clambroth, helios, lavender, marigold, pastel marigold, purple, and smoke.

Forms: vases and whimsies.

Identifying characteristics: This pattern has panels filled with open poppies, foliage, and stems. Production began in 1910 and continued until 1912.

Also known as: Imperial's #488; Imperial's Poppy Show.

Reproductions: The vase has been reproduced.

Poppy Show, Imperial,
vase, 12", marigold, $500-$800.

Poppy Show, Imperial,
vase, 12", purple, $3,000-$5,500 (rare).

Poppy Show

Made by Northwood.

Colors known: amethyst, blue, clambroth, electric blue, green, ice blue, ice green, lime green, marigold, pastel marigold, purple, smoke, and white.

Forms: bowls and plates.

Identifying characteristics: This three-dimensional pattern features a cluster of three open poppies in the center with leaves and poppy buds for an added element. Production began in 1912 and continued until 1914.

Also known as: LaBelle Poppy.

Reproductions: Fenton has reissued vases using the original molds in contemporary colors.

Poppy Show, Northwood, plate, 9", marigold, $900-$1,600.

Poppy Show, Northwood, plate, 9", blue, $1,100-$3,000; outstanding condition, $8,000.

Poppy Show, Northwood, bowl, eight ruffles, 8-1/2", blue, $700-$1,100; outstanding condition, $2,500.

Poppy Show, Northwood, plate, flared, ice blue, $1,700.

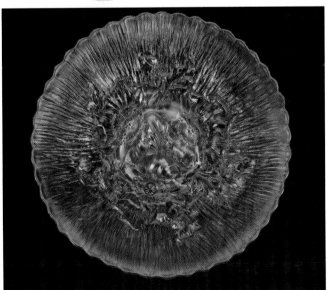

Poppy Show, Northwood, plate, 9", white, $700.

Pulled Loop

Made by Dugan/Diamond.

Colors known: amethyst, aqua, black amethyst, blue, celeste blue, green, marigold, peach opalescent, purple, and white.

Forms: vases.

Identifying characteristics: Six loop panels separated by six wide ribs that extend over the top rim characterize this popular vase pattern. Sizes range from 6" to 16" high.

Also known as: Dugan's #1030; Loop and Column.

Pulled Loop, jack-in-the-pulpit vase, 6-1/2", green, $280.

Pulled Loop, Dugan,
vase, 8-1/2", purple with opal tips, $550.

Quill

Made by Dugan.

Colors known: marigold and purple.

Forms: water sets.

Identifying characteristics: This design incorporates a feather-type quill motif and elongated ovals, flourishes, and a swagged border.

Also known as: Feather and Scroll.

Quill, Dugan, water pitcher and six tumblers, marigold, $1,000.

Raspberry

Made by Northwood.

Colors known: amethyst, blue, green, ice blue, ice green, lavender, marigold, purple, and white.

Forms: milk pitchers, water sets, and whimsies.

Identifying characteristics: Northwood combined realistic looking raspberries and leaves over a basketweave band for this pattern. The pattern was introduced in 1911.

Also known as: Blackberry and Checkerboard.

Raspberry, Northwood,
gravy boat, 6", teal, **$150-$250**.

Raspberry, Northwood,
water pitcher and five tumblers
(four shown), ice blue, **$1,400**.

Ribbon Tie

Made by Fenton.

Colors known: amethyst, black amethyst, blue, green, marigold, purple, and red.

Forms: bowls and plates.

Identifying characteristics: This pattern takes six ribbon segments and swirls them to the perimeter while other ribbons ring the bowl horizontally. Production began in 1911.

Also known as: Comet.

Ribbon Tie, Fenton,
3-in-1 low-ruffled bowl, 9",
blue, **$100-$250**; outstanding
condition, **$800**.

Ribbon Tie, Fenton,
3-in-1 bowl, 8-1/2", electric amethyst, **$125**.

Ripple

Made by Imperial.

Colors known: amber, aqua, blue, clambroth, emerald green, helios, lavender, marigold, olive, powder blue, purple, red, smoke, teal, vaseline, violet, and white.

Forms: vases.

Identifying characteristics: This pattern resembles the ripple created when dropping a pebble into a pond. Production was centered in the 1910 until 1912 period.

Also known as: Ripple Threads.

Reproductions: Marigold, pink, and smoke vases known.

Ripple, Imperial, squat vase, 5-1/2" h x 3-3/8" b, marigold, **$200-$300 (rare)**.

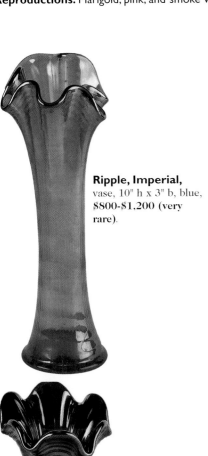

Ripple, Imperial, vase, 10" h x 3" b, blue, **$800-$1,200 (very rare)**.

Ripple, Imperial, vase, 12" h x 2-1/2" b, lime green, **$150-$300 (rare)**.

Ripple, Imperial, funeral vase, 11-1/2", marigold, **$200-$400**.

Ripple, Imperial, vase, 8" h x 2-1/2" b, purple, **$125-$175**.

Ripple, Imperial, squat vase, 4" h x 2-1/2" b, may be the shortest one there is, marigold, **$150-$250**.

Robin

Made by Imperial.

Colors known: marigold, marigold on light green, and smoke.

Forms: mugs and water sets.

Identifying characteristics: A whimsical bird perched on a leafy tree branch is the major design element of this pattern. Production was centered around 1910 to 1911.

Also known as: Imperial's #670; Robin Red Breast.

Reproductions: Imperial reissued the mug in pink and red. They also reissued water sets in cobalt blue, green, red, and white. These pieces are marked with the imposed IG or LIG trademarks.

Robin, Imperial, tumbler, 4-1/4", smoke, $400-$600 (rare).

Rococo

Made by Imperial.

Colors known: lavender, marigold, vaseline, and smoke.

Forms: berry sets, candy dishes, compotes, and vases.

Identifying characteristics: Swagged loops and arches create this interesting pattern. Production began in crystal in 1909 and was soon expanded to carnival colors.

Also known as: Imperial's #248-1/2.

Rococo, Imperial, vase, 4-1/4", marigold, $75.

Rococo, Imperial, vase, 4-1/4", smoke, $95.

Rose Columns

Made by Millersburg.

Colors known: amethyst, aqua, blue, green, and marigold.

Forms: vases.

Identifying characteristics: This molded vase pattern features deeply sculpted vertical roses of rose flowers, topped by leaves.

Rose Column, Millersburg, vase, 10", green, $5,000.

Rose Column, Millersburg,
vase, 10-1/2", dark marigold, $6,500.

Rose Column, Millersburg,
vase, 10", blue, one of two known, $16,000.

Rose Column, Millersburg,
vase, 9-1/2", amethyst, $5,500.

Roses and Ruffles

Made by Consolidated Glass.

Colors known: marigold, marigold on milk glass, and red.

Forms: lamps.

Identifying characteristics: This pattern shows roses, leaves, and ruffles on the ball-shaped lamp shade and matching urn-shaped base, commonly called a "Gone With The Wind" shape.

Roses and Ruffles, lamp, Gone with the Wind, marigold, $2,800.

Rose Show

Made by Northwood.

Colors known: amber, amethyst, aqua, aqua opalescent, blue, emerald green, green, honey amber, horehound, ice blue, ice green, ice green opalescent, lavender, lime green, lime green opalescent, marigold, purple, Renninger blue, sapphire blue, and white.

Forms: bowls and plates.

Identifying characteristics: Northwood designers must have been inspired by beautiful roses when creating this design. The three-dimensional flowers and leaves are very life-like as they are clustered in the center of this design. Production began in 1912 and continued until 1914.

Also known as: LaBelle Rose.

Rose Show, Northwood,
plate, 9", blue, $1,100-$1,600.

Rose Show, Northwood,
plate, marigold over custard, extremely rare, $11,000.

Rose Show, Northwood, bowl, 8-1/2", purple, $150.

Rose Show, Northwood,
plate, 9", pastel marigold, $1,200-$1,800.

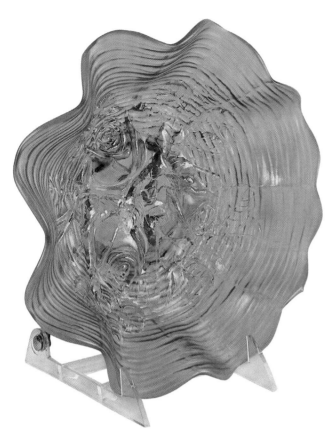

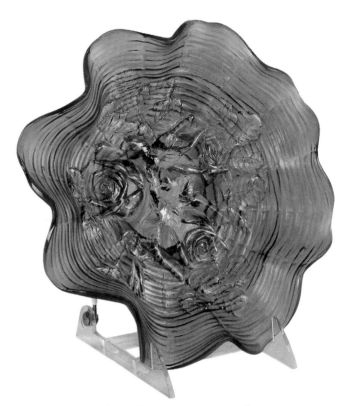

Rose Show, Northwood,
bowl, 8-1/2", eight ruffles, ice green opal, **$2,800-$3,700, (rare)**.

Rose Show, Northwood, bowl, 8-1/2", eight ruffles,
aqua opal, **$900-$1,600**; outstanding condition, **$3,000**.

Round-up

Made by Dugan.

Colors known: amber, blue, lavender, marigold, peach opalescent, purple, and white.

Forms: bowls and plates.

Identifying characteristics: This interesting design features a swirled center flower with stippled highlighted petals, beaded borders, and an additional border with swirled beaded, plain, and floral enhanced petals. Production began in 1910 and ended by 1912.

Also known as: Egyptian Band.

Roundup, Dugan,
ruffled bowl, 8-1/2", purple, **$400-$800**.

Rustic

Made by Fenton.

Colors known: amber, amethyst, blue, electric blue, green, lime green, lime green opalescent, marigold, peach opalescent, red, and white.

Forms: vases.

Identifying characteristics: Elongated teardrops descend from the crown like the top of these vases in evenly spaced rows. Bases of these vases come in three sizes, 3" to 3-1/2" on the standard sizes of 8" to 15" h, 4" to 4-1/4" d on the mid-sized 13" to 18" h vases, and 5" to 5-1/2" on the tallest and funeral sized 17" to 24" h vases. Production began in 1911.

Also known as: Fenton's #507; Maryland.

Rustic, Fenton, jardinière vase, pinched in, 5-2/8" base, 7-1/2" h, blue, **$1,500.**

Rustic, Fenton, funeral vase, 16", plunger base, blue, **$1,500-$2,000.**

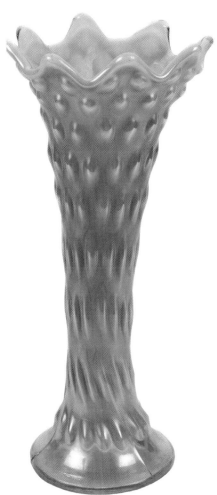

Rustic, Fenton, vase, 9-1/4", lime green opal, **$1,250.**

Rustic, Fenton, vase, peach opal, **$1,400.**

S-Repeat

Made by Dugan.

Colors known: purple.

Forms: creamers and punch sets.

Identifying characteristics: This pattern features scrolling S forms that have a distinctive curl to the top and bottom of each form. Several forms include a beaded border.

Also known as: National.

S Repeat, Dugan, tumbler, marigold, **$210**.

S Repeat, Dugan, punch bowl base and 12 cups, purple, **$8,000**.

Scales

Made Westmoreland.

Colors known: amethyst, aqua, blue opalescent, marigold, marigold over milk glass, and teal.

Forms: bowls and plates.

Identifying characteristics: Rows of scales that diminish in size from the perimeter to the petaled center dominate this design. Production began circa 1909.

Also known as: Peacock Optic; Looped Petals.

Scales, Westmoreland, plate, deep, round, marigold over milk glass, **$250**.

Scroll Embossed

Made by Imperial.

Colors known: aqua, clambroth, emerald green, helios, lavender, marigold, purple, red, and teal.

Forms: bowls, compotes, and plates.

Identifying characteristics: Scroll Embossed has a bull's-eye center plus four additional bull's eyes that are the center of the looping scrolls that make up this interesting pattern. Production began in 1910 and continued until 1917.

Also known as: Embossed Scroll; Peacock Eye.

Reproductions: Fenton has created a vase that resembles this pattern, perhaps because Imperial never made a vase. Imperial has reissued the 9" bowls in amethyst, ice blue, ice green, and pink. These have the LIG mark.

Scroll Embossed, Imperial,
compote, ruffled, 4-1/2" h, marigold, $60-$90.

Scroll Embossed,
Imperial, flat plate, 9-1/2", purple, $350-$600.

Scroll Embossed, Imperial, ruffled compote, 4-1/2" h, purple, $200-$300. A top view of the compote is shown at left.

Scroll Embossed, Imperial,
bowl, six ruffles, 7", purple, $50-$150.

Scroll Embossed, Imperial,
miniature compote, 3", purple, $250-$350.

Seacoast

Made by Millersburg.

Colors known: amethyst, green, marigold, and purple.

Forms: pin trays.

Identifying characteristics: This pattern features an irregularly shaped tray with a lighthouse and other seaside motifs. The American Carnival Glass Association used this pattern as a spittoon for its convention souvenirs. These pieces are now starting to come into the secondary market so that comparable prices can be established.

Also known as: Maine Coast.

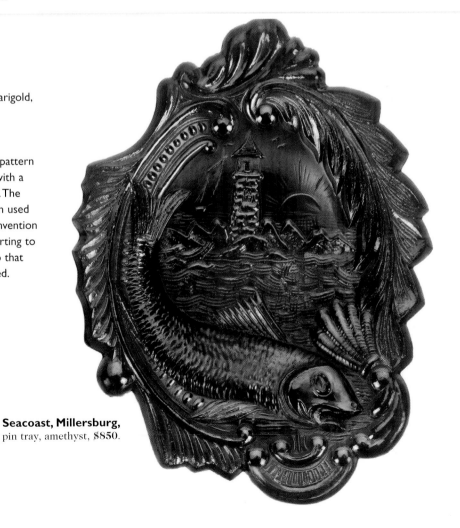

Seacoast, Millersburg,
pin tray, amethyst, $850.

Singing Birds

Made by Northwood.

Colors known: amber, amethyst, aqua opalescent, blue, emerald green, green, horehound, ice blue, ice green, lavender, marigold, olive green, purple, Renninger blue, sapphire blue, smoke, and white.

Forms: berry sets, mugs, table sets, and water sets.

Identifying characteristics: This well-known pattern features a bird that looks like its ready to hop off the flowering branch where it is perched. Production was centered in 1911 to 1912.

Reproductions: Tumblers have been reproduced in amethyst, blue, and vaseline.

Singing Birds, Northwood, mug, aqua opal, **$1,200**.

Singing Birds, Northwood, tumbler, 4", emerald green, **$75-$125**.

Singing Birds, Northwood, water pitcher and six tumblers, marigold, **$275**.

Six Petals

Made by Dugan.

Colors known: lavender, peach opalescent, purple, and white.

Forms: bowls and plates.

Identifying characteristics: Six Petals takes its name from the center six-petaled flower that is surrounded by leaves and a wreath border of additional flower blossoms and leaves. Production was centered between 1910 and 1912.

Also known as: Christmas Rose and Poppy.

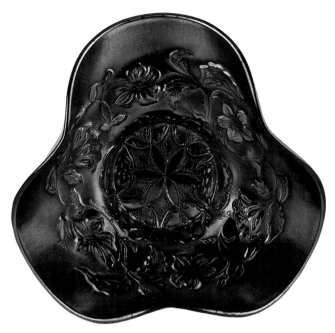

Six Petals, Dugan,
tri-corner bowl, 7-1/2", purple, $100-$200.

Six Petals, Dugan,
tri-corner bowl, peach opal, $20.

Ski Star

Made by Dugan.

Colors known: amethyst, black amethyst, peach opalescent, and purple.

Forms: banana boats, berry sets, bowls, plates, and whimsies.

Identifying characteristics: This interior pattern features stippled rays which form an interesting eight-point star and features a delicate lacy center star design. The Compass pattern is frequently used as an exterior pattern with Ski Star, giving it further interest. Production was centered between 1910 and 1911.

Ski Star, Dugan,
bowl, six ruffles, 10-3/4", purple, $300-$500.

Ski Star, Dugan,
basket with handle, peach opal, $325.

Smooth Panels

Made by Imperial.

Colors known: amber, amethyst, clambroth, lavender, marigold, marigold over milk glass, peach opalescent, red, smoke, teal, white, and wisteria.

Forms: rose bowls and vases.

Identifying characteristics: Convex panels create this design. Many pieces, but not all, include the Imperial iron cross mark on the base. Vase sizes in this pattern range from 4" to 18".

Smooth Panels, Imperial, funeral vase, 12", 10" mouth, marigold, $160.

Smooth Panels, Imperial, funeral vase, 12", 10" mouth, teal, $450.

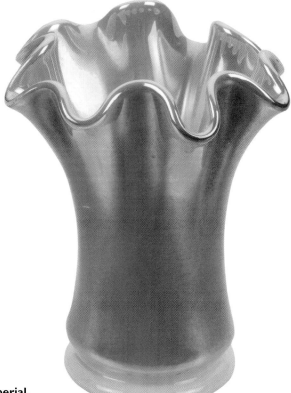

Smooth Panels, Imperial, vase, 4", marigold over milk glass, $200.

Smooth Rays

Made by Dugan, Imperial, Northwood, and Westmoreland.

Colors known: Dugan: amethyst, marigold, peach opalescent; Imperial: amber, clambroth, marigold; Northwood: amethyst, clambroth, green, and marigold, marigold on green; Westmoreland: amber, amethyst, green, marigold, marigold over milk glass, and teal.

Forms: bonbons, bowls, compotes, plates, stemware, and water sets.

Identifying characteristics: This pattern was made by the major manufacturers, each with a slightly different treatment, in different colors, and forms. However, the basic pattern is a ribbed smooth banded type design. Values between the similar patterns are comparable.

Smooth Rays, Westmoreland, compote, 4-1/2", purple, $100-$250. A top view of the compote is shown below.

Soda Gold

Made by Imperial.

Colors known: aqua, light blue, marigold, smoke, and vaseline.

Forms: bowls, candlesticks, chop plates, salts and peppers, and water sets.

Identifying characteristics: This pattern features pronounced random-looking veins which are raised over its stippled surface. This late production pattern first appears in a Butlers Brothers catalog in 1929.

Also known as: Spider Web.

Soda Gold, Imperial, pitcher, 8-1/4", smoke, $200-$350.

Soda Gold, Imperial, tumbler, 4", smoke, $50-$75.

Soutache

Made by Dugan.

Colors known: peach opalescent.

Forms: bowls and plates.

Identifying characteristics: This all-over pattern features a maze of squiggles that surround a flower center.

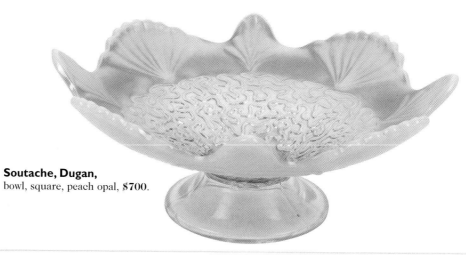

Soutache, Dugan, bowl, square, peach opal, $700.

Springtime

Made by Northwood.

Colors known: amethyst, green, marigold, and purple.

Forms: berry sets, table sets, and water sets.

Identifying characteristics: A ring of spring flowers and leaves dominates this pattern that also includes loops of basketweave, additional larger flowers and leaves. Production dates to 1910-1911. Pieces are sometimes marked.

Also known as: Butterfly and Cable.

Springtime, Northwood, water pitcher and six tumblers, dark marigold, $1,650.

Stag and Holly

Made by Fenton.

Colors known: amber, amberina, amethyst, aqua, black amethyst, blue, green, marigold, marigold on moonstone, pink, pumpkin marigold, red, and vaseline.

Forms: bowls, plates, and rose bowls.

Identifying characteristics: This well-known carnival glass design features a standing stag alternating with a holly tree. The center is a combination of holly berries and leaves. Production began in 1912.

Reproductions: Reproduction bowls are known. By carefully examining details, collectors have identified period pieces as having oval-shaped eyes, while new eyes are found. Original Fenton stags have detailed tongues, an element often missing on reproductions.

Stag and Holly, Fenton, rose bowl, large, marigold, $225.

Stag and Holly, Fenton, chop plate, 11-1/2", sawtooth, marigold, $1,200.

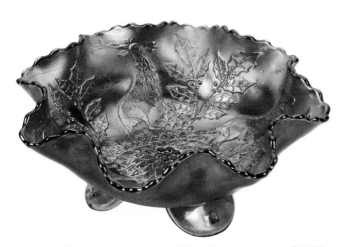

Stag and Holly, Fenton, bowl, 6-1/2", ruffle, spatula, red, $1,500.

Stag and Holly, Fenton, rose bowl, large, ruffled, blue, $700.

Star and File

Made by Imperial.

Colors known: amber, clambroth, helios, ice green, marigold, purple, and smoke.

Forms: bonbons, bowls, celery vases, compotes, milk pitchers, plates, stemware, tumblers, and water sets.

Identifying characteristics: An upright band of filed diamonds creates the "file" of this pattern, both hobstars and rayed stars add the "star" to the name, and areas of caning and fan fill out the rest of this busy pattern. Production began in 1916 and continued until 1929.

Also known as: Imperial's #612; Finecut and Star.

Reproductions: Imperial reissued this pattern as a wine set in marigold and smoke, while re-naming it Peacock. Look for the IG mark on reissues.

Star and File, Imperial,
tumbler, marigold, $100.

Starfish

Made by Dugan.

Colors known: peach opalescent and purple.

Forms: bonbons and compotes.

Identifying characteristics: A large detailed starfish dominates the center of this design, each branch of the starfish end in an embossed fleur-de-lis.

Also known as: Stippled Starfish Medallion.

Starfish, Dugan,
compote, 6", eight ruffles, purple,
$300-$500.

Star Medallion

Made by Imperial.

Colors known: clambroth, marigold, smoke, and smoky blue.

Forms: bowls, celeries, compotes, custard cups, goblets, milk pitchers, plates, and tumblers.

Identifying characteristics: This pattern has a medallion element that is repeated on a caned-type background.

Reproductions: Imperial reissued the compote in amber, helios, ice blue, marigold, and smoke.

Star Medallion, Imperial,
tumbler, marigold, $50.

Star Medallion, Imperial,
milk pitcher, smoke, $75.

Star of David

Made by Imperial.

Colors known: helios, marigold, purple, smoke.

Forms: bowls.

Identifying characteristics: A stippled Star of David dominates the center of this interior pattern. The Arcs pattern is frequently used on the exterior. Production began in 1910.

Also known as: Star of David Medallion.

Star of David, Imperial, bowl, 9", eight ruffles, purple, $200-$350.

Stork and Rushes

Made by Dugan.

Colors known: amethyst, blue, lime green, and marigold.

Forms: berry sets, mugs, punch sets, water sets, and whimsies.

Identifying characteristics: A detailed stork standing among rushes dominates this interesting pattern.

Also known as: Heron and Rushes.

Reproductions: L. G. Wright has created a butter dish, as well as changing the sugar lids. These are known in purple. They also issued water sets in marigold and purple. Reproduction berry sets are known in purple.

Stork and Rushes, Dugan, mug, 4", blue, $1,000-$1,200 (rare).

Stork and Rushes, Diamond, tumbler, lattice banded, marigold, $20.

Strawberry

Made by Northwood.

Colors known: amethyst, blue, green, horehound, ice green, lime green, marigold, marigold with opalescent, pastel marigold, peach opalescent, pumpkin marigold, purple, smoke, and white.

Forms: bowls and plates.

Identifying characteristics: Northwood's Strawberry has four sprigs of berries and leaves, which circle the center that features four leaves.

Strawberry, Northwood,
bowl, stippled, ribbed electric blue, **$650**.

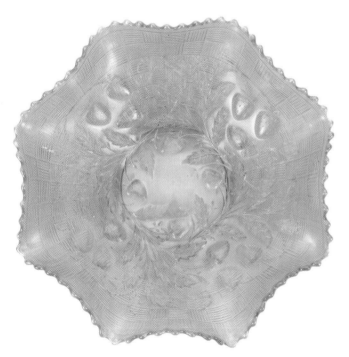

Strawberry, Northwood,
bowl, lime ice green, ruffle/basketweave, **$1,200**.

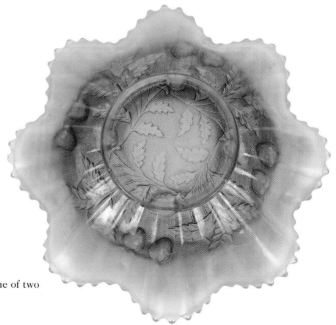

Strawberry, Northwood,
bowl, stippled, ruffle edge, one of two
known, aqua opal, **$15,000**.

Strawberry Scroll

Made by Fenton.

Colors known: amethyst, blue, and marigold.

Forms: water sets.

Identifying characteristics: This pattern features strawberries and a mid band of scrolls.

Also known as: Strawberry and Scroll Band.

Strawberry Scroll, Fenton, water pitcher and six tumblers, marigold, $2,500.

Sunflower

Made by Millersburg.

Colors known: amethyst, green, and marigold.

Forms: pin trays.

Identifying characteristics: This pin tray is shaped as though a large sunflower blossom was just picked and flattened out, the stem twists around with a few leaves to form the handle.

Sunflower, Millersburg,
pin tray, amethyst, $850.

Swirl Hobnail

Made by Millersburg.

Colors known: amethyst, green, marigold, and purple.

Forms: rose bowls, spittoons, and vases.

Identifying characteristics: This pattern features horizontal rows of pointy hobnails with a background of vertical swirls. Production was centered around 1910 to 1911.

Also known as: Hobnail Swirl.

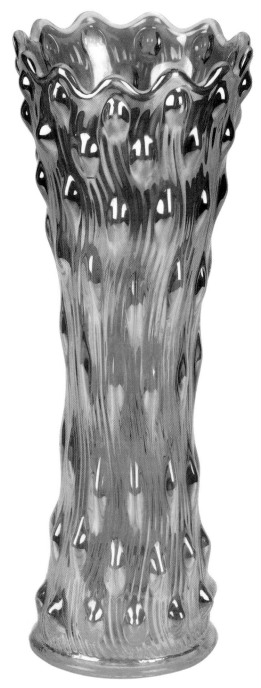

Swirl Hobnail, Millersburg,
vase, 10", marigold, $300.

Target

Made by Dugan.

Colors known: amethyst, blue, marigold, peach opalescent, smoky blue, and white.

Forms: vases.

Identifying characteristics: This pattern features large ribs, which separate vertical rows of raised circles, the top features crown-like points.

Also known as: Loops and Columns.

Target, Fenton,
vase, 6-1/2", blue, $100.

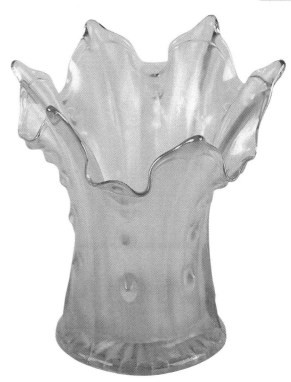

Target, Dugan,
squatty vase, 6", white, $150-$250.

Ten Mums

Made by Fenton.

Colors known: blue, green, marigold, peach opalescent, and white.

Forms: bowls, plates, and water sets.

Identifying characteristics: This interior pattern features a realistic-looking pom-pom chrysanthemum in the center with two leaves. Further leaves form a wreath with additional pom-pom chrysanthemums pointing to the exterior. Production began in 1911.

Also known as: Chrysanthemum Wreath; Double Chrysanthemum.

Ten Mums, Fenton,
3-in-1 bowl, 9-1/2", blue, $350.

Ten Mums, Fenton,
water pitcher and six tumblers, tankard, marigold, $1,550.

Thin Rib

Made by Northwood.

Colors known: amber, amethyst, aqua opalescent, blue, green, emerald green, ice blue, ice green, ice green opalescent, lime green opalescent, marigold, olive, purple, sapphire blue, vaseline, and white.

Forms: vases.

Identifying characteristics: This pattern is found on the exterior and consists of thin rod-type ribs and wider smooth panels. The term "jester cap" is used to describe a style where one point is pulled higher than the rest and the other seven ribs turned outward. Both Dugan and Fenton made similar patterns, which have comparable values.

Thin Rib, Northwood, funeral vase, mid-size, ice green, **$350**.

Thin Rib, Northwood, vase, 10", 10 ribs, electric blue, **$125**.

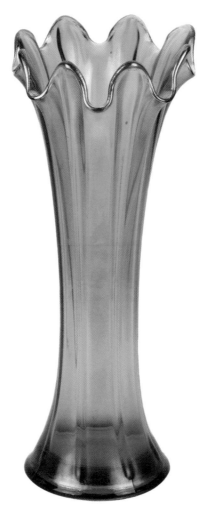

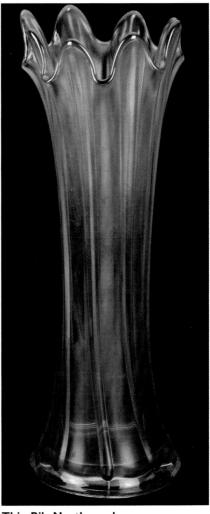

Thin Rib, Northwood,
vase, ice green, **$450**.

Thin Rib, Northwood, funeral vase,
14-1/4", mid-size, sapphire with gold rim,
$600.

Thin Rib, Northwood,
funeral vase, 15", mid-size, white, **$300**.

Thin Rib, Northwood, jardinière vase, 8" h,
4-5/8" base, purple, signed, **$1,450**.

Thistle

Made by Fenton.

Colors known: amber, amethyst, blue, green, lavender, marigold, and vaseline.

Forms: banana boats, bowls, compotes, and plates.

Identifying characteristics: This interesting pattern features four clusters of thistle foliage and flowers each with one leave extending to the center. Production began in 1911.

Also known as: Christmas Cactus.

Reproductions: Joe St. Clair has iridized goblets, never originally issued in carnival.

Thistle, Fenton,
flat plate, 9", green, $4,000-$5,000.

Thistle, Fenton, banana boat, amethyst, $185.

Three Fruits

Made by Northwood.

Colors known: amethyst, aqua, aqua opalescent, black amethyst, blue, clambroth, green, honey amber, horehound, lavender, lime green, marigold, pearlized custard, pumpkin marigold, olive, purple, sapphire blue, smoke, teal, violet, and white.

Forms: bowls.

Identifying characteristics: This pattern features a wreath of peaches, cherries, and pears, leaves, and a bunch of plump cherries in the center. Production of this pattern centered between 1915 and 1916.

Three Fruits, Northwood,
plate, 9", electric blue, $900-$1,200.

Three Fruits, Northwood,
plate, 9", aqua opal, $2,000-$3,000; outstanding condition, $6,500.

Three Fruits, Northwood, bowl, sapphire, $2,200.

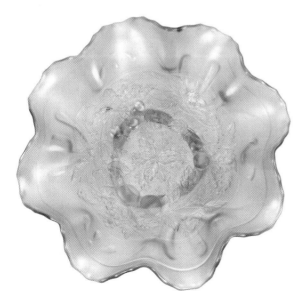

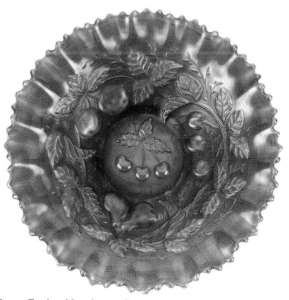

Three Fruits, Northwood,
stippled, bowl, 8-1/2", footed, ice blue, $1,000.

Three Fruits, Northwood,
bowl, pie-crust edge/basketweave, dark marigold, $150.

Tiger Lily

Made by Imperial.

Colors known: amber, aqua, blue, helios, lavender, marigold, olive, purple, teal, and violet.

Forms: water sets.

Identifying characteristics: Tiger Lily is a full pattern featuring detailed open-petaled flowers on a leafy upright stalk alternating with additional buds and stalks. Production began in 1910.

Also known as: Imperial's #484; Amaryllis.

Reproductions: Imperial reissued water sets in ice blue, ice green, marigold, pink, and white. Some are marked IG, others LIG. Riihimaki, Finland, also copied the pattern, with some slight differences, including that their tumblers have a collar base.

Tiger Lily, Imperial, water pitcher, 8-1/2", purple, $800-$1,200 (rare).

Tiger Lily, Imperial, tumbler, 4-1/4", purple, $80-$150 (scarce).

Tiger Lily, Imperial, tumbler, lavender, $100.

Tiger Lily, Imperial, water pitcher and six tumblers, marigold, $540.

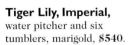

Tornado

Made by Northwood.

Colors known: amethyst, blue, green, ice blue, lavender, marigold, and white.

Forms: vases.

Identifying characteristics: This pattern has a swirling raised tornado-type eye that trails to the base of this vase. It is found with either a rib element on the sides or plain. Production was centered in the 1911 to 1912 period.

Also known as: Tadpole.

Tornado, Northwood,
vase, 6", ribbed flared top, amethyst, $1,800.

Tornado, Northwood,
small vase, 6", purple, $600-$900.

Tornado, Northwood,
small vase, 6", marigold, $600-$900.

Town Pump

Made by Northwood.

Colors known: green, marigold, and purple.

Forms: vases.

Identifying characteristics: Town Pump is a pattern that features ivy on the cylindrical body, a thorn-type handle, and a naturalistic wooden-looking spigot on one side. This is one of the most widely known novelties of the carnival glass world. Production began in 1912 in carnival glass and even earlier in opalescent colors.

Town Pump, Northwood,
town pump, purple, $650.

Tree Trunk

Made by Northwood.

Colors known: amethyst, aqua opalescent, blue, green, ice blue, ice green, lavender, lime green, marigold, marigold on custard, purple, sapphire blue, and white.

Forms: vases.

Identifying characteristics: This pattern is so popular with collectors that they have derived five different names for the sizes: squat, standard, mid-sized funeral, funeral, and elephant foot. The pattern appears as though the designers took a piece of real tree trunk and copied it. By creating the different heights and widths, the pattern extends and expands to cause interesting variations in the design. Heights range from 5" to 22" h. Most have the Northwood trademark. Production began in 1911 and continued until about 1917.

Also known as: Killarney.

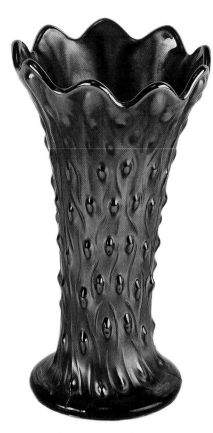

Tree Trunk, Northwood, standard vase, 8", purple, $80-$150.

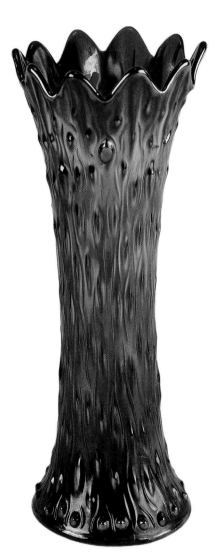

Tree Trunk, Northwood, mid-size vase, 13" h, blue, $550-$950.

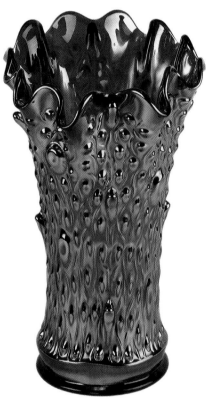

Tree Trunk, Northwood, elephant's foot funeral vase, 13" h, purple, $1,800-$3,400; outstanding condition, $11,000.

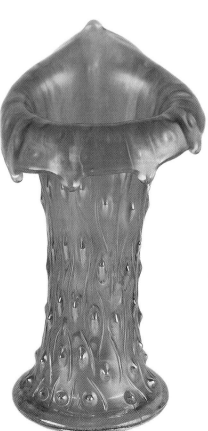

Tree Trunk, Northwood, jester's cap vase, 7-1/2", marigold, $3,000-$4,500 (rare).

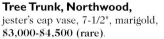

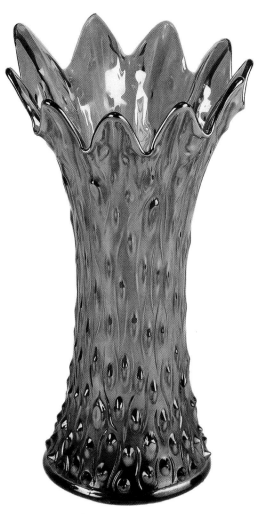

Tree Trunk, Northwood,
mid-size vase, 12" h, green, $350-$650.

Tree Trunk, Northwood,
mid-size vase, $13" h, purple, $350-$550.

Two Flowers

Made by Fenton.

Colors known: amberina, amethyst, aqua, black amethyst, blue, green, lime green, marigold, powder blue, red, sapphire, and white.

Forms: bowls, plates, and rose bowls.

Identifying characteristics: The center of this pattern is dominated by a large detailed chrysanthemum. A wreath of open petaled flowers with oval centers and foliage is further bordered by a band of scales.

Also known as: Dogwood and Marsh Lily.

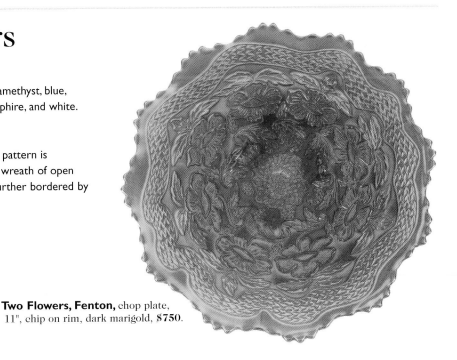

Two Flowers, Fenton, chop plate,
11", chip on rim, dark marigold, $750.

Vineyard

Made by Dugan.

Colors known: marigold, peach opalescent, purple.

Forms: water sets.

Identifying characteristics: This realistic design features a tree bark background topped by grape leaves. Production began in 1910.

Also known as: Grape and Leaf; Peacock Eye and Grape.

Vineyard, Dugan,
tumbler, 3-3/4" h, purple, $50-$150.

Vineyard, Dugan,
water pitcher, peach opal, $1,600.

Vintage

Made by Fenton.

Colors known: amber, amberina, amethyst, amethyst opalescent, aqua opalescent, blue, celeste blue, green, lime green, marigold, peach opalescent, Persian blue, purple, red, vaseline.

Forms: bonbon, bowls, chop plates, compotes, ferners, pitchers, wine glass,

Identifying characteristics: Detailed grape clusters point towards the center where grape leaves are gathered. Additional grape leaves form a wreath around the grapes. Production began in 1912.

Vintage, Fenton,
banana shape, 7-1/2", purple, $500-$700.

Vintage, Fenton,
tri-fold, 6", blue, $100-$150.

Waffle Block

Made by Imperial.

Colors known: clambroth, marigold, purple, smoke, teal.

Forms: baskets, bowls, breakfast sets, parfaits, plates, punch sets, rose bowls, salt and pepper shakers, spittoons, vases, water sets.

Identifying characteristics: This pattern features vertical and horizontal rows of faceted blocks.

Also known as: Imperial's #698.

Waffle Block, Imperial, water pitcher and one tumbler, electric marigold, **$225**.

Water Lily

Made by Fenton.

Colors known: amber slag, amberina, amethyst, aqua, blue, green, lime green, lime green opalescent, marigold, pumpkin marigold, red, reverse amberina, reverse amberina opalescent, sapphire blue, teal, vaseline, vaseline opalescent.

Forms: berry sets, bonbons.

Identifying characteristics: This pattern combines water lily blossoms and poinsettias with a pretty water lily blossom in the center. Production began in 1915.

Also known as: Lotus & Poinsettia; Magnolia and Poinsettia.

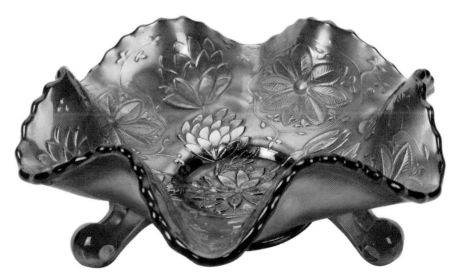

Water Lily, Fenton, bowl, 5", red, **$900**.

Waterlily and Cattails

Made by Fenton.

Colors known: marigold.

Forms: banana boats, bonbons, bowls, hats, plates, spittoons, table sets, water sets.

Identifying characteristics: This water lily pattern has three blossoms that float between cattail, with a center blossom framed by an additional pair of cattails. Production began in 1911.

Also known as: Cattails and Water Lily.

Waterlily and Cattails, Fenton, tumbler, engraved, blue, $1,500.

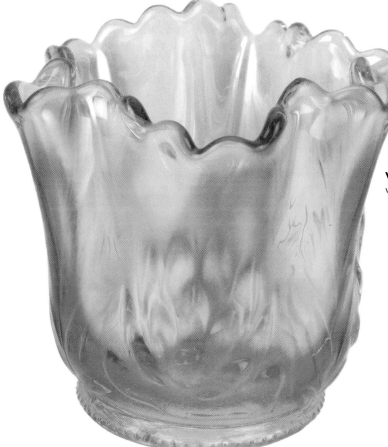

Waterlily and Cattails, Fenton, vase, whimsey, 3-1/2" h, 4" mouth, marigold, $200.

Wide Panel

Made by Fenton, Imperial, Millersburg, and Northwood.

Colors known: amethyst, aqua, black amethyst, blue, celeste blue, clambroth, green, ice blue, ice green, marigold, olive, purple, red, russet, teal, vaseline.

Forms: baskets, bowls, breakfast sets, candlesticks, candy dish, compotes, cruets, epergnes, hats, tumblers, vases.

Identifying characteristics: This pattern was commonly used as an exterior pattern, with it's wide smooth panels being easy to mold. The differences between each maker are hard to distinguish. Values are more dependent upon color and form rather than the maker.

Wide Panel, chop plate, 14-1/2", electric red, $200.

Wide Rib

Made by Dugan/Diamond.

Colors known: amethyst, blue, peach opalescent, white.

Forms: vases.

Identifying characteristics: This ribbed pattern is identified as Dugan/Diamond when the ends of each of the eight ribs have knob-like tips.

Also known as: Dugan's #1016.

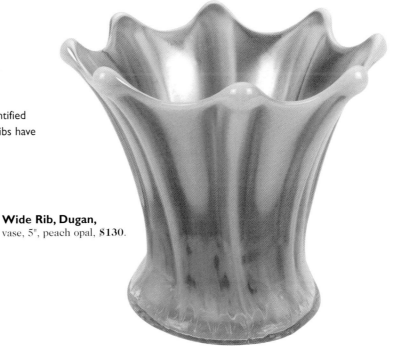

Wide Rib, Dugan, vase, 5", peach opal, $130.

Windmill

Made by Imperial.

Colors: aqua, blue-violet, clambroth, emerald green, helios, lavender, lime green, marigold, marigold on milk glass, olive, purple, smoke.

Forms: bowls, fruit bowls, milk pitchers, pickle dishes, relish trays, water sets.

Identifying characteristics: This lively pattern shows a single windmill within a window scene of trees. Production began in 1910 and continued until 1914.

Also known as: Imperial's #514; Windmill Medallions.

Reproductions: Imperial reissued the water set in marigold, pink, and smoke, as well as marigold with frosted non-iridized panels. Bowls were reissued in marigold, pink, and smoke. Plates were reissued in blue.

Windmill, Imperial, tumbler, 4-1/4", purple, $80-$150.

Windmill, Imperial, water pitcher, smoke, $500.

Windmill, Imperial, bowl, 8", eight ruffles, purple, $150-$300.

Wishbone

Made by Northwood.

Colors known: amethyst, aqua opalescent, blue, green, emerald green, ice blue, ice green, marigold, pumpkin marigold, purple, white.

Forms: bowls, chop plates, epergnes, plates.

Identifying characteristics: This pattern is interesting in that wishbone shapes overlap and alternate with exotic looking orchid blossoms. A multi-petaled flower forms the center. Production began about 1911.

Also known as: Melinda.

Wishbone, Northwood,
footed plate, 8", purple, **$500-$700**.

Wishbone, Northwood,
bowl, 9-1/2", pie-crust edge, electric blue, **$1,900-$2,400**.

Wishbone, Northwood, bowl, 9-1/2", pie-crust edge, purple, **$350-$500**; outstanding condition, **$900**.

Wisteria

Made by Northwood.

Colors known: ice blue, white.

Forms: water sets.

Identifying characteristics: This naturalistic pattern features wisteria flowers and foliate against a lattice background.

Also known as: Wisteria and Lattice.

Wisteria, Northwood, water pitcher and one tumbler, tankard, ice blue, $10,000.

Wreathed Cherries

Made by Dugan/Diamond.

Colors known: amethyst, black amethyst, blue, marigold, peach opalescent, purple, white.

Forms: berry sets, table sets, water sets.

Identifying characteristics: This pattern features a large medallion in which a wreath of leaves encircles a cluster of three hanging cherries. Some pieces exist with enameled red cherries and gilded leaves. Production began in 1911 and continued until 1914.

Also known as: Cherry Wreath; Cherry Wreathed.

Reproductions: Toothpick holders are known while none were ever made in the original production years.

Wreathed Cherries, Dugan, tumbler, white/red cherries, $150.

Wreathed Cherries, Dugan, water pitcher and one tumbler, tankard, white/red cherries, $1,550.

Wreath of Roses

Made by Fenton.

Colors known: amethyst, blue, green, and marigold.

Forms: bonbons, compotes, punch sets, rose bowls.

Identifying characteristics: This delicate pattern features a circle of open roses and leaves with a large rose in the center.

Also known as: American Beauty Roses.

Wreath of Roses, punch bowl base and two cups, Vintage interior, square, green, $650.

Wreath of Roses, Fenton, punch bowl base, six cups, turned up, Vintage interior, amethyst, $650.

Zig Zag

Made by Millersburg.

Colors known: amethyst, green, marigold.

Forms: bowls,

Identifying characteristics: This interior pattern is striking in that rays resembling lightning bolts start closely in the center and radiate to the edges. The exteriors are plain. Production began in 1911.

Zig Zag, Millersburg, bowl, amethyst, $185.

Carnival Glass Price Guide

The following price guide information comes from Tom and Sharon Mordini, Freeport, Ill., two of the most highly respected Carnival Glass people in the United States. Tom and Sharon have been buying, selling and collecting Carnival Glass for 25 years. They create their guide using results from major Carnival Glass auctions throughout the year. For more information about their Carnival Glass Auction Prices guide you can call (815) 235-4407, or email tommordini@aol.com

A Note About the Guide

The description of each item is listed alphabetically. Following each description is a color column followed by a bid amount. This amount reflects the winning bid for that particular item at auction.

The guide attempts to give as much detail about a particular item as necessary. At times, additional comments are made about an item to set it apart from other similar items. This is useful in trying to determine why an item sells for a certain amount. Sometimes, however, there is no way to explain why something sells for much more or much less than it would normally.

When describing bowls, all bowls are ruffled unless otherwise specified. The size of all plates is nine inches unless otherwise specified. When looking up a particular advertising item look first for the word "Advertising" followed by the name of the item. All Northwood, Fenton and Millersburg six-inch bowls and plates in amethyst are listed this way.

Index to Auctions Listed in This Report

DATE	AUCTIONEER	SELLER LOCATION OF SALE	DATE	AUCTIONEER	SELLER LOCATION OF SALE
01-04-03	REICHEL, Consignment	Boonville, MO	06-27-03	BURNS, ACGA/Sharp collection	Pittsburgh, PA
02-01-03	BURNS, S.S.C.G.C./Rissmiller	Deerfield Beach, FL	07-19-03	SEECK, ICGA, Strege, Tilberg, Lough	Indianapolis, IN
02-07-03	BURNS, Tampa Bay, Beedham	Clearwater, FL	07-26-03	WRODA, Baker, Lippay	Greenville, OH
02-15-03	SEECK, Texas C.G.C./Vest	Dallas, TX	08-09-03	REMMEN, PNWCGC/ Private	Beaverton, OR
02-22-03	REICHEL, Burton collection	Boonville, MO	08-23-03	WRODA, Private	Greenville, OH
03-01-03	SEECK, San Diego, So. Cal/Owen	Ontario, CA	09-06-03	BURNS, NECGA/Consignment	Worcester, MA
03-08-03	WRODA, Indiana Collection	Columbus, OH	09-12-03	REICHEL/Consignment	Boonville, MO
03-15-03	REICHEL, Consignment	Boonville, MO	09-13-03	WRODA, Private	Greenville, OH
03-29-03	BURNS, Brandt Collection	Strongsville, OH	09-20-03	SEECK, Farrell Collection	Mason City, IA
04-12-03	REICHEL, WWW.CGA/Kovacs/ Warren	St. Louis, MO	09-27-03	BURNS, NCCGC/Private	Modesto, CA
04-26-03	SEECK, HOACGA/Dooley Coll.	Kansas City, MO	10-11-03	WRODA, Burlew collection	Greenville, OH
05-03-03	WRODA, House Collection	Columbus, OH	10-17-03	REICHEL, ACCGC/ Kovacs/ Warren	Wichita, KS
05-10-03	BURNS, Keystone, Consignment	Morgantown, PA	10-25-03	BURNS, Mid Atlantic/ Vietti Coll.	Hagerstown, MD
05-17-03	SEECK, Owen Collection	Mason City, IA	10-31-03	BURNS, GLCGC/ Ackerman Coll	Lansing, MI
05-24-03	REICHEL, Drabing Collection	Boonville, MO	11-01-03	WRODA, Hatch Collection	Columbus, OH
06-06-03	AYERS, LLCGC, Presbrey/ Goodman	Milwaukee, WI	11-15-03	REICHEL, Shaw Collection	Boonville, MO
06-21-03	WRODA, Yates Collection	Greenville, OH	11-22-03	SEECK, Adams Collection	Wentzville, MO
06-22-03	BURNS, ACGA/Sharp collection	Pittsburgh, PA	12-06-03	WRODA, Gelbach Collection	Greenville, OH

Color Key to Colors in This Report

A	Amethyst	LAV	Lavender, Pale Pastel Amethyst
A.O.	Aqua Opalescent	LIME G	Lime Green, Yellowish Green But Not Vaseline
AMBER	Amber	M	Marigold
AMB O.	Amber Opalescent	M.M.G.	Marigold Flashing Over Milk Glass Base Color
AMRINA	Amberina	MOON	Moonstone, Not Milk Glass, More Opaque
AMY O.	Amethyst Opalescent	O.G.	Olive Green
AQUA	Aqua, Greenish Blue	P	Purple
B	Blue Or Cobalt Blue	P.O.	Peach Opalescent
B.O.	Cobalt Blue Opal	PEARL	Pearlized Milk Glass
B.A.	Black Amethyst	PERS B	Persian Blue, Opaque Like Moonstone
BRK	Red Brick Red, A Brownish Red Fenton Color	PINK	Pink
CELESTE	Celest Blue, Stretchy In Appearance, A Fenton And Dugan Color	POWD B	Powder Blue, Pastel But Not As Lite As Ice Blue
CHOC	Irid. Chocolate Glass	RAO	Red Opalescent
CLAM	Clam Broth, Pale Marigold But Not Pastel Marigold	R/SLAG	Red Slag, Swirl Effect
CLEAR	Clear Base Glass, Not White Or Frosty	RA/OPL	Reverse Amberina Opal
CRYSTAL	Iridised Crystal	RED	Red, True Red, Very Little Or No Yellow In Base
CUSTARD	Iridescent Custard	RENG B	Reningers Blue, An Odd Form Of Blue, Near Teal
E.B.	Electric Blue, Refers To Surface Brilliance	RUBY	Irid. Ruby Flashing
EMR G	Emerald Green, Usualy A Northwood Color	SAPH B	Saphire Blue, Northwood
G	Green	SMOKE	Smokey Gray
HELIOS	A Form Of Green, An Imperial Color	TANGERINE	A Shade Of Marigold
HONAMB	Honey Amber, A U.s. Glass Color	TEAL	Teal Blue/green
HORE	Horehound, Northwoods Form Of Amber	VAS	Vaseline, Yellow/green
I.B.	Ice Blue	VAS O.	Vaseline Opalescent
I.G.	Ice Green	VIOLET	Violet, A Purplish Blue
I.G.O.	Ice Green Opalescent	W	White, Often Frosty
		WISTERIA	A Stretchy Shade Of Lavender

Abbreviations Key

This report contains many abbreviations to describe the characteristics of the glass. This list contains most of the abbreviations used in this report.

ADV	Advertising Item, Sometimes Etched In The Glass	MBRG	Millersburg Glass Company
BW	Basketweave Pattern, Found On Backside Of Item	N	Northwood Glass Company
CR	Candy Ribbon, 3 In 1 Or Tight Crimped Edge	P.C.	Pie Crust Edge
DMG	Damage	PC	Piece, As In 8 Piece Water Set
EA	Each	PITCH	Pitcher, As In Water Cream Or Milk Pitcher
ELEC	Electric Iridescence	PR	Pair, As In Pair Of Candlesticks
EXT	Exterior Or Backside Of Item	PT	Point, Also Could Refer To A Flute
FTD	Footed Item	RAD	Radium Finish
IC	Ice Cream Or Round Shape	SM	Small Size
INT	Interior Of Item	SOUV	Souvenir, Sometimes Etched In The Glass
IRID	Iridescence	SQ	Square Shape
JIP	Jack-in-pulpit Shape	STIP	Stippled, On Front Or Back Surface
LG	Large Size	SZ	Size Of Item, As In Small Or Large Size
LT	Lite, Lack Of Iridescence Or Weak Base Color	VAR	Variant Or Variation Of Pattern

Carnival Glass Auction Prices

DESCRIPTION	COLOR	BID
Acanthus Bowl, Deep Round	P	200
Acanthus Bowl, Deep Round	SMOKE	100
Acanthus Chop Plate	M	105
Acanthus Chop Plate	M	135
Acanthus Milk Pitcher	M	175
Acorn Bowl	AMBER	350
Acorn Bowl	AMY O	375
Acorn Bowl	AQUA	55
Acorn Bowl	AQUA	85
Acorn Bowl	B	65
Acorn Bowl	M	32
Acorn Bowl	MMG	120
Acorn Bowl	RED	310
Acorn Bowl	RED	325
Acorn Bowl	RED	375
Acorn Bowl	RED	375
Acorn Bowl	VAS	400
Acorn Bowl, Ic	AQUA	75
Acorn Bowl, Ic	G	85
Acorn Bowl, Ic	G	110
Acorn Bowl, Ic	RED	225
Acorn Bowl, Ic	RED	300
Acorn Bowl, Ic	RED	300
Acorn Bowl, Ic	RED	300
Acorn Bowl, Ic	RED	325
Acorn Bowl, Ic	RED	350
Acorn Bowl, Ic	RED	900
Acorn Bowl, Ic	RED	1000
Acorn Bowl, Mgold Over Moon.	MOON	425
Acorn Burrs Berry Set, 6 Pc	P	280
Acorn Burrs Berry Set, 7 Pc	M	210
Acorn Burrs Berry Set, 7 Pc	M	225
Acorn Burrs Berry Set, 7 Pc	M	350
Acorn Burrs Berry Set, 7 Pc	P	155
Acorn Burrs Butter Dish	A	245
Acorn Burrs Butter Dish	G	375
Acorn Burrs Butter Dish	M	170

DESCRIPTION	COLOR	BID
Acorn Burrs Butter Dish	M	205
Acorn Burrs Butter Dish	M	375
Acorn Burrs Butter Dish	P	300
Acorn Burrs Pitcher	M	475
Acorn Burrs Pitcher	M	1050
Acorn Burrs Pitcher	P	1000
Acorn Burrs Punch Bowl Only	G	1000
Acorn Burrs Punch Set, 10 Pc	W	5500
Acorn Burrs Punch Set, 8 Pc	G	1600
Acorn Burrs Punch Set, 8 Pc	G	2700
Acorn Burrs Punch Set, 8 Pc	P	1250
Acorn Burrs Punch Set, 8 Pc	P	1500
Acorn Burrs Punch Set, 8 Pc	P	1550
Acorn Burrs Punch Set, 8 Pc, Dark	M	2700
Acorn Burrs Spooner	G	315
Acorn Burrs Sugar	P	200
Acorn Burrs Tumbler	G	100
Acorn Burrs Tumbler	M	60
Acorn Burrs Tumbler	P	35
Acorn Burrs Water Set, 7 Pc	M	700
Acorn Burrs Water Set, 7 Pc	P	600
Acorn Compote, Ruffled, Mbrg	G	3100
Adams Rib Vase, 9"	IG	225
Advertising, Ballard Merced Plate	A	1300
Braziers Candies Plate	A	1100
Advertising, Braziers Candies Plate, Handgrip	A	900
Advertising, Brokers Flour Plate	A	1750
Advertising, Brokers Flour Plate	A	3000
Advertising, Campbell & Beesley Plate, Hgrip	A	750
Advertising, Central Shoe Store Plate	A	1300

DESCRIPTION	COLOR	BID
Advertising, Central Shoe Store Plate, Hndgrip	A	600
Advertising, Davidson Society Card Tray	A	900
Advertising, Davidson Society Card Tray	A	1000
Advertising, Dorsey & Funkenstein Plate	A	2600
Advertising, Dreibus Parfait Bowl, Rfld	A	500
Advertising, Dreibus Parfait Plate, Handgrip	A	1100
Advertising, Eagle Furniture Card Tray	A	1100
Advertising, Eagle Furniture Plate	A	1500
Advertising, Eagle Furniture Plate, Silvery	A	375
Advertising, Exchange Bank Bowl, Ruffled	A	900
Advertising, Exchange Bank Plate	A	1700
Advertising, Exchange Bank Plate, Handgrip	A	1700
Advertising, Fern Brand Choc. Card Tray	A	950
Advertising, Fern Brand Chocolates Card Tray	A	1100
Advertising, Fern Brand Plate, W/metal Adv Box	A	1850
Advertising, George Getts Pianos Bowl, Rfld	A	1100
Advertising, George Getts Pianos Plate	A	1300
Advertising, Gevurtz Bowl, Ruffled	A	1600
Advertising, Gevurtz Plate, Handgrip	A	1700
Advertising, Greengard Furniture Plate, Hndgrp	A	7000
Advertising, Isaac Benesch Bowl	A	260
Advertising, Isaac Benesch Bowl	A	325
Advertising, Isaac Benesch Bowl	A	325
Advertising, Isaac Benesch Bowl	A	375

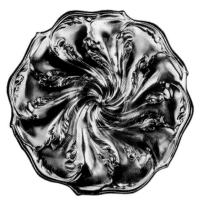

Acanthus, Imperial, chop plate, marigold, pretty and flat, **$135.**

Advertising, Fenton, Gevurtz handgrip plate, spectacular amethyst, has incredible mold work and electric iridescence, very small pinhead on flowers, **$1,700.**

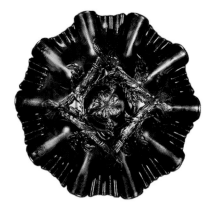

Apple Blossom Twigs, Dugan, bowl, 3-in-1 edge, electric purple, **$700.**

Acorn Burrs, Northwood, punch bowl and base with four cups, green, incredible iridescence, **$1,800.**

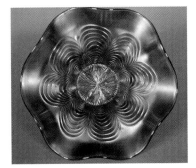

Peacock Tail advertising hat, Fenton, "Hudsons Tahlequah Oklahoma," green, **$130.**

Acorn Burrs, Northwood, covered sugar, green lid with purple bottom and Northwood blue grape, **$30.**

Apple Tree, Fenton, water pitcher and six tumblers, marigold, **$310.**

DESCRIPTION	COLOR	BID
Advertising, Isaac Benesch Bowl	A	375
Advertising, Isaac Benesch Bowl	A	425
Advertising, Isaac Benesch Bowl	A	425
Advertising, Issac Benesch Bowl	A	420
Advertising, Jockey Club Plate	A	1100
Advertising, Jockey Club Plate, Handgrip	A	1100
Advertising, Jockey Club Plate, Looks Mgold	A	1600
Advertising, Norris Smith Bowl, Round	A	1800
Advertising, Norris Smith Plate	A	1400
Advertising, Ogden Furniture Bowl, Rfld	A	700
Advertising, Ogden Furniture Plate, Handgrip	A	1100
Advertising, Paradise Sodas Plate	A	475
Advertising, Paradise Sodas Plate	A	500
Advertising, Roods Chocolates Plate	A	3600
Advertising, Sterling Furniture Bowl, Round	A	750
Advertising, Sterling Furniture Plate, Handgrp	A	1800
Advertising, Utah Liquor Card Tray	A	900
Amaryllis Plate Whimsey From Compote	A	1600
Amaryllis Plate, Tri Corner, Dome Ftd	M	250
Apple & Pear Bowl, 5"	M	40
Apple Blossom Twigs Bowl	P	135
Apple Blossom Twigs Bowl	W	200
Apple Blossom Twigs Bowl, 3/1 Edge	P	375
Apple Blossom Twigs Bowl, 3/1 Edge	P	550
Apple Blossom Twigs Bowl, 3/1 Edge	P	700
Apple Blossom Twigs Bowl, 3/1 Edge	PO	135
Apple Blossom Twigs Bowl, Ic	B	225

DESCRIPTION	COLOR	BID
Apple Blossom Twigs Bowl, Ic	LAV	250
Apple Blossom Twigs Bowl, Low Ruffled	A	130
Apple Blossom Twigs Bowl, Low Rufled	W	115
Apple Blossom Twigs Plate	B	95
Apple Blossom Twigs Plate	B	235
Apple Blossom Twigs Plate	M	95
Apple Blossom Twigs Plate	PO	265
Apple Blossom Twigs Plate	PO	300
Apple Blossom Twigs Plate	W	140
Apple Blossom Twigs Plate, Smooth Edge Var	A	100
Apple Tree Pitcher	M	225
Apple Tree Pitcher, Electric	B	825
Apple Tree Tumbler	B	40
Apple Tree Tumbler	B	95
Apple Tree Tumbler	W	150
Apple Tree Water Set, 7 Pc	W	550
April Showers Vase, 10"	G	35
April Showers Vase, 11"	B	60
April Showers Vase, 11"	RED	1300
Beaded Bullseye Vase, 10"	EMR G	850
Beaded Bullseye Vase, 10"	P	100
Beaded Bullseye Vase, 11"	P	100
Beaded Bullseye Vase, 11"	P	120
Beaded Bullseye Vase, 11"	P	135
Beaded Bullseye Vase, 12"	AMBER	150
Beaded Bullseye Vase, 6"	P	215
Beaded Bullseye Vase, 7"	P	265
Beaded Bullseye Vase, Flared, 8"	P	190
Beaded Shell Butter Dish	M	325
Beaded Shell Mug	P	50
Beaded Shell Mug	W	340
Beaded Shell Mug	W	450
Beaded Shell Tumbler	B	65

DESCRIPTION	COLOR	BID
Big Basketweave Vase, 10"	HORE	350
Big Basketweave Vase, 10"	IB	1300
Big Basketweave Vase, 10"	P	55
Big Basketweave Vase, 10"	P	275
Big Basketweave Vase, 10"	SAPH B	350
Big Basketweave Vase, 10"	W	205
Big Basketweave Vase, 11"	P	250
Big Basketweave Vase, 9"	W	115
Big Basketweave Vase, Squatty	P	215
Big Basketweave Vase, Squatty	P	355
Big Basketweave Vase, Squatty	W	185
Big Fish Bowl	G	750
Big Fish Bowl	G	775
Big Fish Bowl	G	775
Big Fish Bowl, 3/1 Edge	A	400
Big Fish Bowl, 3/1 Edge	A	475
Big Fish Bowl, 3/1 Edge	M	375
Big Fish Bowl, 3/1 Edge	M	425
Big Fish Bowl, Ic	A	600
Big Fish Bowl, Ic	A	675
Big Fish Bowl, Ic	A	750
Big Fish Bowl, Ic	A	750
Big Fish Bowl, Ic	G	475
Big Fish Bowl, Ic, Radium	A	600
Big Fish Bowl, Ic, Radium	M	850
Big Fish Bowl, Square	M	900
Big Fish Bowl, Tri Corner Outstanding Irid.	G	13000
Big Fish Rosebowl Whimsey, 1 In This Color	M	8500
Birds & Cherries Bon Bon	B	110
Birds & Cherries Bon Bon	P	140
Blackberry Block Tankard	G	1100
Blackberry Block Tankard	G	1200
Blackberry Block Tankard	M	240

Blackberry Spray, Fenton, six-ruffled hat, 6-1/2", red, **$300-$500.**

Blackberry Spray, Fenton,
jack-in-the-pulpit hat with a tight crimped
edge, reverse amberina. Has a really neat red
strip around the outer edge, **$275.**

Blackberry Wreath, Millersburg,
bowl with three-in-one edge, marigold, **$80.**

Beaded Bullseye, Imperial,
vase, 8-3/4", electric purple, **$150.**

Butterfly and Berry, Fenton,
vase, 8", top flames, blue, **$75-$150.**

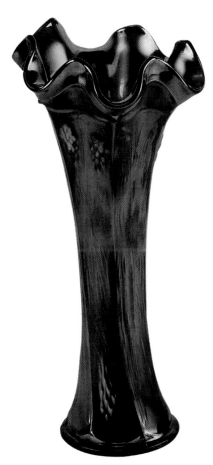

Butterfly and Berry, Fenton,
vase, 8-1/2", top flames, red, **$800-$1,200.**

DESCRIPTION	COLOR	BID
Blackberry Block Tankard	W	4000
Blackberry Block Tumbler	B	47
Blackberry Block Tumbler	G	95
Blackberry Block Water Set, 7 Pc	M	1050
Blackberry Candy Dish, Daisy & Plume Ext.	G	125
Blackberry Candy Dish, Daisy & Plume Ext.	LIME G	275
Blackberry Open Edge Basket	A	40
Blackberry Open Edge Basket	AQUA	275
Blackberry Open Edge Basket	CELEST	1050
Blackberry Open Edge Basket	G	80
Blackberry Open Edge Basket	LIME G	170
Blackberry Open Edge Basket	M	10
Blackberry Open Edge Basket	M	35
Blackberry Open Edge Basket	POWD B	60
Blackberry Open Edge Basket	POWD B	75
Blackberry Open Edge Basket	RED	225
Blackberry Open Edge Basket	RED	280
Blackberry Open Edge Basket	RED	425
Blackberry Open Edge Basket	RED	450
Blackberry Open Edge Basket	W	175
Blackberry Open Edge Basket	W	250
Blackberry Open Edge Basket, Round	B	250
Blackberry Open Edge Basket, Round	W	300
Blackberry Open Edge Basket, Round Whimsey	B	150
Blackberry Open Edge Basket, Square	A	145
Blackberry Open Edge Basket, Square	RED	265
Blackberry Open Edge Basket, Square	W	340
Blackberry Open Edge Basket, Square	B	1650
Blackberry Open Edge Vase Whimsey		

DESCRIPTION	COLOR	BID
Blackberry Open Edge Vase Whimsey	M	1850
Blackberry Open Edge Vase Whimsey	POWD B	1350
Blackberry Open Edge Vase Whimsey, Heat Crack	M	900
Blackberry Spray Hat	AMBER	45
Blackberry Spray Hat	AO	400
Blackberry Spray Hat	B	45
Blackberry Spray Hat	LIME G	45
Blackberry Spray Hat	LIME G	95
Blackberry Spray Hat	RAO	450
Blackberry Spray Hat	RED	195
Blackberry Spray Hat	RED	195
Blackberry Spray Hat	RED	200
Blackberry Spray Hat	RED	210
Blackberry Spray Hat	RED	255
Blackberry Spray Hat, 2 Sides Up	RED	250
Blackberry Spray Hat, 2 Sides Up	RED	275
Blackberry Spray Hat, Crimped, Jip	AO	1300
Blackberry Spray Hat, Crimped, Jip	RED	275
Blackberry Spray Hat, Crimped, Jip	RED	450
Blackberry Wreath Bowl, 10"	B	825
Blackberry Wreath Bowl, 10"	B	900
Blackberry Wreath Bowl, 10"	B	1200
Blackberry Wreath Bowl, 10", Ic	A	180
Blackberry Wreath Bowl, 10", Ic	M	350
Blackberry Wreath Bowl, 10", Ic P 350 01-04 Blackberry Wreath Bowl, 10", Square	M	425
Blackberry Wreath Bowl, 6"	G	250
Blackberry Wreath Bowl, 6", Ic	A	185
Blackberry Wreath Bowl, 7"	G	55
Blackberry Wreath Bowl, 7", Tri-corner	A	125
Blackberry Wreath Bowl, 9", Square	A	275
Blossomtime Compote	M	100
Blossomtime Compote	M	140

DESCRIPTION	COLOR	BID
Blossomtime Compote	P	170
Blossomtime Compote	P	175
Blossomtime Compote	P	250
Blueberry Pitcher	B	650
Blueberry Pitcher	M	275
Blueberry Pitcher	M	500
Blueberry Pitcher	W	4400
Blueberry Pitcher, Elec	B	3800
Blueberry Tumbler	B	70
Blueberry Tumbler	B	75
Blueberry Tumbler	B	135
Blueberry Tumbler	8	180
Blueberry Tumbler	W	70
Bouquet Pitcher	M	135
Bouquet Pitcher, Bright Color	B	525
Bouquet Pitcher, Dark	M	300
Bouquet Tumbler	B	55
Bouquet Tumbler	M	45
Bouquet Tumbler	M	85
Bouquet Water Set, 5 Pc	M	190
Broken Arches Punch Set, 11 Pc	M	450
Broken Arches Punch Set, 6 Pc	M	295
Broken Arches Punch Set, 8 Pc	P	1150
Bushel Basket	AO	175
Bushel Basket	AO	195
Bushel Basket	AO	200
Bushel Basket	AO	250
Bushel Basket	AO	250
Bushel Basket	AO	250
Bushel Basket	AO	250
Bushel Basket	AO	325
Bushel Basket	AO	325
Bushel Basket	AO	325
Bushel Basket	AO	325
Bushel Basket	AQUA	350
Bushel Basket	B	110
Bushel Basket	B	115
Bushel Basket	B	125
Bushel Basket	B	125
Bushel Basket	B	140
Bushel Basket	B	150
Bushel Basket	B	165
Bushel Basket	G	275
Bushel Basket	G	275

Chatalaine, Imperial, water pitcher and six tumblers, electric purple, $2,500.

Captive Rose, Fenton, plate, green, very pretty and even, **$1,200.**

Captive Rose, Fenton, bowl with three-in-one edge, electric blue, super piece, **$500.**

Concord, Fenton, ruffled bowl, marigold, **$200.**

Concord, Fenton, ruffled bowl, green, beautiful multi-color iridescence, **$350.**

DESCRIPTION	COLOR	BID	DESCRIPTION	COLOR	BID	DESCRIPTION	COLOR	BID
Bushel Basket	G	300	Butterfly & Berry Bowl, Lg Berry	W	875	Butterfly & Tulip Bowl, Four Sides Up	M	410
Bushel Basket	G	350	Butterfly & Berry Bowl, Lg Berry, Plain Int	A	170	Butterfly & Tulip Bowl, Ftd, Silvery	P	1050
Bushel Basket	IG	140	Butterfly & Berry Hatpin Holder	B	1200	Butterfly & Tulip Bowl, Square	P	2600
Bushel Basket	IG	145	Butterfly & Berry Hatpin Holder	B	1600	Butterfly Bon Bon	A	75
Bushel Basket	IG	145	Butterfly & Berry Hatpin Holder	B	2200	Butterfly Bon Bon	G	65
Bushel Basket	IG	155	Butterfly & Berry Hatpin Holder	M	900	Butterfly Bon Bon	G	130
Bushel Basket	IG	155	Butterfly & Berry Hatpin Holder	M	1100	Butterfly Bon Bon	G	185
Bushel Basket	IG	210	Butterfly & Berry Hatpin Holder	M	1400	Butterfly Bon Bon, Ribbed Ext	B	525
Bushel Basket	IG	400	Butterfly & Berry Pitcher	B	625	Butterfly Bon Bon, Ribbed Ext	M	375
Bushel Basket	LAV	200	Butterfly & Berry Rosebowl Whimsey	A	350	Captive Rose Bowl	G	105
Bushel Basket	M	55	Butterfly & Berry Vase, 9"	RED	925	Captive Rose Bowl, 3/1 Edge	B	100
Bushel Basket	M	65	Butterfly & Berry Water Set, 7 Pc	A	4750	Captive Rose Bowl, 3/1 Edge	B	120
Bushel Basket	M	75	Butterfly & Berry Water Set, 7 Pc	B	700	Captive Rose Bowl, 3/1 Edge	B	500
Bushel Basket	M	95	Butterfly & Berry Water Set, 7 Pc	M	425	Captive Rose Bowl, 3/1 Edge	G	70
Bushel Basket	M	95	Butterfly & Berry Water Set, 7 Pc, Tumb. Damg.	M	105	Captive Rose Bowl, 3/1 Edge	M	125
Bushel Basket	M	375	Butterfly & Berry Whimsey From Tumbler	M	800	Captive Rose Bowl, Ic	G	110
Bushel Basket	P	60	Butterfly & Fern Pitcher	A	250	Captive Rose Bowl, Tight Ribbon Edge	G	100
Bushel Basket	P	85	Butterfly & Fern Pitcher	A	450	Captive Rose Compote	A	75
Bushel Basket	P	115	Butterfly & Fern Pitcher	B	225	Captive Rose Compote	W	110
Bushel Basket	P	155	Butterfly & Fern Pitcher	G	375	Captive Rose Plate	A	725
Bushel Basket	SAPH B	1600	Butterfly & Fern Pitcher	G	450	Captive Rose Plate	A	850
Bushel Basket	SMOKE	300	Butterfly & Fern Pitcher	M	140	Captive Rose Plate	B	135
Bushel Basket	VIOLET	325	Butterfly & Fern Tumbler	A	55	Captive Rose Plate	B	225
Bushel Basket	W	105	Butterfly & Fern Tumbler	M	50	Captive Rose Plate	B	285
Bushel Basket	W	125	Butterfly & Fern Tumblers X 3	G	60	Captive Rose Plate	B	450
Bushel Basket	W	130	Butterfly & Fern Tumblers, Set Of 6	B	180	Captive Rose Plate	B	1050
Bushel Basket	W	145	Butterfly & Fern Water Set, 7 Pc	B	725	Captive Rose Plate	G	575
Bushel Basket	W	145	Butterfly & Fern Water Set, 7 Pc	B	725	Captive Rose Plate	G	650
Bushel Basket, 8 Sided	A	70	Butterfly & Tulip Bowl, Deep Round	M	425	Captive Rose Plate	G	775
Bushel Basket, 8 Sided	IG	175	Butterfly & Tulip Bowl, Deep Square	M	250	Captive Rose Plate	G	800
Bushel Basket, 8 Sided	M	55				Captive Rose Plate	G	925
Bushel Basket, 8 Sided	P	135				Captive Rose Plate	G	950
Bushel Basket, 8 Sided	W	125				Captive Rose Plate	G	1200
Bushel Basket, 8 Sided	W	130				Captive Rose Plate	G	1200
Bushel Basket, 8 Sided, Elec	B	425				Captive Rose Plate	M	160
Bushel Basket, Slag	A	100				Captive Rose Plate	M	275
Butterfly & Berry Berry Set, 7 Pc	A	225				Captive Rose Plate	M	280
Butterfly & Berry Bowl, Lg Berry	A	100				Captive Rose Plate	M	350
Butterfly & Berry Bowl, Lg Berry	A	120				Captive Rose Plate	M	500
Butterfly & Berry Bowl, Lg Berry	A	130						
Butterfly & Berry Bowl, Lg Berry	A	200						
Butterfly & Berry Bowl, Lg Berry	G	400						

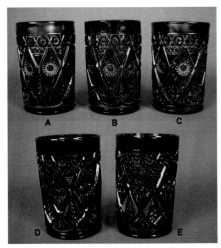

Diamond Lace, Imperial, five tumblers, purple, (sold choice), $125 for the set.

Diamond Lace, Imperial, ruffled bowl, purple, $25.

Dragon and Lotus, Fenton, bowl, vaseline with marigold overlay, $600.

Dragon and Strawberry, Fenton, footed ruffled bowl marigold, scarce and pretty, $425.

Dragon and Strawberry, Fenton, ice-cream shaped bowl, blue, exceptional color, $700.

Embroidered Mums, Northwood, ruffled bowl, blue, covered with electric highlights, $500.

Embroidered Mums, Northwood, ruffled bowl, ice blue, beautiful pastel iridescence, $950.

DESCRIPTION	COLOR	BID
Captive Rose Plate, Light	M	180
Captive Rose Plate, Silvery	G	180
Chatelaine Tumbler	P	195
Chatelaine Tumbler	P	275
Chatelaine Tumbler	P	375
Checkerboard Pitcher	A	750
Checkerboard Pitcher	A	1100
Checkerboard Tumbler	A	85
Checkerboard Tumbler	A	200
Cherries Bowl, 10", Dugan	BA	300
Cherries Bowl, 8", Dugan	P	175
Cherries Bowl, 9", Dugan	P	175
Cherries Bowl, 9", Dugan	P	195
Cherries Bowl, 9", Dugan	P	350
Cherries Bowl, 9", Dugan	P	425
Cherries Bowl, Ftd, Dugan	P	250
Cherries Bowl, Ftd, Dugan	P	280
Cherries Bowl, Ic, 8", Dugan	PO	270
Cherries Bowl, Tri Corner, Crimped, Dugan	P	255
Cherries Plate, 6", Dugan, Crimped Edge	P	175
Cherries Plate, 6", Dugan, Crimped Edge	P	195
Cherry & Cable Butter Dish	M	200
Cherry Chain Bowl	B	140
Cherry Chain Bowl	B	320
Cherry Chain Bowl, 3/1 Edge, 10"	G	200
Cherry Chain Bowl, Lg	W	120
Cherry Chain Bowl, Lg Ic	A	325
Cherry Chain Plate, 6"	B	135
Cherry Chain Plate, 6"	M	40
Cherry Chain Plate, Orange Tree Ext, 6" Emr	G	2500
Chrysanthemum Bowl, 10"	B	155
Chrysanthemum Bowl, 10"	VAS	114
Chrysanthemum Bowl, Lg Ic	B	300

DESCRIPTION	COLOR	BID
Chrysanthemum Bowl, Lg, Ftd	B	115
Chrysanthemum Bowl, Lg, Ftd	B	175
Chrysanthemum Bowl, Lg, Ftd	B	275
Chrysanthemum Bowl, Lg, Ftd	G	245
Chrysanthemum Bowl, Ruffled, Outstanding	RED	4100
Chrysanthemum Chop Plate	P	1750
Chrysanthemum Chop Plate	SMOKE	750
Chrysanthemum Chop Plate, Nuart	SMOKE	800
Circle Scroll Hat, Jip	M	60
Circle Scroll Tumbler	M	100
Circle Scroll Tumbler	M	310
Circle Scroll Tumbler	P	210
Circle Scroll Vase, 7"	P	225
Circle Scroll Vase, 9"	BA	370
Colonial Lady Variant Vase, 8"	M	125
Colonial Lady Vase	M	450
Colonial Lady Vase	P	530
Colonial Lady Vase, Electric	P	2300
Concord Bowl	B	275
Concord Bowl	G	275
Concord Bowl	G	350
Concord Bowl	M	150
Concord Bowl	M	185
Concord Bowl	M	200
Concord Bowl, 3/1 Edge	A	300
Concord Bowl, 3/1 Edge	M	170
Concord Bowl, Ic	B	75
Concord Bowl, Ic	M	135
Concord Plate	A	1350
Concord Plate	A	1400
Concord Plate	M	1100
Concord Plate	M	1800
Constellation Compote	M	140
Constellation Compote	W	65
Coral Bowl	M	90
Coral Bowl	M	225
Coral Bowl, 3/1 Edge, Base Chip	M	210
Coral Bowl, Ic	G	175
Coral Bowl, Ic	G	240
Coral Plate	M	1050

DESCRIPTION	COLOR	BID
Corinth Vase, 8", Small Crack	BO	175
Corinth Vase, Jip	P	100
Corinth Vase, Jip	TEAL	100
Corinth Vase, Jip	TEAL	105
Corn Bottle	G	175
Corn Bottle	G	250
Corn Bottle	G	525
Corn Bottle	HELIOS	150
Corn Bottle	M	150
Corn Bottle	M	175
Corn Bottle	M	290
Corn Bottle	M	375
Corn Bottle	M	375
Corn Bottle	M	400
Corn Bottle	SMOKE	325
Corn Bottle	SMOKE	385
Corn Bottle	SMOKE	450
Corn Bottle	SMOKE	550
Corn Bottle, Clear	W	350
Corn Vase	G	275
Corn Vase	G	375
Corn Vase	G	550
Corn Vase	G	600
Corn Vase	IB	900
Corn Vase	IG	235
Corn Vase	IG	250
Corn Vase	IG	325
Corn Vase	IG	325
Corn Vase	IG	375
Corn Vase	IG	525
Corn Vase	LIME G	400
Corn Vase	LIME G	450
Corn Vase	M	450
Corn Vase	M	500
Corn Vase	M	650
Corn Vase	P	350
Corn Vase	P	450
Corn Vase	W	200
Corn Vase	W	225
Corn Vase	W	225
Corn Vase	W	295
Corn Vase	W	350
Corn Vase, (2) One Has Pinhead, One Has Flaw	M	600
Corn Vase, Glued Back Together At Bottom	AO	3750
Corn Vase, Nicks	TEAL	1450

Floral and Optic, Imperial, rose bowl, marigold over milk glass, footed, **$100**.

Floral and Grape, Fenton,
two tumblers, blue (sold choice),
$50 and **$40**.

Fluffy Peacock, Fenton,
three tumblers, amethyst (sold choice), **$55, $45** and **$25**.

DESCRIPTION	COLOR	BID
Cosmos & Cane Chop Plate	HON AM	425
Cosmos & Cane Compote, 4"	W	200
Cosmos & Cane Compote, Flared	W	110
Cosmos & Cane Compote, Punch Bowl Shape	W	120
Cosmos & Cane Compote, Tall	M	325
Cosmos & Cane Compote, Very Rare Color	P	300
Cosmos & Cane Rosebowl, Headdress Int, 6"	AMBER	725
Cosmos & Cane Tumbler	HON AM	40
Cosmos & Cane Tumbler	HON AM	65
Cosmos & Cane Tumbler	W	270
Cosmos & Cane Tumbler, J.r. Milner Adv	HON AM	110
Cosmos & Cane Tumbler, J.r. Milner Adv	HON AM	130
Cosmos & Cane Water Set, 5 Pc	W	1700
Curved Star Epergne, 3 Pc, European	M	1100
Dahlia Bowl, 7"	AQUA	130
Dahlia Pitcher	W	400
Dahlia Spooner	P	95
Dahlia Tumbler	M	80
Dahlia Tumbler	M	165
Dahlia Tumbler	P	100
Dahlia Tumbler	W	75
Dahlia Tumbler	W	130
Dahlia Tumbler	W	135
Dahlia Water Set, 7 Pc	M	1700
Daisy & Drape Vase	AO	300
Daisy & Drape Vase	AO	425
Daisy & Drape Vase	AO	575
Daisy & Drape Vase	AO	600
Daisy & Drape Vase	AO	600
Daisy & Drape Vase	AO	625
Daisy & Drape Vase	B	450
Daisy & Drape Vase	B	750
Daisy & Drape Vase	IB	2250
Daisy & Drape Vase	M	200
Daisy & Drape Vase	M	225

DESCRIPTION	COLOR	BID
Daisy & Drape Vase	M	400
Daisy & Drape Vase	M	450
Daisy & Drape Vase	M	550
Daisy & Drape Vase	M	550
Daisy & Drape Vase	P	850
Daisy & Drape Vase	W	125
Daisy & Drape Vase	W	130
Daisy & Drape Vase	W	130
Daisy & Drape Vase	W	130
Daisy & Drape Vase	W	150
Daisy & Drape Vase	W	165
Daisy & Drape Vase	W	180
Daisy & Drape Vase	W	185
Daisy & Drape Vase	W	195
Daisy & Drape Vase	W	200
Daisy & Drape Vase	W	200
Daisy & Lattice Tumbler	B	65
Daisy & Plume Rosebowl, Chips On Legs	IB	325
Daisy & Plume Rosebowl, Ft Nicks, Butterscotch	AO	1500
Daisy & Plume Rosebowl, Raspberry Int	AO	7000
Daisy & Plume Rosebowl, Raspberry Int	G	155
Daisy & Plume Rosebowl, Raspberry Int	IG	1150
Daisy & Plume Rosebowl, Raspberry Int	M	55
Daisy & Plume Rosebowl, Raspberry Int	P	175
Daisy & Plume Rosebowl, Raspberry Int	W	525
Daisy & Plume Rosebowl, Raspberry Int, Cracked	HORE	125
Daisy Wreath Bowl	BO	200
Daisy Wreath Bowl	MMG	85
Daisy Wreath Bowl	MMG	90
Daisy Wreath Bowl, Ic	MMG	60
Dandelion Mug	A	275
Dandelion Mug	AO	350
Dandelion Mug	AO	375
Dandelion Mug	AO	375
Dandelion Mug	AO	375
Dandelion Mug	AO	400
Dandelion Mug	AO	425
Dandelion Mug	AO	450
Dandelion Mug	AO	650

DESCRIPTION	COLOR	BID
Dandelion Mug	B	275
Dandelion Mug	B	325
Dandelion Mug	LAV	200
Dandelion Mug	M	170
Dandelion Mug	M	225
Dandelion Mug	M	275
Dandelion Mug	M	320
Dandelion Mug	P	200
Dandelion Mug, Butterscotch	AO	300
Dandelion Mug, Electric	B	650
Dandelion Mug, Knights Templar	IB	475
Dandelion Mug, Knights Templar	IB	950
Dandelion Mug, Knights Templar	IG	675
Dandelion Mug, Knights Templar	IG	850
Dandelion Mug, Knights Templar	IG	925
Dandelion Mug, Knights Templar	M	210
Dandelion Mug, Knights Templar	M	225
Dandelion Mug, Knights Templar	M	355
Dandelion Tankard	G	850
Dandelion Tankard	HORE	400
Dandelion Tankard, Engraved Ella Kress, 1910	P	600
Dandelion Tumbler	A	125
Dandelion Tumbler	G	75
Dandelion Tumbler	G	90
Dandelion Tumbler	IB	155
Dandelion Tumbler	IB	160
Dandelion Tumbler	SMOKE	950
Dandelion Tumbler	W	95
Dandelion Tumbler	W	130
Dandelion Water Set, 3 Pc	G	910
Dandelion Water Set, 7 Pc	P	1300
Dandelion Water Set, 8 Pc	P	750
Diamond & Rib Jardiniere, 6 1/2"	G	1300
Diamond & Rib Vase, 9"	W	95
Diamond & Rib Vase, Whimsey Shape, 5"	G	1000

Grape and Cable, Northwood, punch set, mid-size, white, $6,500.

Grape and Cable, Northwood, punch bowl base, master, 10 cups, white, $9,000.

Grape and Cable, Northwood, punch bowl base, small, white, $6,000.

DESCRIPTION	COLOR	BID
Diamond Lace Pitcher	P	285
Diamond Lace Pitcher	P	325
Diamond Lace Rosebowl Whimsy, Bubble Burst	M	1100
Diamond Lace Tumbler, Cracked	M	175
Diamond Lace Water Set, 7 Pc	P	400
Diamond Lace Water Set, 7 Pc	P	425
Diamond Lace Water Set, 7 Pc	P	475
Diamond Lace Water Set, 7 Pc	P	550
Diamond Point Columns Vase, 12" Lime	G	40
Diamond Points Basket	M	425
Diamond Points Basket	M	2100
Diamond Points Basket, Some Nicks On Base	B	375
Diamond Points Rosebowl	M	675
Diamond Points Vase, 10"	AO	1025
Diamond Points Vase, 10"	B	675
Diamond Points Vase, 10"	LIME G	360
Diamond Points Vase, 10", Base Chip	AO	650
Diamond Points Vase, 11"	AO	900
Diamond Points Vase, 11"	B	125
Diamond Points Vase, 11"	G	105
Diamond Points Vase, 11"	IG	200
Diamond Points Vase, 11"	IG	225
Diamond Points Vase, 11"	IG	275
Diamond Points Vase, 11"	LAV	110
Diamond Points Vase, 11"	M	190
Diamond Points Vase, 11"	SAPH B	1700
Diamond Points Vase, 11"	W	65
Diamond Points Vase, 12"	G	145
Diamond Points Vase, 7"	IB	450

DESCRIPTION	COLOR	BID
Diamond Points Vase, 7"	IG	400
Diamond Points Vase, 7"	P	155
Diamond Points Vase, 9"	A	80
Diamond Points Vase, 9"	G	70
Diamond Points Vase, Squatty, 7"	B	235
Diamond Ring Bowl	P	25
Diamond Spindle Candlesticks, Pr	CELEST	110
Diamonds Pitcher	G	325
Diamonds Pitcher	M	150
Diamonds Tumbler	A	57
Diamonds Tumbler	A	80
Diamonds Tumbler	AQUA	110
Diamonds Tumbler	G	100
Diamonds Tumbler	M	60
Diamonds Tumbler	M	70
Diamonds Tumbler	M	75
Diamonds Tumbler	P	90
Diamonds Tumbler	TEAL	65
Diamonds Tumblers, 3, None Are Iridised	P	525
Diamonds Water Set, 7 Pc	G	575
Dianthus Water Set, 7 Pc, Enameled	W	700
Double Star Pitcher	G	115
Double Star Water Set, 7 Pc	G	600
Dozen Roses Bowl, Ftd	A	900
Dragon & Lotus Bowl	AMBER	110
Dragon & Lotus Bowl	AMBER	225
Dragon & Lotus Bowl	AMBERI	450
Dragon & Lotus Bowl	AMBERI	950
Dragon & Lotus Bowl	AMY O	875
Dragon & Lotus Bowl	AO	2600
Dragon & Lotus Bowl	B	105
Dragon & Lotus Bowl	B	120
Dragon & Lotus Bowl	B	125
Dragon & Lotus Bowl	B	165
Dragon & Lotus Bowl	LGO	350
Dragon & Lotus Bowl	LGO	475
Dragon & Lotus Bowl	LIME G	135
Dragon & Lotus Bowl	LIME G	350
Dragon & Lotus Bowl	M	105
Dragon & Lotus Bowl	PO	145

DESCRIPTION	COLOR	BID
Dragon & Lotus Bowl	PO	200
Dragon & Lotus Bowl	PO	450
Dragon & Lotus Bowl	VAS	120
Dragon & Lotus Bowl, 3/1 Edge	A	135
Dragon & Lotus Bowl, 3/1 Edge	B	110
Dragon & Lotus Bowl, 3/1 Edge	G	130
Dragon & Lotus Bowl, 3/1 Edge	PO	200
Dragon & Lotus Bowl, 3/1 Edge	PO	275
Dragon & Lotus Bowl, Buffed Point	RED	850
Dragon & Lotus Bowl, Ftd	PO	180
Dragon & Lotus Bowl, Ic	AMBER	110
Dragon & Lotus Bowl, Ic	AMBERI	525
Dragon & Lotus Bowl, Ic	AMBERI	775
Dragon & Lotus Bowl, Ic	B	175
Dragon & Lotus Bowl, Ic	G	165
Dragon & Lotus Bowl, Ic	G	200
Dragon & Lotus Bowl, Ic	MOON	900
Dragon & Lotus Bowl, Ic	RED	675
Dragon & Lotus Bowl, Ic	RED	700
Dragon & Lotus Bowl, Ic	RED	725
Dragon & Lotus Bowl, Ic	RED	800
Dragon & Lotus Bowl, Ic	RED	825
Dragon & Lotus Bowl, Ic, Flake On Underside	RED	700
Dragon & Lotus Bowl, Pale Color	B	100
Dragon & Lotus Plate	M	2100
Dragon & Lotus Plate, Collar Base, One Known	G	10000
Dragon & Lotus Plate, Scratches	B	800
Dragon & Strawberry Bowl	G	1300
Dragon & Strawberry Bowl	M	600

Grape and Cable, Northwood, plate, footed, ice green, $850.

Grape and Cable, Northwood,
water pitcher, table size, one tumbler, ice green, very few known, $9,500.

Grape and Cable, Northwood,
water pitcher, tankard, ice green, $7,500.

DESCRIPTION	COLOR	BID
Dragon & Strawberry Bowl, Ftd	M	425
Dragon & Strawberry Bowl, Ic	B	700
Dragon & Strawberry Bowl, Ic	M	250
Dragon & Strawberry Bowl, Ic	M	325
Dragon & Strawberry Bowl, Ic	M	550
Dragon & Strawberry Bowl, Round	M	275
Dragon & Strawberry Bowl, Round	M	350
Dragon & Strawberry Bowl, Round, Some Spots	A	300
Drapery Candy Dish	AQUA	175
Drapery Candy Dish	B	245
Drapery Candy Dish	IB	95
Drapery Candy Dish	IB	95
Drapery Candy Dish	IB	120
Drapery Candy Dish	IB	125
Drapery Candy Dish	IB	225
Drapery Candy Dish	IB	300
Drapery Candy Dish	IG	350
Drapery Candy Dish	LIME G	250
Drapery Candy Dish	M	135
Drapery Candy Dish	P	135
Drapery Candy Dish, Pumpkin	M	205
Drapery Rosebowl	A	250
Drapery Rosebowl	AO	180
Drapery Rosebowl	AO	225
Drapery Rosebowl	AO	250
Drapery Rosebowl	AO	270
Drapery Rosebowl	AO	275
Drapery Rosebowl	AO	275
Drapery Rosebowl	AO	300
Drapery Rosebowl	AO	315
Drapery Rosebowl	AO	325
Drapery Rosebowl	AO	425
Drapery Rosebowl	B	180
Drapery Rosebowl	B	250
Drapery Rosebowl	IB	550
Drapery Rosebowl	LAV	225
Drapery Rosebowl	M	265
Drapery Rosebowl	M	275
Drapery Rosebowl	M	275
Drapery Rosebowl	M	375

DESCRIPTION	COLOR	BID
Drapery Rosebowl	P	110
Drapery Rosebowl	P	150
Drapery Rosebowl	P	200
Drapery Rosebowl	W	250
Drapery Rosebowl, Elec	AO	350
Drapery Rosebowl, Elec	B	350
Drapery Rosebowl, Mfg Defect On Edge	G	450
Drapery Rosebowl, Plain Edge	W	60
Drapery Variant Vase, 9"	B	165
Drapery Variant Vase, 9"	G	350
Drapery Variant Vase, 9"	P	155
Drapery Variant Vase, 9", Elec	B	650
Drapery Vase, 7"	IB	800
Drapery Vase, 7"	IG	205
Drapery Vase, 7"	M	135
Drapery Vase, 7"	W	175
Drapery Vase, 7", Electric	P	1400
Drapery Vase, 7", Flake On Foot	SAPH B	1500
Drapery Vase, 8"	IG	275
Drapery Vase, 8"	P	450
Drapery Vase, 8" Reng	B	675
Drapery Vase, 8"	W	88
Embroidered Mums Bowl	AO	3600
Embroidered Mums Bowl	AO	6500
Embroidered Mums Bowl	B	225
Embroidered Mums Bowl	B	310
Embroidered Mums Bowl	B	465
Embroidered Mums Bowl	B	500
Embroidered Mums Bowl	B	525
Embroidered Mums Bowl	HORE	750
Embroidered Mums Bowl	IB	280
Embroidered Mums Bowl	IB	400
Embroidered Mums Bowl	IB	475
Embroidered Mums Bowl	IB	675
Embroidered Mums Bowl	IB	950

DESCRIPTION	COLOR	BID
Embroidered Mums Bowl	IG	1400
Embroidered Mums Bowl	LAV	575
Embroidered Mums Bowl	M	185
Embroidered Mums Bowl	M	280
Embroidered Mums Bowl	M	325
Embroidered Mums Bowl	M	325
Embroidered Mums Bowl	M	500
Embroidered Mums Bowl	P	200
Embroidered Mums Bowl	P	225
Embroidered Mums Bowl	P	250
Embroidered Mums Bowl	P	275
Embroidered Mums Bowl	P	275
Embroidered Mums Bowl, Elec	B	425
Embroidered Mums Bowl, Pc Edge	B	950
Embroidered Mums Bowl, Pc Edge	SAPH B	2700
Embroidered Mums Bowl, Poor Iridescence	AO	1500
Embroidered Mums Plate	IG	1700
Embroidered Mums Plate, Little Crooked	A, IG	1350
Embroidered Mums Plate, Light Irid.	W	1200
Enameled Cherries Water Set, 5 Pc	B	185
Enameled Cherries Water Set, 7 Pc	B	170
Enameled Cherries Water Set, 7 Pc	B	175
Enameled Cherries Water Set, 7 Pc	B	220
Enameled Freesia Water Set, 7 Pc	M	235
Enameled Swallow Lemonade Tumbler, Decorated	M	300
Estate Vase, 5"	SMOKE	195
Fan Gravy Boat	PO	105
Fanciful Bowl	P	135
Fanciful Bowl	W	95

Grape and Cable, Fenton, footed bowl, green, super iridescence, $85.

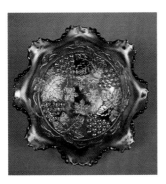

Grape and Cable, Fenton, footed bowl, smoke, rare color, $65.

Grape Leaves, Northwood, bowl with three-in-one edge, marigold, rare early edge, $45.

Greek Key, Northwood, ruffled bowl, electric blue, $1,100.

Grape and Cable, Northwood, punch bowl base, 10 cups (eight shown), mid-size, blue, $3,500.

DESCRIPTION	COLOR	BID
Fanciful Bowl	W	100
Fanciful Bowl, Low Ruffled	B	140
Fanciful Bowl, Low Ruffled, Elec.	P	1300
Fanciful Plate	A	195
Fanciful Plate	B	240
Fanciful Plate	B	325
Fanciful Plate	P	250
Fanciful Plate	W	130
Fanciful Plate	W	130
Fanciful Plate, Elec.	P	1300
Fantail Bowl, Ic	B	125
Fantail Bowl, Ic	B	225
Fantail Bowl, Lg Berry, Rare Color	G	350
Farmyard Bowl, 3/1 Edge	P	4600
Farmyard Bowl, 3/1 Edge, Fair Color	P	2200
Farmyard Bowl, 3/1 Edge, Lite Irid In Center	P	2750
Farmyard Bowl, 6 Ruffle	P	2250
Farmyard Bowl, 6 Ruffle	P	2700
Farmyard Bowl, 6 Ruffle	P	2900
Farmyard Bowl, 6 Ruffle, Electric	P	7000
Farmyard Bowl, 8 Ruffle, Chip On Edge	P	575
Farmyard Bowl, Square, Small Rub On Edge	P	4000
Fashion Creamer & Sugar	SMOKE	175
Fashion Pitcher	M	160
Fashion Pitcher	P	1000
Fashion Punch Set, 10 Pc	M	180
Fashion Punch Set, 14 Pc	M	155
Fashion Punch Set, 8 Pc	M	145
Fashion Punch Set, 8 Pc	M	160
Fashion Punch Set, 8 Pc, Chips	SMOKE	1950
Fashion Rosebowl	M	70
Fashion Rosebowl	M	135
Fashion Rosebowl	M	175
Fashion Tumbler	SMOKE	120
Fashion Water Set, 3 Pc	M	105
Fashion Water Set, 6 Pc	SMOKE	1000
Feather & Heart Hair Receiver Whimsy From Tumb	M	1600

DESCRIPTION	COLOR	BID
Feather & Heart Pitcher	A	350
Feather & Heart Pitcher	G	600
Feather & Heart Pitcher, Nick	A	300
Feather & Heart Pitcher, Nicks On Edge	G	250
Feather & Heart Tumbler	A	75
Feather & Heart Tumbler	A	85
Feather & Heart Tumbler	A	115
Feather & Heart Tumbler	G	80
Feather & Heart Tumbler	G	165
Feather & Heart Tumbler	M	50
Feather & Heart Tumbler	M	60
Feather & Heart Water Set, 7 Pc	M	455
Feathered Serpent Bowl, 3/1 Edge	A	130
Feathered Serpent Bowl, 3/1 Edge	A	150
Feathered Serpent Bowl, Ic	M	175
Fentonia Pitcher, Lighter At Base	M	200
Fentonia Tumbler	B	75
Fentonia Tumbler	M	40
Fentons Flowers Rosebowl	A	135
Fentons Flowers Rosebowl	G	255
Fentons Flowers Rosebowl	LGO	200
Fentons Flowers Rosebowl	LGO	450
Fentons Flowers Rosebowl	W	140
Fentons Flowers Rosebowl	W	195
Fentons Flowers Rosebowl, Nick On Feet	PO	350
Fern Panels Hat, Crimped, Jip	M	20
Field Flower Pitcher	G	85
Field Flower Pitcher	SMOKE	700
Field Flower Tumbler	B	110
Field Flower Tumbler	G	50
Field Flower Tumbler	M	50
Field Flower Tumbler	P	100

DESCRIPTION	COLOR	BID
Fine Rib Vase, 10"	AMBERI	185
Fine Rib Vase, 10"	RED	270
Fine Rib Vase, 10"	RED	300
Fine Rib Vase, 10"	RED	350
Fine Rib Vase, 10"	SAPH B	150
Fine Rib Vase, 10"	SAPH B	225
Fine Rib Vase, 11"	SAPH B	230
Fine Rib Vase, 11"	VO	210
Fine Rib Vase, 7"	G	80
Fine Rib Vase, 9"	A	40
Fine Rib Vase, 9"	AMBERI	270
Fine Rib Vase, 9"	AQUA	475
Fine Rib Vase, 9"	B	25
Fine Rib Vase, 9"	B	210
Fine Rib Vase, 9"	RED	220
Fishermans Mug	M	90
Fishermans Mug	M	105
Fishermans Mug	M	140
Fishermans Mug	M	700
Fishermans Mug	P	90
Fishermans Mug	P	105
Fishscale & Beads Bowl, 7"	P	145
Fishscale & Beads Plate, 7"	A	425
Fishscale & Beads Plate, 7"	P	400
Fishscale & Beads Plate, 7"	W	85
Fishscale & Beads Plate, 8"	W	110
Fleur De Lis Bowl, 10"	G	200
Fleur De Lis Bowl, 10", Ic	P	600
Fleur De Lis Bowl, 9", Round	M	475
Fleur De Lis Bowl, Dome Ftd, Square	VAS	5000
Floral & Grape Pitcher	B	150
Floral & Grape Pitcher	B	250
Floral & Grape Pitcher	M	85
Floral & Grape Pitcher	M	125
Floral & Grape Pitcher	P	325
Floral & Grape Tumbler	A	35
Floral & Grape Tumbler	B	25
Floral & Grape Tumbler	B	27
Floral & Grape Tumbler	LAV	45
Floral & Grape Tumbler	W	50
Floral & Grape Water Set, 6 Pc	W	500

**Hanging Cherries,
Millersburg,**
milk pitcher, marigold,
base roughness,
$1,700.

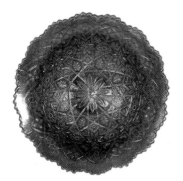

Hattie, Imperial,
bowl ice cream shape, 9", deep
smoke, **$65**.

Hearts and Flowers, Northwood,
compote, frosty white, **$175**.

Hearts and Flowers, Northwood,
compote, marigold, covered with
pink highlights, **$175**.

DESCRIPTION	COLOR	BID
Floral & Grape Water Set, 7 Pc	B	475
Floral & Optic Bowl	RED	125
Floral & Sunburst Vase, Cupped In, 6", Eda	B	1250
Flowers & Frames Bowl	P	425
Flowers & Frames Bowl, 7"	P	200
Flowers & Frames Bowl, Dome Ftd	P	150
Flowers & Frames Bowl, Dome Ftd, Elec	P	225
Flowers & Frames Bowl, Dome Ftd, Tri Corner	PO	185
Fluffy Peacock Hatshape Whimsey From Tumb,chip	A	225
Fluffy Peacock Pitcher	A	900
Fluffy Peacock Pitcher	B	850
Fluffy Peacock Tumbler	A	100
Fluffy Peacock Tumbler	B	105
Fluffy Peacock Water Set, 7 Pc	A	800
Flute & Cane Milk Pitcher	M	155
Flute & Cane Pitcher	M	80
Flute & Cane Pitcher, 8"	M	250
Flute Compote, 8", A Millersburg Blank Pattern	M	1600
Flute Compote, Ruffled, Mbrg, Blank From Acorn	P	400
Flute Toothpick	B	1050
Flute Toothpick	LIME G	115
Flute Toothpick	M	35
Flute Toothpick	P	40
Flute Toothpick	P	70
Flute Toothpick	P	85
Flute Toothpick	P	1095
Flute Tumbler, #1, Imperial	P	130
Flute Tumbler, #3, Imperial	TEAL	100
Flute Vase, Mid Size, 14"	M	80
Flute Water Set, N, 6 Pc	M	150
Formal Hatpin Holder	M	350
Formal Hatpin Holder	M	500
Formal Hatpin Holder	P	350
Formal Hatpin Holder	P	625
Formal Hatpin Holder	P	950
Formal Vase, Jip	M	450
Four Flowers Bowl	G	145
Four Flowers Chop Plate	PO	250
Four Flowers Chop Plate	PO	275
Four Flowers Chop Plate	PO	325
Four Flowers Chop Plate	PO	650
Four Flowers Chop Plate, Soda Gold Back	PO	250
Four Flowers Comp Plate, Silvery	P	125
Four Flowers Plate Emr	G	575
Four Flowers Plate	G	300
Four Flowers Plate	P	145
Four Flowers Plate, 6"	PO	60
Four Flowers Plate, 6"	PO	105
Four Flowers Plate, 6"	PO	130
Four Pillars Variant Vase, 8"	TEAL	325
Four Pillars Vase	AO	135
Four Pillars Vase	AO	155
Four Pillars Vase	AO	235
Four Pillars Vase	AO	300
Four Pillars Vase	B	220
Four Pillars Vase	LGO	825
Four Pillars Vase, Butterscotch	AO	525
Four Seventy Four Milk Pitcher	P	800
Four Seventy Four Punch Bowl & Base	M	180
Four Seventy Four Punch Bowl & Base	M	275
Four Seventy Four Tumbler	AQUA	185
Four Seventy Four Vase, 8"	M	700
Fruits & Flowers Berry Set, 7 Pc	A	140
Fruits & Flowers Bon Bon	A	65
Fruits & Flowers Bon Bon	A	75
Fruits & Flowers Bon Bon	AO	300
Fruits & Flowers Bon Bon	AO	350
Fruits & Flowers Bon Bon	AO	385
Fruits & Flowers Bon Bon	AO	410
Fruits & Flowers Bon Bon	AO	500
Fruits & Flowers Bon Bon	AO	575
Fruits & Flowers Bon Bon	B	100
Fruits & Flowers Bon Bon	B	110
Fruits & Flowers Bon Bon	B	110
Fruits & Flowers Bon Bon	B	120
Fruits & Flowers Bon Bon	B	125
Fruits & Flowers Bon Bon	B	145
Fruits & Flowers Bon Bon	B	150
Fruits & Flowers Bon Bon	B	150
Fruits & Flowers Bon Bon	B	190
Fruits & Flowers Bon Bon	B	205
Fruits & Flowers Bon Bon	B	275
Fruits & Flowers Bon Bon	G	95
Fruits & Flowers Bon Bon	IB	400
Fruits & Flowers Bon Bon	IB	400
Fruits & Flowers Bon Bon	IB	400
Fruits & Flowers Bon Bon	IB	425
Fruits & Flowers Bon Bon	IB	450
Fruits & Flowers Bon Bon	IG	325 02-07
Fruits & Flowers Bon Bon	LAV	100
Fruits & Flowers Bon Bon	LIME G	450
Fruits & Flowers Bon Bon	M	35
Fruits & Flowers Bon Bon	M	55
Fruits & Flowers Bon Bon	OG	85
Fruits & Flowers Bon Bon	OG	165
Fruits & Flowers Bon Bon	P	75
Fruits & Flowers Bon Bon	P	75

**Hearts and Flowers,
Northwood,** flared plate,
marigold, $1,200.

Hearts and Flowers, Northwood,
plate, ice blue, has a small flake on the
marie, $850.

Hearts and Flowers, Northwood,
compote, purple, great iridescence, $350.

Hearts and Flowers, Northwood,
compote, dark marigold, real pretty, $95.

DESCRIPTION	COLOR	BID	DESCRIPTION	COLOR	BID	DESCRIPTION	COLOR	BID
Fruits & Flowers Bon Bon	P	100	Good Luck Bowl	B	335	Good Luck Bowl, Pc Edge	B	135
Fruits & Flowers Bon Bon	P	100	Good Luck Bowl	B	350	Good Luck Bowl, Pc Edge	B	295
Fruits & Flowers Bon Bon	P	105	Good Luck Bowl	B	375	Good Luck Bowl, Pc Edge	B	350
Fruits & Flowers Bon Bon	P	175	Good Luck Bowl	B	400	Good Luck Bowl, Pc Edge	B	360
Fruits & Flowers Bon Bon Reng	B	525	Good Luck Bowl	B	400	Good Luck Bowl, Pc Edge	B	475
Fruits & Flowers Bon Bon	W	175	Good Luck Bowl	B	425	Good Luck Bowl, Pc Edge	G	250
Fruits & Flowers Bon Bon, Elec	B	275	Good Luck Bowl	G	250	Good Luck Bowl, Pc Edge	G	255
Fruits & Flowers Bon Bon, Elec, Stippled	B	575	Good Luck Bowl	G	300	Good Luck Bowl, Pc Edge	G	325
Fruits & Flowers Bon Bon, Elec, Stippled	G	350	Good Luck Bowl	G	625	Good Luck Bowl, Pc Edge	G	350
Fruits & Flowers Bon Bon, Elec, Stippled	M	70	Good Luck Bowl	G	650	Good Luck Bowl, Pc Edge	G	350
Fruits & Flowers Bowl	B	155	Good Luck Bowl	LAV	400	Good Luck Bowl, Pc Edge	G	350
Fruits & Flowers Bowl	IG	325	Good Luck Bowl	M	130	Good Luck Bowl, Pc Edge	G	350
Fruits & Flowers Bowl	IG	1200	Good Luck Bowl	M	145	Good Luck Bowl, Pc Edge	M	150
Fruits & Flowers Bowl, 10"	P	140	Good Luck Bowl	M	145	Good Luck Bowl, Pc Edge	M	150
Fruits & Flowers Card Tray, 8"	G	120	Good Luck Bowl	M	155	Good Luck Bowl, Pc Edge	M	155
Fruits & Flowers Plate, 7"	M	115	Good Luck Bowl	P	130	Good Luck Bowl, Pc Edge	M	175
Fruits & Flowers Plate, 7"	P	225	Good Luck Bowl	P	225	Good Luck Bowl, Pc Edge	M	185
Fruits & Flowers Plate, 7", Handgrip	P	100	Good Luck Bowl	P	225	Good Luck Bowl, Pc Edge	P	200
Fruits & Flowers Plate, 7", Handgrip	P	150	Good Luck Bowl	P	250	Good Luck Bowl, Pc Edge	P	210
Garden Path Plate, 6"	W	165	Good Luck Bowl	P	255	Good Luck Bowl, Pc Edge	P	250
Garden Path Plate, 6"	W	350	Good Luck Bowl	P	275	Good Luck Bowl, Pc Edge	P	275
Garden Path Variant Bowl, Lg	P	625	Good Luck Bowl	P	325	Good Luck Bowl, Pc Edge	P	285
Gay Nineties Tumbler	A	700	Good Luck Bowl	P	355	Good Luck Bowl, Pc Edge	P	300
Gay Nineties Tumbler	M	800	Good Luck Bowl	P	450	Good Luck Bowl, Pc Edge	P	325
God & Home Tumbler	B	135	Good Luck Bowl Reng	B	500	Good Luck Bowl, Pc Edge	P	350
God & Home Tumbler	B	145	Good Luck Bowl	SAPH B	2100	Good Luck Bowl, Pc Edge	P	395
God & Home Tumbler	B	280	Good Luck Bowl	SAPH B	2600	Good Luck Bowl, Pc Edge	P	425
Good Luck Bowl	A	300	Good Luck Bowl, Butterscotch Irid	AO	1600	Good Luck Bowl, Pc Edge	P	450
Good Luck Bowl	A	310	Good Luck Bowl, Butterscotch Irid	AO	2600			
Good Luck Bowl	B	200	Good Luck Bowl, Bw Back	G	230			
Good Luck Bowl	B	235	Good Luck Bowl, Bw Back	G	300			
Good Luck Bowl	B	250	Good Luck Bowl, Bw Back	M	135			
Good Luck Bowl	B	275	Good Luck Bowl, Bw Back	M	160			
Good Luck Bowl	B	300	Good Luck Bowl, Bw Back	P	325			
Good Luck Bowl	B	300	Good Luck Bowl, Bw Back, Pc Edge	G	225			
			Good Luck Bowl, Chip	AO	1300			
			Good Luck Bowl, Elec	B	400			
			Good Luck Bowl, Elec	B	450			
			Good Luck Bowl, Pastel, Sm Spot Of Ext. Glass	AO	2400			
			Good Luck Bowl, Pc Edge	A	275			

Heavy Grape, Imperial,
plate, 8", purple, pretty with electric
highlights, $90.

Heavy Grape, Imperial,
chop plate, marigold, has very heavy stretch
effect, neat plate, $550.

Heavy Grape, Imperial,
punch cup, electric purple, $95.

Heavy Grape, Imperial,
bowl, 6-1/4", purple, $25.

Heavy Iris, Dugan,
three tumblers. marigold (sold choice), $90
for all three.

Hobnail Swirl, Millersburg,
vase, green, $225.

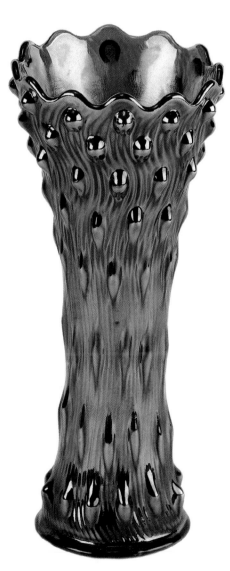

Hobnail Swirl,
Millersburg, vase, 9", green, $300-$450.

Hobnail Swirl,
Millersburg, vase, 9", amethyst, $350-$500.

DESCRIPTION	COLOR	BID
Good Luck Bowl, Pc Edge, Elec	B	450
Good Luck Bowl, Pc Edge, Stippled	B	300
Good Luck Bowl, Pc Edge, Stippled	B	425
Good Luck Bowl, Pc Edge, Stippled	B	650
Good Luck Bowl, Pc Edge, Stippled	B	700
Good Luck Bowl, Pc Edge, Stippled	M	275
Good Luck Bowl, Pc Edge, Stippled	M	500
Good Luck Bowl, Stippled	B	235
Good Luck Bowl, Stippled	B	300
Good Luck Bowl, Stippled	B	625
Good Luck Bowl, Stippled	M	225
Good Luck Bowl, Stippled	M	300
Good Luck Bowl, Stippled, Pastel	M	175
Good Luck Bowl, Variant With Smaller Pattern	M	2700
Good Luck Plate	A	310
Good Luck Plate	G	400
Good Luck Plate	G	575
Good Luck Plate	G	600
Good Luck Plate	M	210
Good Luck Plate	M	325
Good Luck Plate	M	325
Good Luck Plate	P	325
Good Luck Plate	P	400
Good Luck Plate Reng	B	2000
Good Luck Plate, Bw Back	G	600
Good Luck Plate, Bw Back	G	775
Good Luck Plate, Bw Back	HORE	575
Good Luck Plate, Bw Back	HORE	2000
Good Luck Plate, Bw Back	M	350
Good Luck Plate, Bw Back	M	375
Good Luck Plate, Bw Back	M	400

DESCRIPTION	COLOR	BID
Good Luck Plate, Stippled	B	750
Good Luck Plate, Stippled, Flake On Horseshoe	M	475
Good Luck Plate, Stippled, Narrow Base	P	1700
Good Luck Plate, Wear On Tips	G	875
Gothic Arches Vase, 11"	M	1200
Gothic Arches Vase, 11"	SMOKE	900
Grape & Cable Banana Bowl	B	400
Grape & Cable Banana Bowl	G	300
Grape & Cable Banana Bowl	G	350
Grape & Cable Banana Bowl	IB	475
Grape & Cable Banana Bowl	IB	625
Grape & Cable Banana Bowl	IG	575
Grape & Cable Banana Bowl	M	90
Grape & Cable Banana Bowl	M	170
Grape & Cable Banana Bowl, Stip, Band	LIME G	1700
Grape & Cable Berry Bowl, Lg	P	225
Grape & Cable Berry Set, 7 Pc	G	205
Grape & Cable Berry Set, 7 Pc	G	335
Grape & Cable Bon Bon	B	110
Grape & Cable Bon Bon	B	225
Grape & Cable Bon Bon	B	290
Grape & Cable Bon Bon	W	200
Grape & Cable Bon Bon, Stippled	G	275
Grape & Cable Bowl, Bw Back, N, Opal On Tips	PO	300
Grape & Cable Bowl, Fenton, 7"	MOON	200
Grape & Cable Bowl, Fenton, 7"	RED	270
Grape & Cable Bowl, Fenton, 7"	RED	325
Grape & Cable Bowl, Fenton, 7"	VAS	140
Grape & Cable Bowl, Fenton, Ic, 7"	RED	335

DESCRIPTION	COLOR	BID
Grape & Cable Bowl, Ftd, Deep Round, Fenton	CELEST	1650
Grape & Cable Bowl, Ftd, Fenton	VAS	150
Grape & Cable Bowl, Large Fruit	M	250
Grape & Cable Bowl, Large Fruit, Fenton	G	235
Grape & Cable Bowl, Lg Fruit, Banded, Stippled	B	450
Grape & Cable Bowl, Lg Fruit, Banded, Stippled	B	750
Grape & Cable Bowl, Lg Fruit, Banded, Stippled Reng	B	600
Grape & Cable Bowl, Lg Fruit, Fenton	A	450
Grape & Cable Bowl, Lg Fruit, N	G	650
Grape & Cable Bowl, Lg Fruit, N	P	300
Grape & Cable Bowl, Lg Ic, N	B	1150
Grape & Cable Bowl, Lg Ic, N	G	375
Grape & Cable Bowl, Lg Ic, N	IG	1000
Grape & Cable Bowl, Lg Ic, N	M	230
Grape & Cable Bowl, Lg Ic, N	P	275
Grape & Cable Bowl, Lg Ic, N	W	195
Grape & Cable Bowl, Lg Ic, N	W	325
Grape & Cable Bowl, Lg Ic, N, Stippled	B	1400
Grape & Cable Bowl, Lg Ruffled	P	265
Grape & Cable Bowl, Lg, Stippled	B	375
Grape & Cable Bowl, Master Berry	P	150
Grape & Cable Bowl, Pc Edge	B	210
Grape & Cable Bowl, Pc Edge	B	350
Grape & Cable Bowl, Pc Edge	G	210
Grape & Cable Bowl, Pc Edge	IB	850
Grape & Cable Bowl, Pc Edge, Lg, Salad Bowl	M	115
Grape & Cable Bowl, Pc Edge, Lg, Salad Bowl	W	300

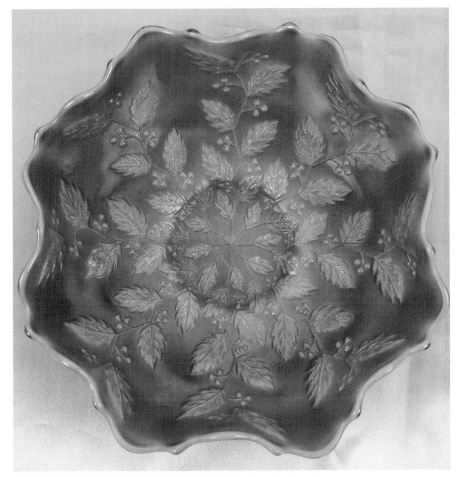

Holly, Fenton, ruffled bowl, marigold over moonstone, $1,000.

Holly, Fenton, deep ice-cream shaped bowl, vaseline, scarce color and shape, $65.

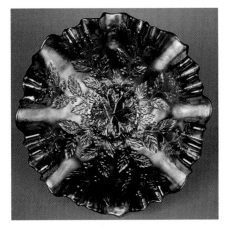

Holly, Fenton, bowl with 3-in-1 edge, amethyst, beautiful color, $145.

Holly, Fenton, plate, blue, really nice, $300.

Holly, Fenton, plate, marigold with spectacular color, $300.

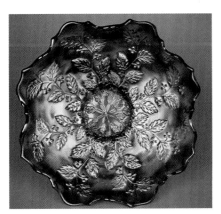

Holly, Fenton, ruffled bowl, $65.

DESCRIPTION	COLOR	BID	DESCRIPTION	COLOR	BID	DESCRIPTION	COLOR	BID
Grape & Cable Bowl, Pc Edge, Stippled, Elec	B	925	Grape & Cable Perfume Bottle	P	335	Grape & Cable Plate, Stippled	G	500
Grape & Cable Bowl, Plain Back	A	200	Grape & Cable Perfume Bottle	P	400	Grape & Cable Plate, Stippled	G	500
Grape & Cable Bowl, Plain Back	G	125	Grape & Cable Perfume Bottle & Stopper	P	475	Grape & Cable Plate, Stippled	M	400
Grape & Cable Bowl, Sm Berry	B	105	Grape & Cable Pin Dish From Punch Cup	M	85	Grape & Cable Plate, Stippled	M	1200
Grape & Cable Bowl, Small Fruit	B	250	Grape & Cable Pin Tray	A	200	Grape & Cable Plate, Stippled	SAPH B	1800
Grape & Cable Bowl, Small Fruit	B	375	Grape & Cable Pin Tray	IB	600	Grape & Cable Plate, Stippled	SAPH B	2200
Grape & Cable Bowl, Small Fruit	G	325	Grape & Cable Pin Tray	M	100	Grape & Cable Plate, Stippled	SAPH B	2700
Grape & Cable Bowl, Small Fruit	IB	1200	Grape & Cable Pin Tray	P	275	Grape & Cable Powder Jar	M	30
Grape & Cable Bowl, Small Fruit	IG	825	Grape & Cable Pin Tray	P	300	Grape & Cable Powder Jar	P	120
Grape & Cable Bowl, Small Fruit	P	145	Grape & Cable Pin Tray, Oval	M	245	Grape & Cable Powder Jar	P	155
Grape & Cable Bowl, Small Fruit	P	145	Grape & Cable Pin Tray, Oval Banded	P	400	Grape & Cable Powder Jar Base Only, No Lid	AO	725
Grape & Cable Bowl, Small Fruit	P	180	Grape & Cable Pitcher	G	200	Grape & Cable Powder Jar Bottom Only	IB	70
Grape & Cable Bowl, Small Fruit	W	700	Grape & Cable Pitcher	G	400	Grape & Cable Powder Jar, Chip On Edge	A	115
Grape & Cable Bowl, Small Fruit, Flared	B	525	Grape & Cable Pitcher	M	110	Grape & Cable Punch Bowl & Base, Master	P	1500
Grape & Cable Bowl, Stippled	SAPH B	1700	Grape & Cable Pitcher	P	155	Grape & Cable Punch Bowl & Base, Small	M	850
Grape & Cable Candle Lamp	M	475	Grape & Cable Pitcher	P	220	Grape & Cable Punch Bowl & Base, Small	P	445
Grape & Cable Card Tray, 2 Sides Up	P	150	Grape & Cable Pitcher	P	275	Grape & Cable Punch Bowl & Base, Small	P	500
Grape & Cable Centerpiece Bowl, Points Turned	M	225	Grape & Cable Pitcher	P	350	Grape & Cable Punch Bowl & Base, Small Size	P	625
			Grape & Cable Pitcher	SMOKE	800			
Grape & Cable Cologne Bottle	P	155	Grape & Cable Pitcher, Table Size	IG	9000	Grape & Cable Punch Bowl & Base, Tips Point Up	G	1800
Grape & Cable Compote, Large Open	G	1100	Grape & Cable Plate	G	170	Grape & Cable Punch Cup	AO	850
Grape & Cable Cracker Jar	IG	800	Grape & Cable Plate	G	225	Grape & Cable Punch Set, Master, 10 Pc	P	2700
Grape & Cable Cracker Jar	P	325	Grape & Cable Plate	M	250	Grape & Cable Punch Set, Master, 12 Pc	M	2700
			Grape & Cable Plate	OG	175			
Grape & Cable Dresser Tray	IB	800	Grape & Cable Plate	P	125	Grape & Cable Punch Set, Master, 13 Pc	B	8000
Grape & Cable Dresser Tray	P	325	Grape & Cable Plate	P	135	Grape & Cable Punch Set, Master, 14 Pc	P	2300
Grape & Cable Fernery	M	650	Grape & Cable Plate	P	350	Grape & Cable Punch Set, Master, 8 Pc	B	7000
Grape & Cable Hatpin Holder	IB	2000	Grape & Cable Plate	P	400			
Grape & Cable Hatpin Holder	P	260	Grape & Cable Plate, 7"	AMY O	375	Grape & Cable Punch Set, Master, 8 Pc	M	700
			Grape & Cable Plate, 7"	P	105			
Grape & Cable Perfume Bottle	M	170	Grape & Cable Plate, Bw Back	P	135	Grape & Cable Punch Set, Master, 9 Pc	P	2600
			Grape & Cable Plate, Plain Back	P	175			
			Grape & Cable Plate, Plain Back	P	325			
			Grape & Cable Plate, Stippled	B	1000			
			Grape & Cable Plate, Stippled	G	325			
			Grape & Cable Plate, Stippled	G	350			
			Grape & Cable Plate, Stippled	G	450			

Holly Sprig, Millersburg, ruffled sauce, purple with radium iridescence, **$55**.

Horse Head Medallion, Fenton, incredible footed bowl, green. One of the best, loaded with color, **$425**.

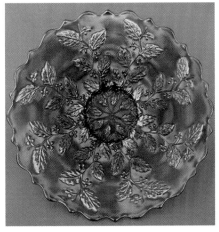

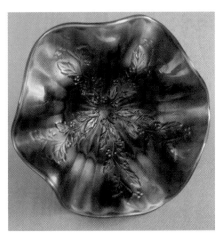

Horse Head Medallion, Fenton, plate, 7-1/2", marigold. Great color and mold strike, **$140**.

Holly, Fenton, plate, amethyst, a super plate, **$1,200**.

Holly, Fenton, compote, green, **$110**.

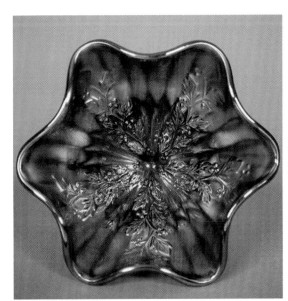

Holly, Fenton, ruffled bowl, red, **$800**.

Holly, Fenton, compote, blue, **$80**.

DESCRIPTION	COLOR	BID
Grape & Cable Punch Set, Mid Size, 10 Pc	B	1950
Grape & Cable Punch Set, Mid Size, 8 Pc	B	2800
Grape & Cable Punch Set, Mid Size, 8 Pc	IB	15000
Grape & Cable Punch Set, Mid Size, 8 Pc	IG	8000
Grape & Cable Punch Set, Small, 10 Pc	M	650
Grape & Cable Punch Set, Small, 8 Pc	M	475
Grape & Cable Punch Set, Small, 8 Pc	P	350
Grape & Cable Punch Set, Small, 8 Pc	P	450
Grape & Cable Punch Set, Small, 8 Pc	P	750
Grape & Cable Punch Set, Small, 9 Pc	M	425
Grape & Cable Shot Glass	M	175
Grape & Cable Shot Glass, The Price Is Correct	P	825
Grape & Cable Spooner	P	95
Grape & Cable Sugar	P	95
Grape & Cable Sugar	P	115
Grape & Cable Sugar Bowl & Lid	P	185
Grape & Cable Sweetmeat	P	160
Grape & Cable Sweetmeat	P	165
Grape & Cable Sweetmeat	P	165
Grape & Cable Sweetmeat	P	175
Grape & Cable Sweetmeat	P	185
Grape & Cable Sweetmeat	P	200
Grape & Cable Sweetmeat	P	210
Grape & Cable Sweetmeat, Chip On Lid	B	1025
Grape & Cable Table Set, 4 Pc	G	190
Grape & Cable Table Set, 4 Pc	G	450
Grape & Cable Tankard	P	750
Grape & Cable Tobacco Jar	M	550
Grape & Cable Tumbler	G	45

DESCRIPTION	COLOR	BID
Grape & Cable Tumbler	M	30
Grape & Cable Tumbler	SMOKE	75
Grape & Cable Tumbler	SMOKE	105
Grape & Cable Tumbler, Stippled	P	185
Grape & Cable Water Set, 5 Pc	P	275
Grape & Cable Water Set, 7 Pc	G	425
Grape & Cable Water Set, 7 Pc	G	475
Grape & Cable Water Set, 7 Pc	M	175
Grape & Cable Water Set, 7 Pc	M	250
Grape & Cable Water Set, 7 Pc	P	350
Grape & Cable Water Set, 7 Pc	P	350
Grape & Cable Water Set, 7 Pc	P	355
Grape & Cable Water Set, 7 Pc	P	415
Grape & Cable Water Set, 7 Pc	P	575
Grape & Cable Water Set, 7 Pc	P	650
Grape & Cable Water Set, Tankard Size, 7 Pc	M	675
Grape & Cable Whiskey Decanter	M	275
Grape & Cable Whiskey Set, 8 Pc	M	850
Grape & Gothic Arches Butter Dish	B	175
Grape & Gothic Arches Butter Dish	M	170
Grape & Gothic Arches Creamer	B	65
Grape & Gothic Arches Pitcher	B	375
Grape & Gothic Arches Pitcher	M	145
Grape & Gothic Arches Pitcher, Chip	M	140
Grape & Gothic Arches Spooner	B	40
Grape & Gothic Arches Spooner	B	100
Grape & Gothic Arches Sugar	B	65
Grape & Gothic Arches Table Set, 4 Pc	M	175
Grape & Gothic Arches Tumbler	B	40

DESCRIPTION	COLOR	BID
Grape & Gothic Arches Tumbler	G	65
Grape & Gothic Arches Tumbler	M	20
Grape & Gothic Arches Tumbler	PEARL	27
Grape & Gothic Arches Tumbler	PEARL	45
Grape & Lattice Tumbler	B	55
Grape & Lattice Tumbler	M	20
Grape & Lattice Tumbler	W	70
Grape & Leaves Spittoon	M	600
Grape & Palisade Tumbler	M	117
Grape Arbor Fruit Bowl	M	110
Grape Arbor Tankard	IB	2100
Grape Arbor Tankard	M	185
Grape Arbor Tankard	M	225
Grape Arbor Tankard	M	260
Grape Arbor Tankard	W	450
Grape Arbor Tankard	W	575
Grape Arbor Tankard	W	575
Grape Arbor Tumbler	IB	130
Grape Arbor Tumbler	IB	145
Grape Arbor Tumbler	IB	250
Grape Arbor Tumbler	IG	325
Grape Arbor Tumbler	M	30
Grape Arbor Tumbler	M	40
Grape Arbor Tumbler	W	65
Grape Arbor Tumbler	W	75
Grape Arbor Tumbler, Elec	B	475
Grape Arbor Tumbler, Electric	B	240
Grape Arbor Water Set, 5 Pc	M	185
Grape Arbor Water Set, 7 Pc	P	750
Grape Arbor Water Set, 7 Pc	W	700
Grape Arbor Water Set, 7 Pc, Rim Flake	W	525
Grape Delight Nut Bowl	B	25
Grape Delight Nut Bowl	P	130
Grape Delight Rosebowl	LAV	145
Grape Delight Rosebowl	W	120
Grape Leaves Bowl, 3/1 Edge, Radium, Mbrg	A	775

Imperial Grape, Imperial, eight-ruffled bowl, 8-1/2", purple, $150-$250.

Imperial Grape, Imperial, carafe, 9", purple, $200-$400.

Imperial Grape, Imperial, wine decanter, 12", purple, $250-$350.

Inverted Strawberry, Cambridge, milk pitcher, amethyst, supposedly one of three known, $4,500.

DESCRIPTION	COLOR	BID
Grape Leaves Bowl, 3/1 Edge, Radium, Mbrg	M	650
Grape Leaves Bowl, Mbrg	A	775
Grape Leaves Bowl, Mbrg	M	675
Grape Leaves Bowl, N	P	85
Grape Leaves Bowl, Radium, Blue Irid, Rfld, Mbrg	G	4600
Grapevine Lattice Hat Whimsey, From Tumbler	W	150
Grapevine Lattice Tumbler	W	180
Grapevine Lattice Tumbler	W	185
Grapevine Lattice Water Set, 7 Pc	M	185
Greek Key Bowl	B	1100
Greek Key Bowl	G	135
Greek Key Bowl	G	165
Greek Key Bowl	P	100
Greek Key Bowl	P	190
Greek Key Bowl, Pc Edge	M	125
Greek Key Bowl, Pc Edge	P	145
Greek Key Pitcher	P	425
Greek Key Plate	M	500
Greek Key Plate, Bruise On Base	M	900
Greek Key Plate, Bw Back	G	600
Greek Key Plate, Pastel	M	650
Greek Key Plate, Ribbed Back	M	550
Greek Key Tumbler	A	80
Greek Key Tumbler	A	105
Greek Key Tumbler	G	155
Greek Key Tumbler	M	55
Greek Key Tumbler	M	90
Greek Key Tumbler	P	75
Greek Key Tumbler	P	95
Greek Key Tumbler	P	155
Hand Vase, Left Hand, 9"	M	60
Hanging Cherries Berry Set, 7 Pc	M	350
Hanging Cherries Bowl, 3/1 Edge, 9"	A	175
Hanging Cherries Bowl, 7", Ic	M	110

DESCRIPTION	COLOR	BID
Hanging Cherries Bowl, 7", Ic	M	200
Hanging Cherries Bowl, 8", Ic	A	275
Hanging Cherries Bowl, Hobnail Ext.	M	875
Hanging Cherries Bowl, Hobnail Ext.	P	900
Hanging Cherries Bowl, Lg	A	210
Hanging Cherries Bowl, Lg	G	210
Hanging Cherries Bowl, Lg	G	275
Hanging Cherries Bowl, Lg Ic	A	130
Hanging Cherries Bowl, Lg Ic	A	165
Hanging Cherries Bowl, Lg Ic	A	200
Hanging Cherries Bowl, Lg Ic	A	275
Hanging Cherries Bowl, Lg Ic	G	195
Hanging Cherries Bowl, Lg Ic	G	245
Hanging Cherries Bowl, Lg Ic	G	275
Hanging Cherries Bowl, Lg Ic	LAV	350
Hanging Cherries Bowl, Lg Ic	M	135
Hanging Cherries Bowl, Lg Ic	M	135
Hanging Cherries Bowl, Lg Ic	P	225
Hanging Cherries Bowl, Lg, 3/1 Edge	G	150
Hanging Cherries Chop Plate	G	3700
Hanging Cherries Compote	A	750
Hanging Cherries Compote	A	1425
Hanging Cherries Compote	M	1100
Hanging Cherries Compote, Small Chip	A	750
Hanging Cherries Pitcher	A	500
Hanging Cherries Pitcher	G	675
Hanging Cherries Pitcher	G	1000
Hanging Cherries Pitcher	M	1800

DESCRIPTION	COLOR	BID
Hanging Cherries Pitcher	P	1700
Hanging Cherries Pitcher, Chip On Base	M	450
Hanging Cherries Plate, 6"	M	3400
Hanging Cherries Sauce, 3/1 Edge	B	1700
Hanging Cherries Table Set, 4 Pc	A	500
Hanging Cherries Table Set, 4 Pc	A	595
Hanging Cherries Tumbler	G	105
Hanging Cherries Tumbler	G	115
Hanging Cherries Tumbler	G	210
Hanging Cherries Tumbler	G	280
Hanging Cherries Tumbler	M	230
Hanging Cherries Tumbler, Mfg Ground Base	M	75
Hattie Bowl	SMOKE	110
Hattie Bowl, Electric	P	275
Hattie Chop Plate	AMBER	3500
Hattie Chop Plate	M	1050
Hattie Chop Plate	P	1850
Heart & Vine Bowl, 3/1 Edge	G	50
Heart & Vine Bowl, Cr Edge	A	130
Heart & Vine Plate	A	250
Heart & Vine Plate	A	285
Heart & Vine Plate	A	300
Heart & Vine Plate	A	700
Heart & Vine Plate	B	200
Heart & Vine Plate	B	225
Heart & Vine Plate	B	325
Heart & Vine Plate	B	350
Heart & Vine Plate	B	475
Heart & Vine Plate	B	500
Heart & Vine Plate	B	525
Heart & Vine Plate	B	600
Heart & Vine Plate	B	900
Hearts & Flowers Bowl	A	280
Hearts & Flowers Bowl	AQUA	1400
Hearts & Flowers Bowl	B	1150
Hearts & Flowers Bowl	EMR G	600
Hearts & Flowers Bowl	G	1300

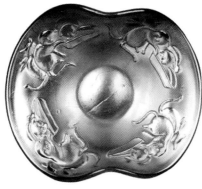

Kittens, Fenton, plate with two sides up, marigold, **$125**.

Lattice and Points, Dugan, squatty vase, electric amethyst, $80.

Lattice and Daisy, Dugan, tankard, marigold, $90.

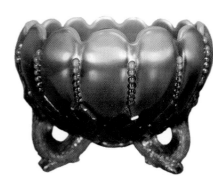

Leaf and Beads, Northwood, aqua opal rose bowl, beautiful butterscotch iridescence, $325.

Leaf and Beads, Northwood, nut bowl with fancy interior, green, $50.

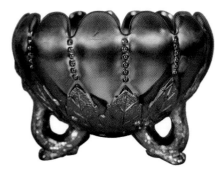

Leaf and Beads, Northwood, rose bowl, purple, $90.

Leaf and Little Flowers, Millersburg, compote, 3" h, amethyst, $400-$550.

DESCRIPTION	COLOR	BID
Hearts & Flowers Bowl	G	1450
Hearts & Flowers Bowl	G	1500
Hearts & Flowers Bowl	IB	250
Hearts & Flowers Bowl	IB	295
Hearts & Flowers Bowl	IB	300
Hearts & Flowers Bowl	IG	475
Hearts & Flowers Bowl	IG	500
Hearts & Flowers Bowl	IG	550
Hearts & Flowers Bowl	M	300
Hearts & Flowers Bowl	M	400
Hearts & Flowers Bowl	M	750
Hearts & Flowers Bowl	P	475
Hearts & Flowers Bowl	P	550
Hearts & Flowers Bowl	P	575
Hearts & Flowers Bowl	W	100
Hearts & Flowers Bowl	W	200
Hearts & Flowers Bowl	W	200
Hearts E Flowers Bowl, Elec.	B	1200
Hearts & Flowers Bowl, Opal Tips	AO	1550
Hearts & Flowers Bowl, Pc Edge	B	300
Hearts & Flowers Bowl, Pc Edge	B	1000
Hearts & Flowers Bowl, Pc Edge	G	1300
Hearts & Flowers Bowl, Pc Edge	IB	750
Hearts & Flowers Bowl, Pc Edge	LIME G	850
Hearts & Flowers Bowl, Pc Edge	LIME G	1800
Hearts & Flowers Bowl, Pc Edge	LIME G	2100
Hearts & Flowers Bowl, Pc Edge	M	375
Hearts & Flowers Bowl, Pc Edge	M	525
Hearts & Flowers Bowl, Pc Edge	M	1600
Hearts & Flowers Bowl, Pc Edge	W	350
Hearts & Flowers Bowl, Pc Edge	W	425
Hearts & Flowers Bowl, Pc Edge, Chip	B	900
Hearts & Flowers Bowl, Sm Chip On Edge	G	550
Hearts & Flowers Bowl, Small Amt. Of Opal	AO	1000
Hearts & Flowers Compote	AO	385
Hearts & Flowers Compote	AO	395
Hearts & Flowers Compote	B	325
Hearts & Flowers Compote	B	350
Hearts & Flowers Compote	B	375
Hearts & Flowers Compote	B	475
Hearts & Flowers Compote	B	500
Hearts & Flowers Compote	G	1300
Hearts & Flowers Compote	G	1400
Hearts & Flowers Compote	G	1600
Hearts & Flowers Compote	IB	450
Hearts & Flowers Compote	IB	575
Hearts & Flowers Compote	IB	600
Hearts & Flowers Compote	IB	825
Hearts & Flowers Compote	IG	600
Hearts & Flowers Compote	IG	625
Hearts & Flowers Compote	IG	700
Hearts & Flowers Compote	IG	725
Hearts & Flowers Compote	IG	725
Hearts & Flowers Compote	IG	1200
Hearts & Flowers Compote	M	105
Hearts & Flowers Compote	M	105
Hearts & Flowers Compote	M	110
Hearts & Flowers Compote	P	275
Hearts & Flowers Compote	P	425
Hearts & Flowers Compote	W	90
Hearts & Flowers Compote	W	95
Hearts & Flowers Compote	W	105
Hearts & Flowers Compote	W	115
Hearts & Flowers Compote	W	175
Hearts & Flowers Compote	W	185
Hearts & Flowers Compote	W	285
Hearts & Flowers Compote, Elec.	B	200
Hearts & Flowers Compote, Pastel	M	90
Hearts & Flowers Compote, Pastel	M	185
Hearts & Flowers Compote, Pinheads	AO	265
Hearts & Flowers Compote, Points Flaw	G	1075
Hearts & Flowers Compote, Some Opal On Edge	B	400
Hearts & Flowers Plate	IB	1100
Hearts & Flowers Plate	M	650
Hearts & Flowers Plate	M	725
Hearts & Flowers Plate	M	750
Hearts & Flowers Plate	M	1300
Hearts & Flowers Plate	P	550
Hearts & Flowers Plate	P	600
Hearts & Flowers Plate	P	850
Hearts & Flowers Plate	P	1200
Hearts & Flowers Plate	W	2500
Hearts & Flowers Plate, Pastel	M	650
Hearts & Flowers Plate, Small Flake	IB	850
Hearts & Trees Bowl	M	225
Hearts & Trees Bowl	M	360
Heavy Grape Bowl, 11", Dugan, Compas Ext	P	175
Heavy Grape Bowl, 6", Imperial	SMOKE	50
Heavy Grape Chop Plate	AMBER	105
Heavy Grape Chop Plate	AMBER	125
Heavy Grape Chop Plate	P	400
Heavy Grape Chop Plate	P	650
Heavy Grape Chop Plate, Silvery	P	115
Heavy Grape Chop Plate, Stretchy Finish	SMOKE	1500
Heavy Grape Nappy	P	40
Heavy Grape Plate, 8"	P	110

Leaf Chain, Fenton, plate, 9", white, has incredible color, **$550.**

Leaf Chain, Fenton, plate, 9", electric blue, fantastic, **$2,300.**

Leaf Chain, Fenton, plate, 9", marigold, super iridescence, **$1,400.**

Little Flowers, Fenton, ruffled bowl, green, **$25.**

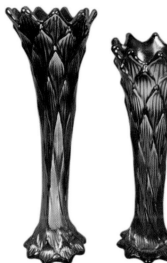

Lined Lattice, Dugan, two purple vases, one has flake on point (sold choice), **$25.**

Lined Lattice, Dugan, vase, 11", white, **$60.**

Little Flowers, Fenton, bowl, ice cream shape, 10", marigold, pretty and scarce, **$60.**

Leaf Tiers, Fenton, covered sugar and creamer, marigold, **$200.**

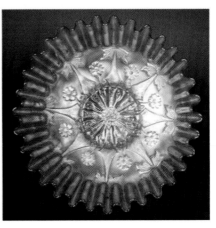

Little Flowers, Fenton, bowl, 9", with candy ribbon edge, marigold, **$50.**

DESCRIPTION	COLOR	BID	DESCRIPTION	COLOR	BID	DESCRIPTION	COLOR	BID
Heavy Grape Plate, 8"	P	145	Hobnail Swirl Spittoon	A	325	Holly Bowl	BO	1300
Heavy Grape Plate, 8"	P	155	Hobnail Swirl Spittoon	A	500	Holly Bowl	BO	1900
Heavy Grape Plate, 8"	P	155	Hobnail Swirl Spittoon	M	475	Holly Bowl	G	85
Heavy Grape Plate, 8"	P	225	Hobnail Swirl Spittoon	M	625	Holly Bowl	G	130
Heavy Grape Plate, 8"	P	275	Hobnail Swirl Spittoon	M	650	Holly Bowl	LIME G	130
Heavy Grape Plate, 8"	SMOKE	165	Hobnail Swirl Spittoon	M	850	Holly Bowl	M	25
Heavy Iris Tankard	M	150	Hobnail Swirl Spittoon	P	400	Holly Bowl	M	115
Heavy Iris Tankard	M	250	Hobnail Swirl Spittoon	P	650	Holly Bowl	MMG	2700
Heavy Iris Tankard	W	850	Hobnail Swirl Vase, 10"	A	250	Holly Bowl	MOON	575
Heavy Iris Tankard, Elec	P	2000	Hobnail Swirl Vase, 10"	A	400	Holly Bowl	MOON	600
Heavy Iris Tumbler	LAV	80	Hobnail Swirl Vase, 10"	G	225	Holly Bowl	MOON	800
Heavy Iris Tumbler	M	105	Hobnail Swirl Vase, 10"	G	300	Holly Bowl	P	70
Heavy Iris Tumbler	M	125	Hobnail Swirl Vase, 10"	G	500	Holly Bowl	RED	650
Heavy Iris Tumbler	P	85	Hobnail Swirl Vase, 10"	LAV	325	Holly Bowl	RED	800
Heavy Iris Tumbler	P	100	Hobstar & Feather Bowl, 10", Irid Crystal	CRYSTA	700	Holly Bowl	RED	950
Heavy Iris Water Set, 7 Pc	A	1000	Hobstar & Feather Card Tray, 2 Sides Up	W	800	Holly Bowl	RED	1000
Heavy Iris Water Set, 7 Pc	M	350	Hobstar & Feather Compote, 6", Very Rare	M	1800	Holly Bowl	RED	1800
Heron Mug	P	135	Hobstar & Feather Diamond Shape Dish	M	1000	Holly Bowl	TEAL	160
Heron Mug	P	165	Hobstar & Feather Dish, Heart Shape	M	300	Holly Bowl	W	95
Hobnail Cordial, 2	M	220	Hobstar & Feather Giant Rosebowl	G	1700	Holly Bowl	W	175
Hobnail Decanter	M	130	Hobstar & Feather Giant Rosebowl	G	2500	Holly Bowl, 3/1 Edge	A	100
Hobnail Jardiniere, Mbrg, Very Rare	A	4200	Hobstar & Feather Punch Base Only, Mbrg	VAS	800	Holly Bowl, 3/1 Edge	A	135
Hobnail Rosebowl	A	185	Hobstar & Feather Punch Set, 14 Pc, Mgold Base	G	2400	Holly Bowl, 3/1 Edge	AQUA	395
Hobnail Rosebowl	A	210				Holly Bowl, 3/1 Edge	B	85
Hobnail Rosebowl	G	525	Hobstar & Feather Punch Set, 15 Pc	M	750	Holly Bowl, 3/1 Edge	B	120
Hobnail Rosebowl	M	125	Hobstar Butter Dish	P	260	Holly Bowl, 3/1 Edge	BA	165
Hobnail Rosebowl	M	150	Hobstar Flower Compote	G	80	Holly Bowl, 3/1 Edge	G	90
Hobnail Rosebowl	M	150	Hobstar Flower Compote	P	180	Holly Bowl, 3/1 Edge	G	100
Hobnail Rosebowl	M	155	Hobstar Flower Compote	VIOLET	255	Holly Bowl, 3/1 Edge	LIME G	100
Hobnail Rosebowl	M	195	Hobstar Pickle Caster	M	475	Holly Bowl, 3/1 Edge	LIME G	140
Hobnail Rosebowl, Cracked	G	225	Holly Bowl	A	55	Holly Bowl, 3/1 Edge	M	55
Hobnail Salt, Oval, English	M	110	Holly Bowl	A	80	Holly Bowl, 3/1 Edge	OG	75
Hobnail Spittoon	A	350	Holly Bowl	A	155	Holly Bowl, 3/1 Edge	P	165
Hobnail Spittoon	G	2000	Holly Bowl	AMBER	105	Holly Bowl, 3/1 Edge	POWD B	115
Hobnail Spittoon	P	600	Holly Bowl	AQUA	115	Holly Bowl, 3/1 Edge	TEAL	185
Hobnail Spittoon, Nick	M	400	Holly Bowl	B	65	Holly Bowl, 3/1 Edge	W	190
Hobnail Swirl Rosebowl	A	150	Holly Bowl	B	150	Holly Bowl, Buffed	MOON	325
Hobnail Swirl Rosebowl	A	215	Holly Bowl	BO	1050	Holly Bowl, Deep	B	45
Hobnail Swirl Rosebowl	A	325				Holly Bowl, Deep	LIME G	95
Hobnail Swirl Rosebowl	M	165				Holly Bowl, Deep	M	40
Hobnail Swirl Rosebowl	M	170				Holly Bowl, Ic	AMBER	120
Hobnail Swirl Rosebowl	M	200				Holly Bowl, Ic	B	100
Hobnail Swirl Rosebowl	P	300				Holly Bowl, Ic	CELEST	5250
Hobnail Swirl Spittoon	A	195				Holly Bowl, Ic	G	130
						Holly Bowl, Ic	G	160
						Holly Bowl, Ic	M	160
						Holly Bowl, Ic	M	225

Morning Glory, Imperial, funeral vase, 17-1/4" h, 4-3/4" base, **$400**.

Maple Leaf, Dugan, seven tumblers marigold (sold choice), **$10 each.**

Memphis, Northwood, six Tumblers, green with gold decoration, non-carnival, **$50**.

Morning Glory, Imperial,
funeral vase, purple, 14-1/4" h, 8-1/2" mouth, **$700**.

Morning Glory, Millersburg,
water pitcher and four tumblers, tankard, amethyst, **$18,000**.

DESCRIPTION	COLOR	BID
Holly Bowl, Ic	POWD B	135
Holly Bowl, Ic	TEAL	75
Holly Bowl, Ic	W	175
Holly Bowl, Ic, Elec	B	200
Holly Bowl, Nick On Edge	BO	550
Holly Bowl, Some Slag	G	175
Holly Compote	A	45
Holly Compote	AQUA	90
Holly Compote	AQUA	215
Holly Compote	B	55
Holly Compote	BA	95
Holly Compote	BA	175
Holly Compote	G	45
Holly Compote	G	110
Holly Compote	G	125
Holly Compote	LAV	105
Holly Compote	LIME G	50
Holly Compote	M	25
Holly Compote	OG	85
Holly Compote	RED	210
Holly Compote	RED	325
Holly Compote	RED	425
Holly Compote	VAS	95
Holly Compote, 2 Sides Up	M	15
Holly Compote, 2 Sides Up	M	100
Holly Compote, 2 Sides Up	P	200
Holly Compote, 2 Sides Up	VIOLET	150
Holly Goblet	AQUA	140
Holly Goblet	B	20
Holly Goblet	G	120
Holly Goblet	G	125
Holly Goblet	LGO	425
Holly Goblet	LGO	600
Holly Goblet	LIME G	70
Holly Goblet	M	20
Holly Goblet	RED	275
Holly Goblet	RED	500
Holly Goblet	VAS	125
Holly Goblet	VAS	170
Holly Hat	A	165
Holly Hat	AMBER	80
Holly Hat	AMY O	235
Holly Hat	AO	700
Holly Hat	AQUA	75

DESCRIPTION	COLOR	BID
Holly Hat	G	50
Holly Hat	MMG	155
Holly Hat	MOON	125
Holly Hat	MOON	140
Holly Hat	RED	180
Holly Hat, 2 Sides Up	RED	525
Holly Hat, Crimped	RED	215
Holly Hat, Elec	RED	550
Holly Hat, Jip	M	100
Holly Hat, Jip, Crimped	AMBER	80
Holly Hat, Jip, Crimped	AQUA	115
Holly Hat, Jip, Crimped	B	115
Holly Hat, Jip, Crimped	LIME G	120
Holly Hat, Jip, Crimped	M	40
Holly Hat, Jip, Crimped	P	50
Holly Hat, Jip, Crimped	POWD B	40
Holly Hat, Jip, Crimped	RED	250
Holly Hat, Square	AMBER I	125
Holly Plate	A	250
Holly Plate	A	300
Holly Plate	A	400
Holly Plate	A	525
Holly Plate	A	1200
Holly Plate	B	145
Holly Plate	B	200
Holly Plate	B	225
Holly Plate	B	300
Holly Plate	BA	600
Holly Plate	CLAM	110
Holly Plate	CLAM	155
Holly Plate	G	375
Holly Plate	G	400
Holly Plate	G	500
Holly Plate	G	525
Holly Plate	LAV	185
Holly Plate	M	105
Holly Plate	M	120
Holly Plate	M	130
Holly Plate	M	135
Holly Plate	M	155
Holly Plate	M	195
Holly Plate	M	200
Holly Plate	M	275
Holly Plate	M	300
Holly Plate	M	400
Holly Plate	P	400
Holly Plate	TEAL	2400

DESCRIPTION	COLOR	BID
Holly Plate	W	150
Holly Plate	W	155
Holly Plate	W	185
Holly Plate	W	200
Holly Plate	W	215
Holly Plate	W	275
Holly Rosebowl	B	195
Holly Rosebowl	M	135
Holly Sherbet	RED	450
Holly Sprig Bon Bon, Isaac Benesch Adv.	M	140
Holly Sprig Bowl	A	105
Holly Sprig Bowl, 6" Ic	G	180
Holly Sprig Bowl, 6", 3/1 Edge	A	145
Holly Sprig Bowl, 6", 3/1 Edge	VAS	875
Holly Sprig Bowl, 6", Tri Corner	A	150
Holly Sprig Bowl, 6", Tri Corner	G	175
Holly Sprig Bowl, 6", Tri Corner	M	105
Holly Sprig Bowl, 7", Ic	A	180
Holly Sprig Bowl, 8"	A	140
Holly Sprig Bowl, 8"	A	210
Holly Sprig Bowl, 8", Crimped Edge	A	575
Holly Sprig Bowl, 8", Tri Corner	A	175
Holly Sprig Card Tray	A	85
Holly Sprig Nappy	M	85
Homestead Chop Plate	AMBER	1700
Homestead Chop Plate	M	450
Homestead Chop Plate	M	450
Homestead Chop Plate	P	1400
Homestead Chop Plate	P	2700
Homestead Chop Plate	SMOKE	500
Homestead Chop Plate	SMOKE	625
Homestead Chop Plate	W	600
Homestead Chop Plate	W	950
Homestead Chop Plate, Flakes In Pattern	P	1100
Homestead Chop Plate, Nick On Edge	P	650
Homestead Chop Plate, Nuart	M	450
Homestead Chop Plate, Nuart	P	2200
Homestead Chop Plate, Nuart	SMOKE	575

Octagon, Dugan,
decanter including five cordials, $90.

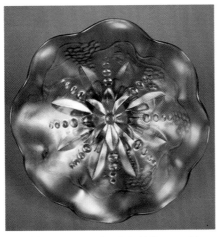

Octet, Northwood, bowl, 8-1/4", emerald
green, tough to find, $175.

Open Edge, Fenton,
jack-in-the-pulpit basket, red, $250.

Open Edge, Fenton, basket, banana-boat shape with
factory applied metal base, 9", celeste blue, some checks in
webbing, $625.

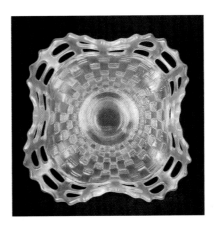

Open Edge, Fenton, square basket, ice
green, really pretty and scarce, $230.

Nesting Swan, Millersburg, bowl, green, radium
and covered with blue and pink iridescence, $275.

Open Edge, Fenton, two-row basket, 7", ice green, $250.

DESCRIPTION	COLOR	BID
Homestead Chop Plate, Nuart	W	450
Homestead Chop Plate, Nuart, Flake In Pattern	AMBER	2100
Horse Medallion Bowl	B	180
Horse Medallion Bowl	B	235
Horse Medallion Bowl	G	165
Horse Medallion Bowl	G	250
Horse Medallion Bowl, Ftd	A	415
Horse Medallion Nut Bowl	AMBER	185
Horse Medallion Nut Bowl	AQUA	400
Horse Medallion Nut Bowl	B	40
Horse Medallion Nut Bowl	M	50
Horse Medallion Nut Bowl	M	75
Horse Medallion Plate	M	300
Horse Medallion Plate	POWD B	1375
Horse Medallion Rosebowl	B	245
Horse Medallion Rosebowl	B	250
Imperial Compote, No Pattern	P	80
Imperial Grape Bowl	P	80
Imperial Grape Bowl	SMOKE	245
Imperial Grape Bowl, 10"	P	150
Imperial Grape Bowl, Elec.	P	175
Imperial Grape Bowl, Low Ruffled	LAV	245
Imperial Grape Bowl, Low Ruffled	M	145
Imperial Grape Bowl, Low Ruffled	P	100
Imperial Grape Bowl, Low Ruffled	P	300
Imperial Grape Carafe	M	105
Imperial Grape Carafe	P	145
Imperial Grape Carafe	P	150
Imperial Grape Carafe	P	175
Imperial Grape Carafe	P	205
Imperial Grape Carafe	P	225
Imperial Grape Carafe	P	235
Imperial Grape Carafe	P	250
Imperial Grape Carafe	P	350
Imperial Grape Carafe	P	390

DESCRIPTION	COLOR	BID
Imperial Grape Carafe	P	400
Imperial Grape Carafe	SMOKE	900
Imperial Grape Compote	G	40
Imperial Grape Compote	P	125
Imperial Grape Cup & Saucer	G	135
Imperial Grape Goblet	M	30
Imperial Grape Goblet	P	140
Imperial Grape Goblet	P	175
Imperial Grape Goblet	SMOKE	20
Imperial Grape Pitcher	M	95
Imperial Grape Pitcher	SMOKE	425
Imperial Grape Pitcher & 1 Tumbler	SMOKE	500
Imperial Grape Pitcher, Electric	P	700
Imperial Grape Plate	P	1900
Imperial Grape Plate, 6"	M	75
Imperial Grape Plate, 6"	TEAL	35
Imperial Grape Plate, 6"	TEAL	750
Imperial Grape Punch Set, 15 Pc	M	155
Imperial Grape Tumbler	P	85
Imperial Grape Water Set, 7 Pc	M	115
Imperial Grape Wine	SMOKE	35
Imperial Grape Wine Decanter	P	275
Imperial Grape Wine Decanter	SMOKE	280
Imperial Grape Wine Set, 5 Pc	SMOKE	225
Imperial Grape Wine Set, 7 Pc	G	135
Imperial Grape Wine Set, 7 Pc	M	75
Imperial Grape Wine Set, 7 Pc	M	180
Imperial Grape Wine Set, 7 Pc	P	260
Imperial Grape Wine Set, 8 Pc	G	170
Imperial Grape Wine Set, 8 Pc	M	180
Imperial Grape Wine Set, 8 Pc	P	250
Inverted Feather Cracker Jar	G	175
Inverted Feather Creamer	A	375

DESCRIPTION	COLOR	BID
Inverted Feather Tumbler	G	700
Inverted Strawberry Bowl, Round, Dome Ftd	M	225
Inverted Strawberry Candle Sticks, Sm Chip	M	425
Inverted Strawberry Compote, 9"	P	475
Inverted Strawberry Compote, Lg	A	350
Inverted Strawberry Creamer	M	65 09-13
Inverted Strawberry Pitcher	M	775
Inverted Strawberry Powder Jar	G	135
Inverted Strawberry Powder Jar	G	185
Inverted Strawberry Powder Jar	G	210
Inverted Strawberry Powder Jar	G	225
Inverted Strawberry Powder Jar	M	175
Inverted Strawberry Powder Jar	M	210
Inverted Strawberry Powder Jar	M	225
Inverted Strawberry Spittoon	M	650
Inverted Strawberry Tumbler	A	250
Inverted Strawberry Tumbler	G	130
Inverted Strawberry Tumbler	M	105
Inverted Strawberry Tumbler	M	130
Inverted Strawberry Tumbler	M	150
Jeweled Heart Pitcher	M	145
Jeweled Heart Pitcher	M	695
Jeweled Heart Tumbler	M	55
Jeweled Heart Tumbler	M	75
Kittens Bowl	B	250
Kittens Bowl	B	350
Kittens Bowl	M	110
Kittens Bowl	M	125
Kittens Bowl	M	135
Kittens Bowl	M	145
Kittens Bowl	M	155
Kittens Bowl, 2 Sides Up	B	250
Kittens Bowl, 2 Sides Up	B	250

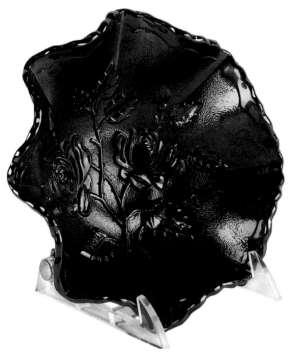

Open Rose, Imperial,
six-ruffled sauce, 5-1/2", violet blue, $600-$900 (rare).

Open Rose, Imperial,
round sauce, 5", violet blue, $500-$800 (rare).

Orange Tree Orchard, Fenton, two tumblers, marigold
with dark radium iridescence (sold choice), **$50 and $35**.

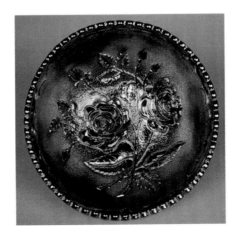

Open Rose, Imperial,
super plate, 9", flakes on roses, **$450**.

Open Rose, Imperial,
bowl, 6", electric purple, super, **$85**.

Orange Tree, Fenton,
loving cup, amethyst, one of the best, **$500**.

Description	Color	Bid
Kittens Bowl, 2 Sides Up	B	250
Kittens Bowl, 2 Sides Up	M	85
Kittens Bowl, 2 Sides Up	M	110
Kittens Bowl, 2 Sides Up	M	125
Kittens Bowl, 2 Sides Up	M	125
Kittens Bowl, 2 Sides Up	M	145
Kittens Bowl, 4 Sides Up	M	135
Kittens Bowl, 4 Sides Up	M	165
Kittens Bowl, 4 Sides Up	POWD B	185
Kittens Bowl, 4 Sides Up	POWD B	475
Kittens Cereal Bowl	B	295
Kittens Cereal Bowl	B	425
Kittens Cereal Bowl	M	130
Kittens Cereal Bowl	M	160
Kittens Cup	B	310
Kittens Cup	B	375
Kittens Cup	B	475
Kittens Cup & Saucer	M	125
Kittens Cup & Saucer	M	185
Kittens Cup & Saucer	M	195
Kittens Cup & Saucer, Saucer Has Chip	B	550
Kittens Plate	M	105
Kittens Plate	M	135
Kittens Plate	M	170
Kittens Plate	POWD B	260
Kittens Plate	POWD B	265
Kittens Spittoon, Chip On Base	M	1100
Kittens Toothpick	B	225
Kittens Toothpick	B	250
Kittens Toothpick	B	250
Kittens Toothpick	M	65
Kittens Toothpick	M	75
Kittens Toothpick	M	115
Kittens Toothpick	M	125
Kittens Toothpick	M	150
Kittens Vase	B	205
Kittens Vase	B	250
Kittens Vase	M	100
Knotted Beads Vase, Crimped Top, 10"	AMBER	110
Lattice & Grape Tankard	M	195
Lattice & Grape Tankard	W	275
Lattice & Grape Water Set, 7 Pc	M	125
Lattice & Grape Water Set, 7 Pc	M	145
Lattice & Grape Water Set, 7 Pc	M	160
Lattice & Grape Water Set, 7 Pc	M	170
Lattice & Points Vase, 8"	P	100
Leaf & Beads Nut Bowl	AO	1000
Leaf & Beads Nut Bowl	LAV	180
Leaf & Beads Nut Bowl	P	110
Leaf & Beads Rosebowl	AO	135
Leaf & Beads Rosebowl	AO	185
Leaf & Beads Rosebowl	AO	195
Leaf & Beads Rosebowl	AO	205
Leaf & Beads Rosebowl	AO	220
Leaf & Beads Rosebowl	AO	225
Leaf & Beads Rosebowl	AO	225
Leaf & Beads Rosebowl	AO	250
Leaf & Beads Rosebowl	AO	275
Leaf & Beads Rosebowl	AO	300
Leaf & Beads Rosebowl	AO	325
Leaf & Beads Rosebowl	AO	350
Leaf & Beads Rosebowl	AO	425
Leaf & Beads Rosebowl	AO	450
Leaf & Beads Rosebowl	AO	450
Leaf & Beads Rosebowl	AO	475
Leaf & Beads Rosebowl	AO	800
Leaf & Beads Rosebowl	B	100
Leaf & Beads Rosebowl	B	100
Leaf & Beads Rosebowl	B	150
Leaf & Beads Rosebowl	B	275
Leaf & Beads Rosebowl	IB	1000
Leaf & Beads Rosebowl	IG	1500
Leaf & Beads Rosebowl	IG	2600
Leaf & Beads Rosebowl	M	105
Leaf & Beads Rosebowl	P	105
Leaf & Beads Rosebowl	P	125
Leaf & Beads Rosebowl Reng	B	315
Leaf & Beads Rosebowl Reng	B	350
Leaf & Beads Rosebowl Reng	B	400
Leaf & Beads Rosebowl	W	245
Leaf & Beads Rosebowl	W	375
Leaf & Beads Rosebowl, Some Damage To Foot	IG	450
Leaf & Beads Rosebowl, Sunflower Int	G	75
Leaf & Beads Rosebowl, Sunflower Int	G	155
Leaf & Beads Rosebowl, Sunflower Int	G	215
Leaf & Beads Rosebowl, Sunflower Int	P	230
Leaf Chain Bowl	RED	450
Leaf Chain Bowl, 8"	IG	1800
Leaf Chain Plate	CLAM	185
Leaf Chain Plate	CLAM	250
Leaf Chain Plate	G	1300
Leaf Chain Plate	M	115
Leaf Chain Plate	M	155
Leaf Chain Plate	M	275
Leaf Chain Plate	M	300
Leaf Chain Plate	M	355
Leaf Chain Plate	M	400
Leaf Chain Plate	M	575
Leaf Chain Plate	M	1400
Leaf Chain Plate	W	130
Leaf Chain Plate	W	140
Leaf Chain Plate	W	550
Leaf Chain Plate, 7"	B	100
Leaf Chain Plate, 7"	B	100
Leaf Chain Plate, 7"	M	75
Leaf Chain Plate, 8"	B	90
Leaf Chain Plate, Dark Pumpkin	M	2050
Leaf Chain Plate, Elec.	B	2300
Leaf Columns Vase, 10"	G	100
Leaf Columns Vase, 10"	G	190
Leaf Columns Vase, 10"	W	300
Leaf Columns Vase, 11"	IB	300
Leaf Columns Vase, 12"	HORE	425
Leaf Columns Vase, 5"	P	245
Leaf Columns Vase, 6"	P	110
Leaf Ray Nappy	LIME G	120
Leaf Tiers Butter Dish, Light	M	55
Leaf Tiers Tumbler	M	52
Leaf Tiers Tumbler	M	65
Leaf Tiers Tumbler	M	75
Lincoln Drape Mini Lamp	M	725
Lined Lattice Vase, 10"	M	45
Lined Lattice Vase, 10"	P	105
Lined Lattice Vase, 10"	P	140
Lined Lattice Vase, 10"	P	195
Lined Lattice Vase, 10"	W	75

Orange Tree, Fenton,
punch bowl and base including eight
punch cups, blue, $300.

Orange Tree, Fenton,
footed fruit bowl, blue, $160.

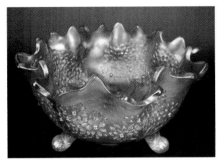

Orange Tree, Fenton,
footed fruit bowl, marigold, $60.

Oriental Poppy, Northwood,
tankard, white, very frosty with great
iridescence; has usual manufacturer's
roughness around rim, $1,400.

Oriental Poppy, Northwood,
pair of tumblers, white (sold choice), $60 each.

Oriental Poppy, Northwood,
six tumblers, marigold, (sold choice),
three are $25 each; three are $45 each.

Oriental Poppy, Northwood,
tankard, purple, $425.

Oriental Poppy, Northwood,
five tumblers, purple (sold choice),
two are $55 each; three are $45 each.

DESCRIPTION	COLOR	BID
Lined Lattice Vase, 11"	M	55
Lined Lattice Vase, 14"	P	225
Lined Lattice Vase, 5"	P	500
Lined Lattice Vase, 7"	P	105
Lined Lattice Vase, 8"	P	350
Lined Lattice Vase, 8'	P	150
Lined Lattice Vase, 9"	LAV	95
Lined Lattice Vase, 9"	P	135
Lined Lattice Vase, 9"	W	100
Lined Lattice Vase, Slight Opal In Tips	M	155
Little Fishes Bowl, Ftd	M	170
Little Fishes Bowl, Ic	M	140
Little Fishes Bowl, Lg	B	250
Little Fishes Sauce, Ftd	AQUA	255
Little Flowers Berry Set, 7 Pc	A	135
Little Flowers Bowl	AMBERI	1400
Little Flowers Bowl	B	100
Little Flowers Bowl, 10", Ruffled	RED	4100
Little Flowers Bowl, Ic	B	135
Little Flowers Bowl, Lg Ic	B	175
Little Flowers Bowl, Lg, Elec	B	105
Little Flowers Chop Plate	M	1400
Little Stars Bowl, 10"	AQUA	1300
Little Stars Bowl, 7"	G	105
Little Stars Bowl, 7"	G	185
Little Stars Bowl, 7"	M	100
Little Stars Bowl, 7"	P	150
Little Stars Bowl, 8"	A	295
Little Stars Bowl, 8"	G	100
Little Stars Bowl, 8"	G	255
Little Stars Bowl, 8"	G	325
Little Stars Bowl, 8"	M	155
Little Stars Bowl, 8", 3/1 Edge	M	300
Little Stars Bowl, 8", Ic	M	290
Little Stars Bowl, 8", Ic	M	350
Loganberry Vase	AMBER	375
Loganberry Vase	AMBER	425
Loganberry Vase	AMBER	550
Loganberry Vase	AMBER	700
Loganberry Vase	G	295
Loganberry Vase	M	300
Loganberry Vase	M	300

DESCRIPTION	COLOR	BID
Loganberry Vase	M	650
Loganberry Vase	P	1700
Loganberry Vase, Pumpkin Irid	M	425
Long Thumbprint Variant Vase, 5 1/4", Mbrg.	A	900
Lotus & Grape Bon Bon	RED	450
Lotus & Grape Bon Bon	RED	600
Lotus & Grape Bowl	G	150
Lotus & Grape Bowl	M	120
Lotus & Grape Plate	A	1200
Lotus & Grape Plate	A	1300
Lotus & Grape Plate	G	1000
Lotus & Grape Plate	G	1600
Lotus & Grape Plate, Poor Color	B	500
Luster Rose Butterdish	P	275
Luster Rose Spooner	P	55
Lustre Rose Bowl, Centerpiece	P	135
Lustre Rose Bowl, Low Ic, 9 1/2"	P	625
Lustre Rose Fernery	B	115
Lustre Rose Fernery	B	125
Lustre Rose Pitcher	G	150
Lustre Rose Table Set, 4 Pc	M	110
Lustre Rose Tumbler	OG	40
Lustre Rose Tumbler	P	75
Lustre Rose Tumbler	TEAL	80
Lustre Rose Water Set, 7 Pc	P	1600
Many Fruits Punch Set, 6 Pc	P	1100
Many Fruits Punch Set, 7 Pc	M	300
Many Fruits Punch Set, 7 Pc	P	1050
Many Fruits Punch Set, 8 Pc	M	450
Many Fruits Punch Set, 8 Pc	P	425
Many Stars Bowl	A	400
Many Stars Bowl	A	500
Many Stars Bowl	A	600
Many Stars Bowl	A	600
Many Stars Bowl	A	750
Many Stars Bowl	A	875
Many Stars Bowl	M	700

DESCRIPTION	COLOR	BID
Many Stars Bowl, 3/1 Edge	G	625
Many Stars Bowl, 3/1 Edge, Light Color	M	375
Many Stars Bowl, Flaw On Edge	B	875
Many Stars Bowl, Ic	A	550
Many Stars Bowl, Ic	G	850
Many Stars Bowl, Ic	G	900
Many Stars Bowl, Ic	G	900
Maple Leaf Butter Dish	P	45
Maple Leaf Pitcher	M	210
Maple Leaf Spooner	P	75
Maple Leaf Water Set, 7 Pc	A	250
Mary Ann Loving Cup, Crack In Handle, 3 Handle	M	165
Mary Ann Vase	M	75
Mary Ann Vase	M	85
Mary Ann Vase, Odd Lime Green/vaseline	LIME G	175
Memphis Fruit Bowl & Base	M	350
Memphis Fruit Bowl & Base	P	400
Memphis Fruit Bowl & Base & 6 Cups	P	675
Memphis Fruit Bowl & Base & 6 Cups	P	750
Memphis Fruit Bowl, Base, 6 Cups, Bad Crack	IB	825
Memphis Punch Base Only	P	135
Memphis Punch Cups, 5	P	125
Memphis Punch Set, 8 Pc	M	1100
Morning Glory Funeral Vase, 12"	P	650
Morning Glory Funeral Vase, 13"	M	375
Morning Glory Funeral Vase, 14", 9" Mouth	P	350
Morning Glory Funeral Vase, 16"	P	300
Morning Glory Funeral Vase, Peeling On Top	AMBER	400
Morning Glory Tumbler	A	700
Morning Glory Tumbler	A	800
Morning Glory Tumbler	A	2100
Morning Glory Tumbler	M	2700
Morning Glory Tumbler, Silvery	G	1000

Peacock at the Fountain, Northwood, water pitcher and six tumblers, ice blue, **$3,600**.

Peacock and Grape, Fenton,
ice-cream shaped bowl, electric blue, **$135**.

Peacock and Grape, Fenton,
plate with collar base, marigold, absolutely
incredible, **$750**.

Pansy, Imperial,
ruffled bowl, electric purple, **$180**.

DESCRIPTION	COLOR	BID
Morning Glory Vase, 3 3/4"	P	220
Morning Glory Vase, 4 3/4"	G	155
Morning Glory Vase, 4 3/4"	P	195
Morning Glory Vase, 6 1/2"	SMOKE	115
Morning Glory Vase, 6"	LAV	200
Morning Glory Vase, 6"	M	70
Morning Glory Vase, 6"	P	110
Morning Glory Vase, 6"	P	200
Morning Glory Vase, 6"	SMOKE	135
Morning Glory Vase, 6", 4" Opening	SMOKE	135
Morning Glory Vase, 7"	SMOKE	55
Multi Fruits & Flowers Pitcher, Collar Base	A	8000
Multi Fruits & Flowers Punch Base Only	A	425
Multi Fruits & Flowers Punch Bowl & Base	A	1600
Multi Fruits & Flowers Punch Set, 6 Pc	A	1800
Multi Fruits & Flowers Sherbet	A	475
Multi Fruits & Flowers Tumbler	G	550
Nautilus Creamer	P	225
Nautilus Creamer	P	255
Nautilus Creamer	PO	125
Nautilus Creamer	PO	175
Nautilus Vase, 6"	M	165
Nautilus Vase, 6"	P	200
Nautilus Vase, 9"	P	175
Near Cut Creamer, Souv. Amana, Iowa	M	125
Near Cut Creamer, Souv. Big Stone City, Sd	M	175
Near Cut Creamer, Souv. Vesta, Minnesota	M	175
Near Cut Tumbler	M	650
Nesting Swan Bowl	A	250
Nesting Swan Bowl	A	300
Nesting Swan Bowl	A	500
Nesting Swan Bowl	G	200
Nesting Swan Bowl	G	225
Nesting Swan Bowl	G	225
Nesting Swan Bowl	G	225
Nesting Swan Bowl	G	275
Nesting Swan Bowl	G	450

DESCRIPTION	COLOR	BID
Nesting Swan Bowl	M	140
Nesting Swan Bowl	M	200
Nesting Swan Bowl	M	350
Nesting Swan Bowl	P	250
Nesting Swan Bowl	P	275
Nesting Swan Bowl, Deep Round	G	700
Nesting Swan Bowl, Deep Round, Blue Irid.	M	3700
Nesting Swan Bowl, Nick	G	220
Nesting Swan Bowl, Square Crimped, Edge Flakes	G	900
Nesting Swan Bowl, Square, Crimped Edge	M	1800
Nippon Bowl	G	190
Nippon Bowl	G	220
Nippon Bowl	IB	170
Nippon Bowl	IG	825
Nippon Bowl	M	225
Nippon Bowl	P	475
Nippon Bowl, Dark	M	M 375
Nippon Bowl, Pc Edge	AQUA	3300
Nippon Bowl, Pc Edge	G	250
Nippon Bowl, Pc Edge	IB	155
Nippon Bowl, Pc Edge	IB	180
Nippon Bowl, Pc Edge	IB	225
Nippon Bowl, Pc Edge	IB	230
Nippon Bowl, Pc Edge	IB	475
Nippon Bowl, Pc Edge	IG	675
Nippon Bowl, Pc Edge	LIME G	775
Nippon Bowl, Pc Edge	M	180
Nippon Bowl, Pc Edge	M	500
Nippon Bowl, Pc Edge	P	180
Nippon Bowl, Pc Edge	P	275
Nippon Bowl, Pc Edge	P	675
Nippon Bowl, Pc Edge	W	125
Nippon Bowl, Pc Edge	W	135
Nippon Bowl, Pc Edge	W	225
Nippon Bowl, Pc Edge	W	350
Nippon Bowl, Pc Edge	W	450
Nippon Bowl, Pc Edge, Nick On Flute	IB	200
Nippon Bowl, Pc Edge, Pumpkin Marigold	M	800
Nippon Plate	G	1100
Octagon Berry Bowl, Small	LAV	135

DESCRIPTION	COLOR	BID
Octagon Bowl, 12", Square	G	240
Octagon Cordial	M	135
Octagon Decanter & Stopper	G	170
Octagon Pitcher, Small	M	65
Octagon Tumbler	P	200
Octagon Vase, 8"	M	55
Octagon Water Set, 7 Pc	M	170
Octagon Wine Glass	AQUA	85
Octagon Wine Set, 6 Pc	M	95
Octagon Wine Set, 7 Pc	M	180
Octet Bowl	G	175
Octet Bowl	G	375
Octet Bowl	M	575
Octet Bowl	P	100
Ohio Star Vase	A	1100
Ohio Star Vase	M	1000
Ohio Star Vase, Chip On Base	G	1250
Ohio Star Vase, Polished Base	M	2400
Ohio Star Vase, Small Flake	P	1700
Open Edge Basket, 2 Sides Up, Lg	B	110
Open Edge Basket, 2 Sides Up, Lg	IB	350
Open Edge Basket, 2 Sides Up, Lg	IB	550
Open Edge Basket, 2 Sides Up, Lg	IG	350
Open Edge Basket, 2 Sides Up, Lg	W	220
Open Edge Basket, 2 Sides Up, Small	AMBER	190
Open Edge Basket, 2 Sides Up, Small	AMBERI	325
Open Edge Basket, 2 Sides Up, Small	AQUA	40
Open Edge Basket, 2 Sides Up, Small	AQUA	190
Open Edge Basket, 2 Sides Up, Small	BA	70
Open Edge Basket, 2 Sides Up, Small	G	300
Open Edge Basket, 2 Sides Up, Small	IB	375
Open Edge Basket, 2 Sides Up, Small	IB	575
Open Edge Basket, 2 Sides Up, Small	IG	225

Peacock at the Fountain, Northwood, punch bowl base and six cups, dark marigold, **$750**.

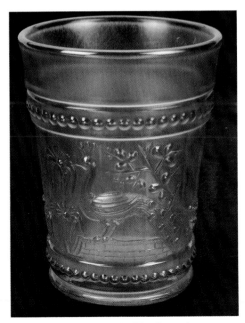

Peacock at the Fountain, Northwood,
tumbler, lavender, **$250**.

Peacock at the Fountain, Northwood,
master berry bowl, three small, ice blue, straight up, **$650**.

DESCRIPTION	COLOR	BID
Open Edge Basket, 2 Sides Up, Small	IG	275
Open Edge Basket, 2 Sides Up, Small	M	20
Open Edge Basket, 2 Sides Up, Small	OG	110
Open Edge Basket, 2 Sides Up, Small	PINK	120
Open Edge Basket, 2 Sides Up, Small	RAO	500
Open Edge Basket, 2 Sides Up, Small	RAO	650
Open Edge Basket, 2 Sides Up, Small	RED	200
Open Edge Basket, 2 Sides Up, Small	RED	225
Open Edge Basket, 2 Sides Up, Small	RED	250
Open Edge Basket, 2 Sides Up, Small	VAS	60
Open Edge Basket, 2 Sides Up, Small, Damaged	RAO	225
Open Edge Basket, 3 Row	CELEST	550
Open Edge Basket, 3 Row	IG	350
Open Edge Basket, 3 Row	IG	600
Open Edge Basket, Ic, Lg	CELEST	350
Open Edge Basket, Ic, Lg	IG	150
Open Edge Basket, Ic, Lg	W	200
Open Edge Basket, Jip, Small	A	135
Open Edge Basket, Jip, Small	AMBER	135
Open Edge Basket, Jip, Small	AMBERI	135
Open Edge Basket, Jip, Small	AQUA	65
Open Edge Basket, Jip, Small	AQUA	120
Open Edge Basket, Jip, Small	AQUA	135
Open Edge Basket, Jip, Small	B	40
Open Edge Basket, Jip, Small	G	60
Open Edge Basket, Jip, Small	G	135
Open Edge Basket, Jip, Small	G	145

DESCRIPTION	COLOR	BID
Open Edge Basket, Jip, Small	G	185
Open Edge Basket, Jip, Small	LIME G	50
Open Edge Basket, Jip, Small	OG	75
Open Edge Basket, Jip, Small	OG	150
Open Edge Basket, Jip, Small	RED	110
Open Edge Basket, Jip, Small	RED	160
Open Edge Basket, Jip, Small	RED	180
Open Edge Basket, Jip, Small	RED	200
Open Edge Basket, Jip, Small	RED	250
Open Edge Basket, Lg	W	550
Open Edge Basket, Lg, Square	CELEST	350
Open Edge Basket, Lg, Square	IG	115
Open Edge Basket, Lg, Square	W	180
Open Edge Basket, Round, Lg	IG	350
Open Edge Basket, Round, Small	IB	425
Open Edge Basket, Round, Small	IG	185
Open Edge Basket, Round, Small	W	135
Open Edge Basket, Ruffled, Lg	CELEST	575
Open Edge Basket, Ruffled, Lg	IG	325
Open Edge Basket, Small	AQUA	60
Open Edge Basket, Small	B	50
Open Edge Basket, Small	BA	70
Open Edge Basket, Small	BA	125
Open Edge Basket, Small	IB	325
Open Edge Basket, Small	IB	350
Open Edge Basket, Small	IB	500
Open Edge Basket, Small	IG	195
Open Edge Basket, Small	IG	375

DESCRIPTION	COLOR	BID
Open Edge Basket, Small	LIME G	55
Open Edge Basket, Small	M	25
Open Edge Basket, Small	RAO	300
Open Edge Basket, Small	RAO	625
Open Edge Basket, Small	RED	175
Open Edge Basket, Small	RED	205
Open Edge Basket, Small	RED	215
Open Edge Basket, Small	RED	220
Open Edge Basket, Small	RED	220
Open Edge Basket, Small	RED	225
Open Edge Basket, Small	RED	235
Open Edge Basket, Small	RED	300
Open Edge Basket, Small	RED	320
Open Edge Basket, Small	RO	675
Open Edge Basket, Small	SAPH B	150
Open Edge Basket, Small	W	160
Open Edge Basket, Small	W	270
Open Edge Basket, Small, John H. Brand Adv	M	65
Open Edge Basket, Square, Lg	IB	275
Open Edge Basket, Square, Lg	W	575
Open Edge Basket, Square, Small	AQUA	80
Open Edge Basket, Square, Small	G	175
Open Edge Basket, Square, Small	IB	375
Open Edge Basket, Square, Small	IG	295
Open Edge Basket, Square, Small	POWD B	150
Open Edge Basket, Square, Small	RED	245
Open Edge Basket, Square, Small	W	300

Peacock at Urn, Northwood,
two ice-cream shaped sauces, electric blue, both
super (sold choice), **$135 each**.

Peacock at Urn, Northwood,
master ice-cream shaped bowl, purple,
$750.

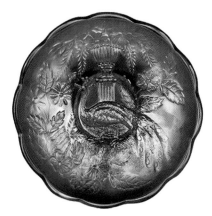

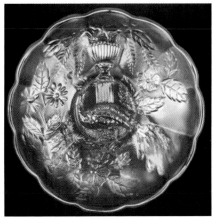

Peacock at Urn, Northwood,
two ice-cream shaped sauces (one shown),
purple (sold choice), **$70 each**.

Peacock at Urn, Northwood,
ice-cream shaped sauce, green, rare and
beautiful, **$800**.

Peacock at Urn, Northwood,
ice-cream shape sauce, pastel marigold, **$75**.

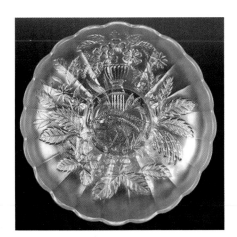

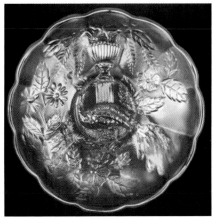

Peacock at Urn, Northwood,
master bowl, ice cream shape, ice blue,
pastel and pretty, **$900**.

Peacock at Urn, Northwood,
stippled master bowl, ice cream shape,
pumpkin marigold, one of the best, **$1,800**.

Peacock at Urn, Northwood,
sauce, ice cream shape, pumpkin marigold,
$350.

DESCRIPTION	COLOR	BID
Open Edge Bowl, 3 Row, Lg	IG	275
Open Edge Bowl, 3 Row, Lg	IG	310
Open Edge Bowl, 3 Row, Lg	W	225
Open Edge Bowl, 3 Rowl, 2 Sides Up, Lg	IB	500
Open Edge Plate Whimsey, 8"	M	950
Open Rose Bowl, Centerpiece, 9"	AMBER	225
Open Rose Bowl, Electric	P	275
Open Rose Plate	AMBER	100
Open Rose Plate	AMBER	130
Open Rose Plate	AMBER	195
Open Rose Plate	AMBER	250
Open Rose Plate	HELIOS	100
Open Rose Plate	M	135
Open Rose Plate	P	1700
Open Rose Rosebowl	SMOKE	55
Orange Tree Bowl	B	85
Orange Tree Bowl	G	130
Orange Tree Bowl, Ic	A	160
Orange Tree Bowl, Ic	G	200
Orange Tree Bowl, Ruffled	RED	4300
Orange Tree Bowl, Tree Trunk Center	B	180
Orange Tree Compote	G	280
Orange Tree Compote	VAS	220
Orange Tree Creamer	W	65
Orange Tree Creamer Whimsey From Punch Cup	W	165
Orange Tree Fruit Bowl, Ftd	B	160
Orange Tree Fruit Bowl, Ftd	B	200
Orange Tree Hatpin Holder	B	170
Orange Tree Hatpin Holder	B	200
Orange Tree Hatpin Holder	B	200
Orange Tree Hatpin Holder	M	85
Orange Tree Hatpin Holder	M	105
Orange Tree Hatpin Holder	M	110

DESCRIPTION	COLOR	BID
Orange Tree Hatpin Holder	M	180
Orange Tree Hatpin Holder	M	245
Orange Tree Hatpin Holder, Damaged Foot	B	180
Orange Tree Hatpin Holder, Feet Roughness	B	125
Orange Tree Hatpin Holder, Irid Choc Glass	CHOL	2700
Orange Tree Loving Cup	A	300
Orange Tree Loving Cup	A	450
Orange Tree Loving Cup	A	500
Orange Tree Loving Cup	A	500
Orange Tree Loving Cup	B	165
Orange Tree Loving Cup	B	300
Orange Tree Loving Cup	G	250
Orange Tree Loving Cup	G	350
Orange Tree Loving Cup	G	1000
Orange Tree Loving Cup	M	140
Orange Tree Loving Cup	M	175
Orange Tree Loving Cup	M	250
Orange Tree Loving Cup	W	175
Orange Tree Loving Cup	W	325
Orange Tree Loving Cup	W	550
Orange Tree Loving Cup, Electric	B	2750
Orange Tree Loving Cup, Electric	W	475
Orange Tree Mug, Lg	AMBER	85
Orange Tree Mug, Lg	AMBER	205
Orange Tree Mug, Lg	AMBERI	225
Orange Tree Mug, Lg	AQUA	150
Orange Tree Mug, Lg	AQUA	325
Orange Tree Mug, Lg	B	40
Orange Tree Mug, Lg	B	85
Orange Tree Mug, Lg	BA	170
Orange Tree Mug, Lg	M	20
Orange Tree Mug, Lg	POWD B	90

DESCRIPTION	COLOR	BID
Orange Tree Mug, Lg	POWD B	135
Orange Tree Mug, Lg	RED	195
Orange Tree Mug, Lg	RED	300
Orange Tree Mug, Lg	RED	350
Orange Tree Mug, Lg	RED	380
Orange Tree Mug, Lg	VAS	150
Orange Tree Mug, Sm	AMBER	75
Orange Tree Mug, Sm	AQUA	130
Orange Tree Mug, Sm	AQUA	200
Orange Tree Mug, Sm	AQUA	210
Orange Tree Mug, Sm	AQUA	225
Orange Tree Mug, Sm	BA	75
Orange Tree Mug, Sm	G	235
Orange Tree Mug, Sm	P	165
Orange Tree Mug, Sm	POWD B	150
Orange Tree Mug, Sm	RED	205
Orange Tree Mug, Sm	VAS	100
Orange Tree Mug, Sm	VAS	105
Orange Tree Mug, Small	R SLAG	275
Orange Tree Orchard Pitcher	M	350
Orange Tree Orchard Pitcher	M	375
Orange Tree Orchard Tumbler	B	105
Orange Tree Orchard Tumbler	W	115
Orange Tree Pitcher	B	285
Orange Tree Pitcher	M	235
Orange Tree Plate	B	245
Orange Tree Plate	B	255
Orange Tree Plate	B	275
Orange Tree Plate	B	450
Orange Tree Plate	B	500
Orange Tree Plate	B	700
Orange Tree Plate	B	800
Orange Tree Plate	CLAM	85
Orange Tree Plate	M	225
Orange Tree Plate	M	250
Orange Tree Plate	W	160
Orange Tree Plate	W	175
Orange Tree Plate	W	210
Orange Tree Plate	W	250
Orange Tree Plate	W	275
Orange Tree Plate, Chip On Base	G	1700
Orange Tree Plate, Elec	B	750
Orange Tree Plate, Elec, Tree Trunk Center	B	1100

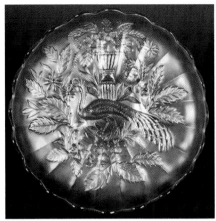

Peacock at Urn, Northwood,
master ice cream shape bowl, marigold,
$400.

Peacock at Urn, Fenton, plate, blue, $700.

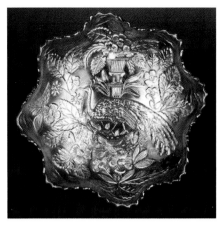

Peacock at Urn, Fenton,
ruffled bowl, marigold, $90.

Peacocks, Northwood,
eight-ruffled bowl,
8-1/2", marigold,
$300-$500.

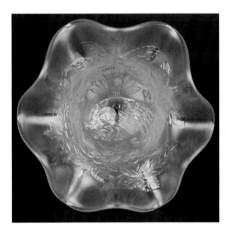

Peacock at Urn, Fenton, compote,
white, $100.

Peacocks, Northwood,
stipled plate,
9", electric blue,
$1,200-$1,800;
outstanding
condition, **$3,500.**

Peacocks, Northwood,
bowl, pie-
crust edge,
8-1/2", purple,
$400-$600;
outstanding,
$1,000.

DESCRIPTION	COLOR	BID	DESCRIPTION	COLOR	BID	DESCRIPTION	COLOR	BID
Orange Tree Plate, Electric	B	550	Orange Tree Tumbler, Ftd	B	80	Palm Beach Rosebowl Whimsey	M	125
Orange Tree Plate, Electric	B	800	Orange Tree Tumbler, Ftd	M	50	Palm Beach Rosebowl Whimsey	M	125
Orange Tree Plate, No Tree Trunk In Center	G	13000	Orange Tree Tumbler, Ftd	M	85	Palm Beach Rosebowl Whimsey	M	130
Orange Tree Plate, Tree Trunk Center	B	325	Orange Tree Tumbler, Ftd	W	120	Palm Beach Tumbler	HON AM	100
Orange Tree Plate, Tree Trunk Center	B	325	Orange Tree Tumbler, Ftd	W	150	Palm Beach Vase Whimsey	M	275
Orange Tree Plate, Tree Trunk Center	B	425	Orange Tree Tumblers, 3	M	66	Palm Beach Vase, 6", From Spooner	W	450
Orange Tree Plate, Tree Trunk Center	M	250	Orange Tree Tumblers, 6	B	300	Palm Beach Vase, 7"	HON AM	325
Orange Tree Plate, Tree Trunk Center	M	275	Orange Tree Water Set, 7 Pc, Ftd	M	400	Palm Beach Vase, Whimsey, 4"	M	400
Orange Tree Plate, Tree Trunk Center, Pastel	M	725	Oriental Poppy Tankard	G	1350	Palm Beach Water Set, 5 Pc	W	500
Orange Tree Powder Jar	A	500	Oriental Poppy Tankard	M	325	Palm Beach, Vase, 5", Bulbous	A	300
Orange Tree Powder Jar	B	100	Oriental Poppy Tankard	M	325	Paneled Cherries Bowl, Ftd, 3/1 Edge	A	140
Orange Tree Punch Bowl & Base	B	290	Oriental Poppy Tankard	M	325	Paneled Dandelion Pitcher, Handle Mtd On Seam	M	325
Orange Tree Punch Bowl & Base	M	220	Oriental Poppy Tankard	P	500	Paneled Dandelion Tankard	A	350
Orange Tree Punch Bowl & Base, Round	B	225	Oriental Poppy Tankard	W	925	Paneled Dandelion Tankard	G	1300
Orange Tree Punch Bowl & Base, Round	B	250	Oriental Poppy Tankard	W	1400	Paneled Dandelion Tankard, Handle Dmg.	G	650
Orange Tree Punch Bowl & Base, Round	M	225	Oriental Poppy Tankard, Elec, Cracked & Glued	B	700	Paneled Dandelion Water Set, 7 Pc	A	675
Orange Tree Punch Set, 10 Pc	B	375	Oriental Poppy Tumbler	G	65	Paneled Dandelion Water Set, 7 Pc	B	450
Orange Tree Punch Set, 8 Pc	B	350	Oriental Poppy Tumbler	IB	115	Pansy Bowl	G	25
Orange Tree Punch Set, 8 Pc	B	375	Oriental Poppy Tumbler	IB	215	Pansy Bowl	M	165
Orange Tree Punch Set, 8 Pc	B	425	Oriental Poppy Tumbler	P	40	Pansy Bowl	P	80
Orange Tree Punch Set, 8 Pc	B	500	Oriental Poppy Tumbler	P	60	Pansy Bowl	P	85
Orange Tree Punch Set, 8 Pc	M	175	Oriental Poppy Tumbler	W	70	Pansy Bowl	P	115
Orange Tree Punch Set, 8 Pc	M	220	Oriental Poppy Tumbler, Ribbed Interior	LIME G	300	Pansy Bowl	P	130
Orange Tree Scroll Tankard	B	825	Oriental Poppy Tumbler, Silvery	B	105	Pansy Bowl	P	135
Orange Tree Scroll Tumbler	B	70	Oriental Poppy Water Set, 6 Pc	IB	2525	Pansy Bowl	P	290
Orange Tree Scroll Tumbler	B	80	Oriental Poppy Water Set, 7 Pc	G	900	Pansy Bowl	P	425
Orange Tree Syrup Whimsey, From Small Mug	B	5000	Oriental Poppy Water Set, 7 Pc	G	950	Pansy Bowl, Low Ruffled	LAV	120
Orange Tree Tumbler	M	95	Oriental Poppy Water Set, 7 Pc	M	600	Pansy Bowl, Low Ruffled	LAV	150
			Oriental Poppy Water Set, 7 Pc	P	900	Pansy Bowl, Low Ruffled	LAV	425
			Oriental Poppy Water Set, 7 Pc	P	1100	Pansy Dresser Tray	M	55
			Palm Beach Berry Set, 7 Pc	W	375	Pansy Dresser Tray	SMOKE	115
			Palm Beach Bowl, Tri Corner	M	100	Pansy Nappy	P	110
			Palm Beach Pitcher	HON AM	375	Pansy Pickle Dish	P	110
			Palm Beach Plate, 7", Applied Goofus	M	350			

Persian Garden, Dugan,
large bowl, ice cream shape, white, $110.

Persian Gardens, Dugan,
master bowl, ice cream shape, white, $150.

Persian Gardens, Dugan,
five small bowls, ice cream shape, white,
$150.

Persian Gardens, Dugan,
fruit bowl and base electric purple, $825.

Persian Gardens, Dugan, fruit bowl and base, peach
opal, base is marigold, $185.

Pine Cone, Fenton, plate, green, $225.

Persian Medallion, Fenton,
plate, 9", white, super and even, and covered
with pastel yellow iridescence, $2,000.

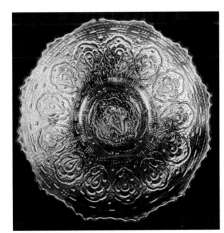

Persian Medallion, Fenton,
plate, 6", marigold, $80.

DESCRIPTION	COLOR	BID
Pansy Pickle Dish	P	120
Pansy Pickle Dish	P	150
Panther Berry Bowl, Lg	B	275
Panther Berry Bowl, Lg	B	450
Panther Berry Set, 7 Pc, Chip	M	205
Panther Sauce	RED	700
Panther Sauce	RED	1050
Peach Spooner	W	65
Peach Sugar Bowl	W	90
Peach Tumbler	B	95
Peach Tumbler	B	100
Peach Tumbler	B	110
Peach Tumbler	B	130
Peach Tumbler	W	65
Peach Water Set, 7 Pc, Elec	B	1500
Peacock & Grape Bowl	AMBERI	600
Peacock & Grape Bowl	AMBERI	875
Peacock & Grape Bowl	B	170
Peacock & Grape Bowl	B	175
Peacock & Grape Bowl	G	95
Peacock & Grape Bowl	G	120
Peacock & Grape Bowl	PO	230
Peacock & Grape Bowl	PO	400
Peacock & Grape Bowl	VAS	175
Peacock & Grape Bowl, 3/1 Edge	G	100
Peacock & Grape Bowl, 3/1 Edge	LGO	675
Peacock & Grape Bowl, Ftd	RED	700
Peacock & Grape Bowl, Ftd	RED	875
Peacock & Grape Bowl, Ic	B	135
Peacock & Grape Bowl, Powder Blue, Smokey	POWD B	350
Peacock & Grape Plate	G	300
Peacock & Grape Plate	M	200
Peacock & Grape Plate	M	275
Peacock & Grape Plate	M	750
Peacock & Grape Plate, Dark Pumpkin Mgold	M	1750
Peacock & Grape Plate, Ftd	B	325
Peacock At Fountain Berry Set, 5 Pc	IB	525
Peacock At Fountain Berry Set, 7 Pc	IB	750

DESCRIPTION	COLOR	BID
Peacock At Fountain Berry Set, 7 Pc	M	260
Peacock At Fountain Bowl, Lg Berry	M	120
Peacock At Fountain Bowl, Lg Berry	M	145
Peacock At Fountain Bowl, Lg Berry	P	185
Peacock At Fountain Butter Dish	M	140
Peacock At Fountain Butter Dish	P	175
Peacock At Fountain Compote	B	975
Peacock At Fountain Compote	IB	500
Peacock At Fountain Compote	IG	1350
Peacock At Fountain Compote	IG	1350
Peacock At Fountain Compote	P	575
Peacock At Fountain Compote, Polished Base	IG	305
Peacock At Fountain Creamer	P	120
Peacock At Fountain Creamer	P	280
Peacock At Fountain Fruit Bowl	A	350
Peacock At Fountain Fruit Bowl	A	750
Peacock At Fountain Fruit Bowl	B	475
Peacock At Fountain Fruit Bowl	B	475
Peacock At Fountain Fruit Bowl	B	600
Peacock At Fountain Fruit Bowl	B	700
Peacock At Fountain Fruit Bowl	B	850
Peacock At Fountain Fruit Bowl	G	2100
Peacock At Fountain Fruit Bowl	M	210
Peacock At Fountain Fruit Bowl	M	215
Peacock At Fountain Fruit Bowl	M	375
Peacock At Fountain Fruit Bowl	P	200
Peacock At Fountain Fruit Bowl, Electric	B	1100
Peacock At Fountain Pitcher	B	450

DESCRIPTION	COLOR	BID
Peacock At Fountain Pitcher	M	230
Peacock At Fountain Pitcher	M	475
Peacock At Fountain Pitcher	P	400
Peacock At Fountain Pitcher	P	2000
Peacock At Fountain Pitcher, Chip Inside	W	150
Peacock At Fountain Pitcher, Elec	B	630
Peacock At Fountain Pitcher, Elec	B	950
Peacock At Fountain Pitcher, Fair Irid.	W	475
Peacock At Fountain Pitcher, White Dye In Base	W	350
Peacock At Fountain Punch Bowl & Base	M	900
Peacock At Fountain Punch Bowl & Base	P	1300
Peacock At Fountain Punch Set, 11 Pc, Pastel	M	950
Peacock At Fountain Punch Set, 8 Pc	M	750
Peacock At Fountain Punch Set, 8 Pc	M	1200
Peacock At Fountain Punch Set, 8 Pc	P	1050
Peacock At Fountain Punch Set, 8 Pc, Round	W	4000
Peacock At Fountain Spooner	P	125
Peacock At Fountain Spooner	P	130
Peacock At Fountain Spooner	W	225
Peacock At Fountain Table Set, 4 Pc	M	300
Peacock At Fountain Table Set, 4 Pc	M	425
Peacock At Fountain Table Set, 4 Pc, Crack	M	230
Peacock At Fountain Tumbler	B	65
Peacock At Fountain Tumbler	B	115
Peacock At Fountain Tumbler	G	100
Peacock At Fountain Tumbler	IB	110
Peacock At Fountain Tumbler	IB	155

Poppy Show, Northwood, bowl, white, ruffle, $400.

Poppy Show, Northwood, plate, 9", electric blue, $5,000.

Poppy Show, Northwood, ruffled bowl, electric blue, $1,500.

Poppy Show, Imperial, funeral vase, dark marigold, $450.

DESCRIPTION	COLOR	BID	DESCRIPTION	COLOR	BID	DESCRIPTION	COLOR	BID
Peacock At Fountain Tumbler	IB	250	Peacock At Urn Bowl, Fenton	P	165	Peacock At Urn Bowl, Lg Ic, N	M	375
Peacock At Fountain Tumbler	IB	260	Peacock At Urn Bowl, Fenton, Ic	B	225	Peacock At Urn Bowl, Lg Ic, N	M	400
Peacock At Fountain Tumbler	P	70	Peacock At Urn Bowl, Lg Ic, Elec, N	B	1200	Peacock At Urn Bowl, Lg Ic, N	M	450
Peacock At Fountain Tumbler, Bright Irid.	G	420	Peacock At Urn Bowl, Lg Ic, Mbrg	A	300	Peacock At Urn Bowl, Lg Ic, N	P	325
Peacock At Fountain Tumbler, Elec	B	110	Peacock At Urn Bowl, Lg Ic, Mbrg	A	500	Peacock At Urn Bowl, Lg Ic, N	P	350
Peacock At Fountain Tumbler, Elec	B	120	Peacock At Urn Bowl, Lg Ic, Mbrg	G	475	Peacock At Urn Bowl, Lg Ic, N	P	400
Peacock At Fountain Water Set, 5 Pc	M	275	Peacock At Urn Bowl, Lg Ic, Mbrg	G	800	Peacock At Urn Bowl, Lg Ic, N	P	725
Peacock At Fountain Water Set, 6 Pc	M	475	Peacock At Urn Bowl, Lg Ic, N	B	500	Peacock At Urn Bowl, Lg Ic, N	RENG B	1900
Peacock At Fountain Water Set, 7 Pc	A	1000	Peacock At Urn Bowl, Lg Ic, N	B	600	Peacock At Urn Bowl, Lg Ic, N	W	300
Peacock At Fountain Water Set, 7 Pc	B	400	Peacock At Urn Bowl, Lg Ic, N	B	750	Peacock At Urn Bowl, Lg Ic, N	W	350
Peacock At Fountain Water Set, 7 Pc	M	260	Peacock At Urn Bowl, Lg Ic, N	B	1200	Peacock At Urn Bowl, Lg Ic, N	W	375
Peacock At Fountain Water Set, 7 Pc	P	700	Peacock At Urn Bowl, Lg Ic, N	B	1300	Peacock At Urn Bowl, Lg Ic, N	W	400
Peacock At Urn Bowl, 10", Mbrg	A	185	Peacock At Urn Bowl, Lg Ic, Clam	N	550	Peacock At Urn Bowl, Lg Ic, N	W	550
Peacock At Urn Bowl, 10", Mbrg	M	120	Peacock At Urn Bowl, Lg Ic, N	G	1400	Peacock At Urn Bowl, Lg Ic, N	W	600
Peacock At Urn Bowl, Fenton	A	185	Peacock At Urn Bowl, Lg Ic, N	IB	850	Peacock At Urn Bowl, Lg Ic, N, 2 Sm Flakes	IB	400
Peacock At Urn Bowl, Fenton	A	250	Peacock At Urn Bowl, Lg Ic, N	IB	875	Peacock At Urn Bowl, Lg Ic, N, Large Cinder	G	2700
Peacock At Urn Bowl, Fenton	B	115	Peacock At Urn Bowl, Lg Ic, N	IB	900	Peacock At Urn Bowl, Lg Ic, N, Out Of Round	AO	14000
Peacock At Urn Bowl, Fenton	B	120	Peacock At Urn Bowl, Lg Ic, N	IB	1000	Peacock At Urn Bowl, Lg Ic, N, Pastel	M	550
Peacock At Urn Bowl, Fenton	B	130	Peacock At Urn Bowl, Lg Ic, N	IG	750	Peacock At Urn Bowl, Lg Ic, N, Silvery	B	450
Peacock At Urn Bowl, Fenton	B	150	Peacock At Urn Bowl, Lg Ic, N	IG	800	Peacock At Urn Bowl, Lg Ic, N, Silvery	IG	550
Peacock At Urn Bowl, Fenton	B	160	Peacock At Urn Bowl, Lg Ic, N	IG	950	Peacock At Urn Bowl, Lg Ic, N, Stippled	B	575
Peacock At Urn Bowl, Fenton	B	170	Peacock At Urn Bowl, Lg Ic, N	IG	950	Peacock At Urn Bowl, Lg Ic, N, Stippled	B	1600
Peacock At Urn Bowl, Fenton	B	185	Peacock At Urn Bowl, Lg Ic, N	IG	1400	Peacock At Urn Bowl, Lg Ic, N, Stippled	B	1600
Peacock At Urn Bowl, Fenton	B	195	Peacock At Urn Bowl, Lg Ic, Lime G	N	1750	Peacock At Urn Bowl, Lg Ic, N, Stippled	B	2200
Peacock At Urn Bowl, Fenton	G	175	Peacock At Urn Bowl, Lg Ic, N	M	175	Peacock At Urn Bowl, Lg Ic, N, Stippled	B	2200
Peacock At Urn Bowl, Fenton	G	225	Peacock At Urn Bowl, Lg Ic, N	M	250	Peacock At Urn Bowl, Lg Ic, N, Stippled	HORE	700
Peacock At Urn Bowl, Fenton	G	270	Peacock At Urn Bowl, Lg Ic, N	M	300	Peacock At Urn Bowl, Lg Ic, N, Stippled	M	375
Peacock At Urn Bowl, Fenton	M	175	Peacock At Urn Bowl, Lg Ic, N	M	350	Peacock At Urn Bowl, Lg Ic, N, Stippled	M	650

Pulled Loops, Dugan,
vase, 9-1/4", amethyst, **$225**.

Raspberry, Northwood,
pitcher, purple, **$150**.

Ribbon Tie, Fenton,
bowl, candy ribbon edge, amethyst, **$150**.

Ripple, Imperial, vase, 11" h, with a
3" base, aqua, **$150-$300 (scarce).**

Ripple, Imperial, squat vase, 6-1/2" h, with a 3"
base, purple, **$150-$250.**

Rococco, Imperial, vase, smoke, **$125**.

DESCRIPTION	COLOR	BID
Peacock At Urn Bowl, Lg Ic, N, Stippled	M	850
Peacock At Urn Bowl, Lg Ic, N, Stippled	M	1800
Peacock At Urn Bowl, Lg Ic, N, Stippled	SMOKE	3500
Peacock At Urn Bowl, Lg Ic, Radium, Mbrg	A	550
Peacock At Urn Bowl, Lg, 3/1 Edge, Mbrg	A	300
Peacock At Urn Bowl, Lg, 3/1 Edge, Mbrg	G	275
Peacock At Urn Bowl, Lg, 3/1 Edge, Mbrg	G	425
Peacock At Urn Bowl, Lg, Mbrg	M	225
Peacock At Urn Bowl, Master Ic, Mbrg	G	1000
Peacock At Urn Bowl, Mystery, 3/1 Edge, Mbrg	G	150
Peacock At Urn Bowl, Mystery, 3/1 Edge, Mbrg	G	200
Peacock At Urn Bowl, Mystery, 3/1 Edge, Mbrg	M	210
Peacock At Urn Bowl, Mystery, Mbrg	A	170
Peacock At Urn Bowl, Mystery, Mbrg	G	400
Peacock At Urn Bowl Mystery Mbrg	M	125
Peacock At Urn Bowl, Mystery, Mbrg	M	325
Peacock At Urn Bowl, N, Lg Ruffled	B	1700
Peacock At Urn Bowl, N, Lg Ruffled	M	310
Peacock At Urn Bowl, Shotgun, 3/1 Edge, Mbrg	G	650
Peacock At Urn Bowl, Shotgun, Mbrg	G	375
Peacock At Urn Bowl, Shotgun, Mbrg	G	575
Peacock At Urn Bowl, Shotgun, Mbrg	M	475
Peacock At Urn Bowl, Sm Ic, Mbrg	B	1800
Peacock At Urn Bowl, Sm Ic, Mbrg	G	275
Peacock At Urn Bowl, Sm Ic, N	B	60
Peacock At Urn Bowl, Sm Ic, N	B	135
Peacock At Urn Bowl, Sm Ic, N	B	135

DESCRIPTION	COLOR	BID
Peacock At Urn Bowl, Sm Ic, N	B	155
Peacock At Urn Bowl, Sm Ic, N	B	225
Peacock At Urn Bowl, Sm Ic, N	G	375
Peacock At Urn Bowl, Sm Ic, N	G	800
Peacock At Urn Bowl, Sm Ic, N	IB	175
Peacock At Urn Bowl, Sm Ic, N	IB	180
Peacock At Urn Bowl, Sm Ic, N	IG	250
Peacock At Urn Bowl, Sm Ic, N	M	250
Peacock At Urn Bowl, Sm Ic, N	M	350
Peacock At Urn Bowl, Sm Ic, N, Elec.	G	1700
Peacock At Urn Bowl, Small Ic, Stippled, N	B	150
Peacock At Urn Chop Plate, N	P	650
Peacock At Urn Chop Plate, N	P	725
Peacock At Urn Compote, Fenton	AQUA	115
Peacock At Urn Compote, Fenton	LIME G	120
Peacock At Urn Compote, Fenton	VAS	110
Peacock At Urn Compote, Fenton	W	100
Peacock At Urn Compote, Fenton	W	125
Peacock At Urn Giant Compote, Mbrg	G	3000
Peacock At Urn Giant Compote, Mbrg, Nick	G	1000
Peacock At Urn Ice Cream Set, 7 Pc, N	A	675
Peacock At Urn Plate, Fenton	B	250
Peacock At Urn Plate, Fenton	B	325
Peacock At Urn Plate, Fenton	B	365
Peacock At Urn Plate, Fenton	B	375
Peacock At Urn Plate, Fenton	B	425
Peacock At Urn Plate, Fenton	B	450
Peacock At Urn Plate, Fenton	B	475

DESCRIPTION	COLOR	BID
Peacock At Urn Plate, Fenton	B	500
Peacock At Urn Plate, Fenton	B	575
Peacock At Urn Plate, Fenton	B	700
Peacock At Urn Plate, Fenton	B	925
Peacock At Urn Plate, Fenton	M	200
Peacock At Urn Plate, Fenton	M	210
Peacock At Urn Plate, Fenton	M	285
Peacock At Urn Plate, Fenton	M	300
Peacock At Urn Plate, Fenton	M	325
Peacock At Urn Plate, Fenton	M	350
Peacock At Urn Plate, Fenton	M	400
Peacock At Urn Plate, Fenton	M	425
Peacock At Urn Plate, Fenton	M	425
Peacock At Urn Plate, Fenton	M	425
Peacock At Urn Plate, Fenton	M	775
Peacock At Urn Plate, Fenton	W	280
Peacock At Urn Plate, Fenton	W	300
Peacock At Urn Plate, Fenton, 1 Amethyst Known	A	12000
Peacock At Urn Proof, Round, Radium, Mbrg	G	1250
Peacock Bowl, Deep Rfld, Mbrg	M	350
Peacock Bowl, Flared, 10", Mbrg	P	275
Peacock Bowl, Lg Berry, Dark Mgold, Mbrg	M	400
Peacock Bowl, Lg Berry, Mbrg	P	350
Peacock Bowl, Lg Berry, Mbrg	P	375
Peacock Bowl, Lg Ic, Mbrg	A	1000
Peacock Bowl, Lg Ic, Mbrg	A	2400
Peacock Bowl, Lg Ic, Mbrg	G	800

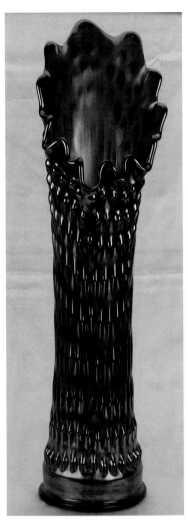

Rustic, Fenton, jack-in-the-pulpit funeral vase, amethyst, 21-3/4", 10" mouth, $1,800.

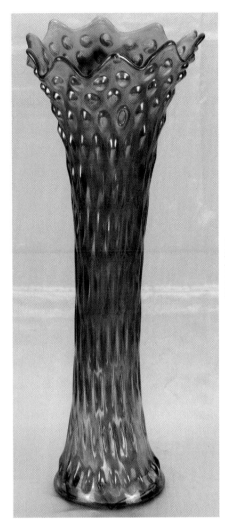

Rustic, Fenton, funeral vase, marigold with amethyst streaks, 19-1/2", 8" mouth, $650.

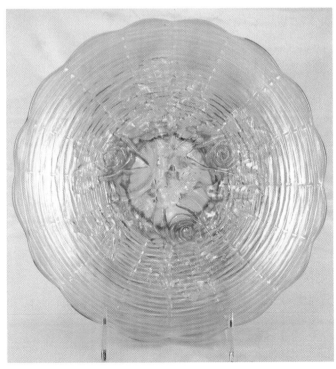

Rose Show, Northwood, plate, ice green opal, $10,000.

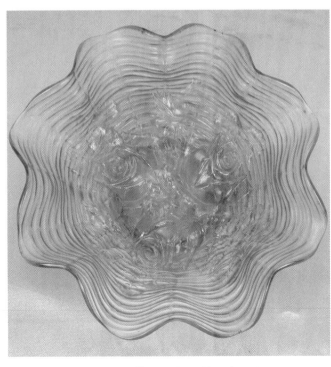

Rose Show, Northwood, ruffled bowl, ice blue, $1,300.

DESCRIPTION	COLOR	BID
Peacock Bowl, Lg Ic, Mbrg	M	3300
Peacock Bowl, Lg Ic, Mbrg	P	525
Peacock Bowl, Sm Berry, Mbrg	P	200
Peacock Lamp	P	875
Peacock Lamp	RED	900
Peacock Lamp With Cloth Shade	P	500
Peacock Plate, 6", Mbrg	A	725
Peacock Plate, 6", Mbrg.	A	700
Peacock Rosebowl Whimsey, Mbrg, One Known	A	2500
Peacock Sauce, 3/1 Edge, Mbrg	B	900
Peacock Sauce, Proof, Mbrg	A	125
Peacock Tail Bowl, 3/1 Edge	A	475
Peacock Tail Bowl, 6"	VAS	310
Peacock Tail Bowl, 6", Ic, Flake On Edge	RED	700
Peacock Tail Bowl, Ic	B	225
Peacock Tail Bowl, Low Ruffled	A	1100
Peacock Tail Chop Plate, 1 Known	M	6000
Peacock Tail Plate	M	1500
Peacock Tail Plate, 6"	M	175
Peacock Tail Plate, 6"	M	825
Peacock Tail Plate, 7", Many Flaws	A	195
Peacock Tail Variant Compote	A	115
Peacock Tail Variant Compote	M	125
Peacock Tail Variant Compote	P	325
Peacocks Bowl	AO	750
Peacocks Bowl	AO	750
Peacocks Bowl	AO	800
Peacocks Bowl	AO	850
Peacocks Bowl	AO	850
Peacocks Bowl	AO	975
Peacocks Bowl	AO	1200
Peacocks Bowl	AO	1250
Peacocks Bowl	AO	1350
Peacocks Bowl	AO	1400
Peacocks Bowl	AO	1450
Peacocks Bowl	AO	1500
Peacocks Bowl	AO	1600
Peacocks Bowl	AQUA	950
Peacocks Bowl	B	300
Peacocks Bowl	B	350
Peacocks Bowl	B	375
Peacocks Bowl	B	400
Peacocks Bowl	B	400
Peacocks Bowl	B	525
Peacocks Bowl	B	575
Peacocks Bowl	G	600
Peacocks Bowl	G	900
Peacocks Bowl	G	975
Peacocks Bowl	IB	675
Peacocks Bowl	IG	575
Peacocks Bowl	IG	1050
Peacocks Bowl	M	155
Peacocks Bowl	M	260
Peacocks Bowl	M	275
Peacocks Bowl	M	275
Peacocks Bowl	P	235
Peacocks Bowl	P	245
Peacocks Bowl	P	255
Peacocks Bowl	P	275
Peacocks Bowl	P	300
Peacocks Bowl	P	325
Peacocks Bowl	P	325
Peacocks Bowl	P	400
Peacocks Bowl	P	425
Peacocks Bowl	P	475
Peacocks Bowl	P	475
Peacocks Bowl	SMOKE	925
Peacocks Bowl	SMOKE	1100
Peacocks Bowl, 3" Crack	POWD B	850
Peacocks Bowl, Butterscotch	AO	1700
Peacocks Bowl, Elec	B	550
Peacocks Plate, Stippled, Elec	B	1200
Peacocks Plate, Stippled, Ribbed Back	RENG B	1700
Penny Match Holder	M	400
Pepper Plant Hat, General Furniture Adv	A	155
Perfection Pitcher	A	5500
Perfection Pitcher, Cracked	G	700
Perfection Tumbler	A	200
Perfection Tumbler	A	400
Perfection Tumbler	A	425
Perfection Tumbler	A	550
Persian Gardens Base To Fruit Bowl	LAV	250
Persian Gardens Bowl, 10, Deep Round	P	185
Persian Gardens Bowl, Lg Ic	LAV	500
Persian Gardens Bowl, Lg Ic	P	1600
Persian Gardens Bowl, Lg Ic	PO	230
Persian Gardens Bowl, Lg Ic	PO	275
Persian Gardens Bowl, Lg Ic	W	185
Persian Gardens Bowl, Lg Ic	W	185
Persian Gardens Bowl, Lg Ic	W	195
Persian Gardens Bowl, Lg Ic	W	200
Persian Gardens Bowl, Lg Ic, Elec	P	1900
Persian Gardens Bowl, Sm Ic	W	42
Persian Gardens Chop Plate, Chip	W	825
Persian Gardens Fruit Bowl & Base	W	400
Persian Gardens Fruit Bowl & Base, Rfld.	W	550
Persian Gardens Plate, 6"	A	130
Persian Gardens Plate, 6"	W	110
Persian Gardens Plate, 6"	W	125
Persian Medallion Bon Bon	A	65
Persian Medallion Bon Bon	AQUA	135
Persian Medallion Bon Bon	AQUA	160
Persian Medallion Bon Bon	AQUA	165
Persian Medallion Bon Bon	AQUQ	110
Persian Medallion Bon Bon	B	45
Persian Medallion Bon Bon	G	235
Persian Medallion Bon Bon	LIME G	120
Persian Medallion Bon Bon	LIME G	125
Persian Medallion Bon Bon	M	65

Scroll Embossed, Imperial,
bowl, ice-cream shaped, purple, $95.

Scroll Embossed, Imperial,
spectacular plate, pastel lavender, with
super pastel color edge to edge, $500.

Scroll Embossed, Imperial,
plate, electric purple, incredible, $625.

Scroll Embossed, Imperial,
bowl, ice cream shape, plain exterior,
electric purple, $170.

Scroll Embossed, Imperial,
large compote, pastel marigold, $20.

Singing Birds, Northwood, mug, blue,
covered with electric highlights, $100.

**Singing Birds,
Northwood,**
mug, dark marigold
and radium, $65.

Shell, Imperial,
plate, smoke,
super and even,
$750.

DESCRIPTION	COLOR	BID
Persian Medallion Bon Bon	RED	260
Persian Medallion Bon Bon	RED	625
Persian Medallion Bon Bon	RED	650
Persian Medallion Bon Bon	RED	800
Persian Medallion Bon Bon	VAS	110
Persian Medallion Bon Bon	VAS	165
Persian Medallion Bowl	A	140
Persian Medallion Bowl	G	130
Persian Medallion Bowl, 10"	G	90
Persian Medallion Chop Plate	B	325
Persian Medallion Compote, Lg	B	300
Persian Medallion Compote, Lg, Crimped Edge	B	55
Persian Medallion Compote, Lg, Crimped Edge	W	550
Persian Medallion Compote, Small	A	115
Persian Medallion Fruit Bowl, G&c Ext.	B	525
Persian Medallion Fruit Bowl, Small Size	B	220
Persian Medallion Hair Receiver	B	150
Persian Medallion Hair Receiver	M	80
Persian Medallion Plate	B	135
Persian Medallion Plate	B	165
Persian Medallion Plate	B	275
Persian Medallion Plate	B	450
Persian Medallion Plate	B	450
Persian Medallion Plate	B	1000
Persian Medallion Plate	G	3750
Persian Medallion Plate	W	2000
Persian Medallion Plate, 6"	A	75
Persian Medallion Plate, 6"	B	115
Persian Medallion Plate, 6"	B	130
Persian Medallion Plate, 6"	B	130
Persian Medallion Plate, 6"	B	195

DESCRIPTION	COLOR	BID
Persian Medallion Plate, 6"	LIME G	115
Persian Medallion Plate, 6"	M	20
Persian Medallion Plate, 6"	M	50
Persian Medallion Plate, 6"	P	125
Persian Medallion Plate, 7"	G	375
Persian Medallion Punch Bowl & Base	A	650
Persian Medallion Punch Bowl & Base	M	400
Persian Medallion Punch Set, 9 Pc	G	625
Persian Medallion Rosebowl	B	80
Persian Medallion Rosebowl	W	100
Persian Medallion Rosebowl	W	105
Persian Medallion Rosebowl	W	110
Petal & Fan Berry Bowl, Lg	P	400
Petal & Fan Bowl, Lg	P	330
Petal & Fan Bowl, Lg	P	395
Petal & Fan Bowl, Lg	P	400
Petal & Fan Bowl, Lg	W	150
Petal & Fan Plate, Crimped Edge, 6"	P	225
Petal & Fan Plate, Crimped Edge, 6"	P	395
Peter Rabbit Bowl	M	1200
Peter Rabbit Bowl	M	1300
Peter Rabbit Bowl, Ic	G	2600
Peter Rabbit Bowl, Ic	M	1800
Peter Rabbit Plate, Chip On Back	G	3200
Peter Rabbit Plate, Tiny Flake On Point	G	2200
Pine Cone Plate, 6"	A	235
Pine Cone Plate, 6"	B	105
Pine Cone Plate, 6"	B	125
Pine Cone Plate, 6"	G	205
Pine Cone Plate, 6"	M	55
Pine Cone Plate, 6"	M	150
Pine Cone Plate, 7"	AMBER	425
Pine Cone Plate, 7"	B	185
Pine Cone Plate, 7"	G	225
Pine Cone Plate, 7"	P	800

DESCRIPTION	COLOR	BID
Plaid Bowl	B	425
Plaid Bowl	G	130
Plaid Bowl	G	300
Plaid Bowl	G	450
Plaid Bowl, Chips	RED	400
Plaid Bowl, Ic	M	160
Plaid Bowl, Low Ic	M	200
Plaid Bowl, Low Ic Plate Shape	A	850
Plaid Bowl, Very Flat Plate Shape	B	1150
Poinsettia Milk Pitcher	G	200
Poinsettia Milk Pitcher	M	70
Poinsettia Milk Pitcher	M	75
Poinsettia Milk Pitcher	M	85
Poinsettia Milk Pitcher	M	115
Poinsettia Milk Pitcher	SMOKE	200
Poinsettia Milk Pitcher	SMOKE	255
Poinsettia Milk Pitcher	SMOKE	300
Poinsettia Milk Pitcher	SMOKE	375
Poinsettia Milk Pitcher	SMOKE	425
Poinsettia Milk Pitcher, Electric	P	4100
Pony Bowl	A	100
Pony Bowl	A	125
Pony Bowl	A	130
Pony Bowl	A	160
Pony Bowl	A	200
Pony Bowl	AQUA	550
Pony Bowl	AQUA	700
Pony Bowl	IG	1400
Pony Bowl	IG	1500
Pony Bowl	M	115
Pony Bowl	P	170
Pony Bowl, 10 Ruffled	IG	1100
Pony Bowl, Cracked	IG	400
Pony Plate, Thought To Be Old	M	950
Poppy Show Bowl	B	800 06-2
Poppy Show Bowl	B	1200
Poppy Show Bowl	IG	1000
Poppy Show Bowl	IG	1700
Poppy Show Bowl	M	340
Poppy Show Bowl	M	700
Poppy Show Bowl	M	725
Poppy Show Bowl	M	775
Poppy Show Bowl	P	350
Poppy Show Bowl	P	775

Singing Birds, Northwood,
mug, aqua opal, super pastel and
spectacular, $1,200.

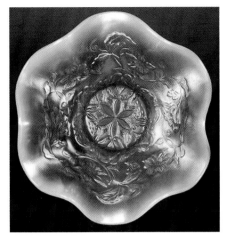

Six Petals, Dugan,
beautiful ruffled bowl, $60.

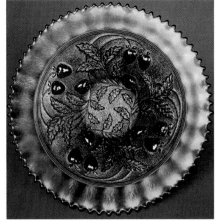

Strawberry, Northwood,
stippled plate with ribbed back, purple, super
plate, $1,400.

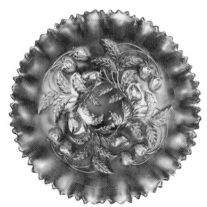

Strawberry, Northwood,
bowl, pie-crust edge, marigold, $50.

Strawberry, Northwood,
ruffled bowl, marigold, $50.

Strawberry, Northwood,
handgrip plate, pastel marigold, $105.

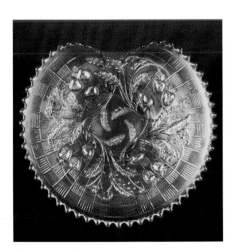

Strawberry Northwood,
handgrip plate, dark marigold, $125.

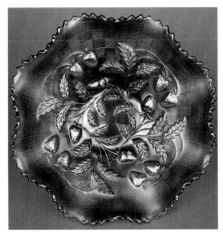

Strawberry, Northwood,
ruffled bowl with basket-weave exterior,
green, very nice, $155.

Strawberry, Northwood,
purple ruffled bowl with basket-weave
exterior, pretty and even, $180.

DESCRIPTION	COLOR	BID	DESCRIPTION	COLOR	BID	DESCRIPTION	COLOR	BID
Poppy Show Bowl	W	275	Poppy Show Vase	M	525	Ripple Vase, 10	AQUA	245
Poppy Show Bowl	W	575	Poppy Show Vase	SMOKE	4400	Ripple Vase, 10", 3 7/8" Base	P	75
Poppy Show Bowl, Chip	M	875	Poppy Show Vase, Light, Sm Crack In Base	SMOKE	550	Ripple Vase, 11"	AMBER	140
Poppy Show Bowl, Pastel	M	280	Poppy Show Vase, Pastel	M	650	Ripple Vase, 11"	AQUA	275
Poppy Show Bowl, Pastel	M	450	Poppy Show Vase, Pastel	M	1500	Ripple Vase, 11"	P	85
Poppy Show Bowl, Pastel	M	750	Pulled Loops Vase, 10"	B	105	Ripple Vase, 11"	P	150
Poppy Show Plate	A	1050	Pulled Loops Vase, 10"	B	215	Ripple Vase, 11"	SMOKE	145
Poppy Show Plate	B	900	Pulled Loops Vase, 12"	CELEST	950	Ripple Vase, 11", Peeling On Edge	AQUA	400
Poppy Show Plate	B	950	Pulled Loops Vase, 5", 7" Mouth	P	125	Ripple Vase, 12"	AMBER	125
Poppy Show Plate	B	1000	Pulled Loops Vase, 5", Variation	A W	300	Ripple Vase, 12"	AQUA	230
Poppy Show Plate	B	1250	Quill Pitcher	M	500	Ripple Vase, 12"	LIME G	145
Poppy Show Plate	B	2400	Quill Tumbler	M	115	Ripple Vase, 12"	P	150
Poppy Show Plate	G	4200	Quill Tumbler	P	170	Ripple Vase, 12"	TEAL	145
Poppy Show Plate	IB	750	Quill Tumbler	P	185	Ripple Vase, 13"	P	210
Poppy Show Plate	IB	1000	Ragged Robin Bowl, 3/1 Edge	M	95	Ripple Vase, 16"	M	105
Poppy Show Plate	IB	1100	Rambler Rose Pitcher	M	475	Ripple Vase, 4 1/2"	M	195
Poppy Show Plate	IB	1200	Ranger Tumbler	M	105	Ripple Vase, 5"	M	140
Poppy Show Plate	IG	1425	Raspberry Gravy Boat	A	200	Ripple Vase, 5"	P	140
Poppy Show Plate	IG	2350	Raspberry Milk Pitcher	LIME G	4000	Ripple Vase, 5",	G	185
Poppy Show Plate	M	600	Raspberry Milk Pitcher	P	205	Ripple Vase, 6"	P	165
Poppy Show Plate	M	600	Raspberry Milk Pitcher	P	250	Ripple Vase, 8 1/2"	AMBER	120
Poppy Show Plate	M	650	Raspberry Milk Pitcher	W	1150	Ripple Vase, 8 1/2"	P	80
Poppy Show Plate	M	650	Raspberry Milk Pitcher, Chip On Edge	IB	600	Ripple Vase, 8"	AMBER	115
Poppy Show Plate	M	650	Raspberry Pitcher	P	400	Ripple Vase, 8"	LAV	80
Poppy Show Plate	M	700	Raspberry Tumbler	AQUA	210	Ripple Vase, 8"	LAV	200
Poppy Show Plate	M	700	Raspberry Tumbler	G	50	Ripple Vase, 8"	P	85
Poppy Show Plate	M	950	Raspberry Tumbler	IB	175	Ripple Vase, 8"	P	195
Poppy Show Plate	M	1000	Raspberry Tumbler	IG	375	Ripple Vase, 9"	P	100
Poppy Show Plate	P	550	Raspberry Tumbler	M	37	Ripple Vase, 9"	P	265
Poppy Show Plate	P	575	Raspberry Tumbler	P	35	Ripple Vase, 9"	SMOKE	200
Poppy Show Plate	W	300	Raspberry Water Set, 7 Pc	G	450	Robin Tumbler	M	70
Poppy Show Plate	W	325	Ribbon Tie Bowl, 3/1 Edge	B	110	Robin Water Set, 7 Pc	M	225
Poppy Show Plate	W	400	Ribbon Tie Bowl, 3/1 Edge	B	160	Robin Water Set, 7 Pc	M	275
Poppy Show Plate	W	525	Ribbon Tie Bowl, 3/1 Edge	B	300	Rococco Vase	M	105
Poppy Show Plate	W	550	Ribbon Tie Bowl, Crimped Edge	A	150	Rococco Vase	M	115
Poppy Show Plate, Chip	B	875	Ribbon Tie Bowl, Crimped Edge	G	105	Rococco Vase	SMOKE	95
Poppy Show Plate, Elec	B	4900	Ribbon Tie Bowl, Ic	G	65	Rococco Vase	SMOKE	110
Poppy Show Plate, Elec	G	4500	Ribbon Tie Bowl, Low Ruffled, 3/1 Edge	B	295	Rococco Vase,	SMOKE	135
Poppy Show Plate, Nick	IB	750	Ripple Funeral Vase, 14"	M	325	Rose Show Bowl	A	300
Poppy Show Plate, Nick On Poppy	M	700				Rose Show Bowl	AO	650
Poppy Show Plate, Pinhead Nick On Poppy	IB	700				Rose Show Bowl	AO	775 12-06
Poppy Show Plate, Small Chip On Pattern	IB	550				Rose Show Bowl	AO	800
Poppy Show Plate, Very Dark	M	2500				Rose Show Bowl	AO	900
Poppy Show Vase	M	500				Rose Show Bowl	AO	950
						Rose Show Bowl	AO	1000

Stretch Imperial, vase, 11-1/2", red, **$270.**

Stretch, Northwood, spiral vase, 9-1/4", celeste blue, **$175.**

Thin Rib, Northwood, mid-size vase, 13-1/2" h, with 5" base, marigold, **$160.**

Thin Rib, Northwood, squatty vase, purple, great color top to bottom, **$210.**

Thistle, Fenton, banana boat, amethyst with great iridescence, **$275.**

Thistle, Fenton, bowl with candy ribbon edge, green, **$150.**

Three Fruits, Northwood, plate with basketweave exterior, pastel marigold, **$90.**

Three Fruits, Northwood, plate with plain back, apple green, **$650.**

DESCRIPTION	COLOR	BID	DESCRIPTION	COLOR	BID	DESCRIPTION	COLOR	BID
Rose Show Bowl	AO	1300	Rose Show Plate	M	575	Rustic Funeral Vase, 18"	M	450
Rose Show Bowl	B	550	Rose Show Plate	M	600	Rustic Funeral Vase, 18"	M	750
Rose Show Bowl	B	700	Rose Show Plate	M	800	Rustic Funeral Vase, 18"	W	900
Rose Show Bowl	B	825	Rose Show Plate	M	900	Rustic Funeral Vase, 18"	W	1025
Rose Show Bowl	B	1000	Rose Show Plate	M	1000	Rustic Funeral Vase, 18", Chip On Tip	W	150
Rose Show Bowl	B	1250	Rose Show Plate	M	1700	Rustic Funeral Vase, 18", Plunger Base	A	1400
Rose Show Bowl	G	600	Rose Show Plate	P	700	Rustic Funeral Vase, 18", Small Flake	W	1100
Rose Show Bowl	G	1250	Rose Show Plate	P	800	Rustic Funeral Vase, 19"	B	675
Rose Show Bowl	G	1300	Rose Show Plate	P	1100	Rustic Funeral Vase, 19"	G	1300
Rose Show Bowl	G	1350	Rose Show Plate	W	225	Rustic Funeral Vase, 19", Plunger Base	A	2300
Rose Show Bowl	G	1600	Rose Show Plate	W	375	Rustic Funeral Vase, 20"	B	850
Rose Show Bowl	IB	750	Rose Show Plate	W	375	Rustic Funeral Vase, 20"	B	1600
Rose Show Bowl	IB	950	Rose Show Plate	W	400	Rustic Funeral Vase, 21"	B	1050
Rose Show Bowl	IG	490	Rose Show Plate	W	500	Rustic Funeral Vase, 21"	M	350
Rose Show Bowl	IG	1150	Rose Show Plate, Chip On Rose	IG	750	Rustic Funeral Vase, 21"	M	550
Rose Show Bowl	IG	1200	Rose Show Plate, Crack In Base	IB	800	Rustic Funeral Vase, 21", Plunger Base	A	875
Rose Show Bowl	IG	1300	Rose Show Plate, Elec	B	1200	Rustic Funeral Vase, 22"	M	600
Rose Show Bowl	M	300	Rose Show Plate, Flaw	A	1100	Rustic Funeral Vase, 22", Plunger Base	EMR G	3600
Rose Show Bowl	M	300	Rose Show Plate, Outstanding Color	A	2500	Rustic Funeral Vase, 23", Plunger Base, Elec.	B	3000
Rose Show Bowl	M	350	Rose Show Plate, Rose Nicks	IB	725	Rustic Vase, 11"	G	45
Rose Show Bowl	M	350	Roses & Ruffles Gwtw Lamp	M	1700	Rustic Vase, Mid Size, 16"	A	100
Rose Show Bowl	M	375	Roses & Ruffles Gwtw Lamp, Spider Crack	M	1400	Rustic Vase, Mid Size, 16"	G	155
Rose Show Bowl	M	400	Round Up Bowl, Ic	A	175	Rustic Vase, Mid Size, 16"	M	85
Rose Show Bowl	M	545	Round Up Bowl, Low Ruffled	P	625	Rustic Vase, Mid Size, 16"	W	150
Rose Show Bowl	M	650	Round Up Plate	A	230	S Repeat Whimsey, Creamer From Punch Cup	P	75
Rose Show Bowl	P	400	Round Up Plate	A	300	Scroll Embossed Bowl	P	195
Rose Show Bowl	P	500	Round Up Plate	A	350	Scroll Embossed Bowl, 7"	P	105
Rose Show Bowl	P	650	Round Up Plate	B	110	Scroll Embossed Bowl, Emerald Irid.	G	110
Rose Show Bowl	P	925	Round Up Plate	B	225	Scroll Embossed Bowl, Emerald Irid.	G	200
Rose Show Bowl	W	225	Round Up Plate	B	260	Scroll Embossed Bowl, File Ext	P	90
Rose Show Bowl	W	275	Round Up Plate	B	260	Scroll Embossed Bowl, File Ext	P	105
Rose Show Bowl, Chip On Base	LIME G	800	Round Up Plate	P	135	Scroll Embossed Bowl, File Ext	SMOKE	265
Rose Show Bowl, Elec	B	900	Round Up Plate	P	975	Scroll Embossed Compote, Lg	B	350
Rose Show Bowl, Pastel	AO	1400	Round Up Plate	PO	300			
Rose Show Bowl, Small Nick	LGO	2200	Rustic Funeral Vase, 17"	A	1500			
Rose Show Plate	B	550	Rustic Funeral Vase, 17"	G	1400			
Rose Show Plate	B	650	Rustic Funeral Vase, 17"	G	4000			
Rose Show Plate	B	1100	Rustic Funeral Vase, 17", Plunger Base	P	1900			
Rose Show Plate	B	1300	Rustic Funeral Vase, 18"	A	1100			
Rose Show Plate	B	1500	Rustic Funeral Vase, 18"	B	575			
Rose Show Plate	IB	1200	Rustic Funeral Vase, 18"	B	650			
Rose Show Plate	IB	1225	Rustic Funeral Vase, 18"	B	675			
Rose Show Plate	IG	2500						
Rose Show Plate	IG	2600						
Rose Show Plate	LAV	900						
Rose Show Plate	M	550						

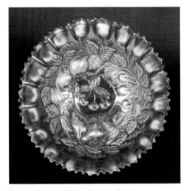

Three Fruit, Northwood,
bowl, pie-crust edge, slight scratches on
fruit, marigold, $40.

Three Fruits, Northwood, domed footed
bowl, marigold, super color, $105.

Tracery, Millersburg, bon bon, green with
satin finish, rare and beautiful, $650.

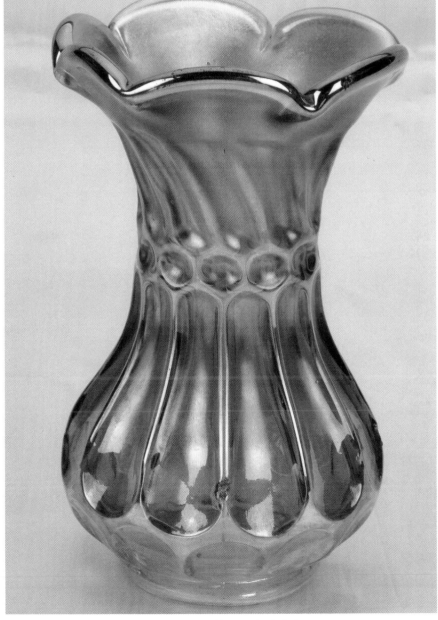

Thumbprint and Oval, Imperial, vase, marigold, scratched, $350.

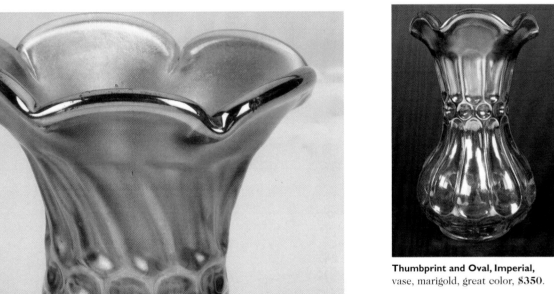

Thumbprint and Oval, Imperial,
vase, marigold, great color, $350.

Tree Trunk, Northwood,
funeral vase, blue, super piece, slight
peeling on edge of ruffles, $2,500.

DESCRIPTION	COLOR	BID
Scroll Embossed Compote, Lg	P	115
Scroll Embossed Compote, Lg	P	145
Scroll Embossed Compote, Lg	P	170
Scroll Embossed Compote, Lg	P	185
Scroll Embossed Compote, Miniature	P	185
Scroll Embossed Compote, Miniature	P	325
Scroll Embossed Compote, Round, Miniature	P	410
Scroll Embossed Compote, Small	P	115
Scroll Embossed Compote, Small	P	200
Scroll Embossed Compote, Small	P	375
Scroll Embossed Plate	LAV	265
Scroll Embossed Plate	LAV	500
Scroll Embossed Plate	LAV	525
Scroll Embossed Plate	P	225
Scroll Embossed Plate	P	270
Scroll Embossed Plate	P	275
Scroll Embossed Plate	P	275
Scroll Embossed Plate	P	275
Scroll Embossed Plate	P	275
Scroll Embossed Plate	P	310
Scroll Embossed Plate	P	325
Scroll Embossed Plate	P	625
Scroll Embossed Sauce	P	105
Scroll Embossed Sauce	P	165
Seacoast Pin Tray	A	1050
Seacoast Pin Tray	G	650
Seacoast Pin Tray, Chip On Back	G	400
Singing Birds Berry Set, 6 Pc	P	210
Singing Birds Butter Dish	M	145
Singing Birds Mug	AO	1200
Singing Birds Mug	AO	1600
Singing Birds Mug	B	65
Singing Birds Mug	B	85
Singing Birds Mug	B	100
Singing Birds Mug	B	105
Singing Birds Mug	B	145
Singing Birds Mug	B	150

DESCRIPTION	COLOR	BID
Singing Birds Mug	B	155
Singing Birds Mug	G	95
Singing Birds Mug	G	100
Singing Birds Mug	G	110
Singing Birds Mug	G	180
Singing Birds Mug	HORE	350
Singing Birds Mug	IB	550
Singing Birds Mug	LAV	185
Singing Birds Mug	LAV	215
Singing Birds Mug	M	40
Singing Birds Mug	M	65
Singing Birds Mug	P	55
Singing Birds Mug	P	75
Singing Birds Mug	P	100
Singing Birds Mug	W	700
Singing Birds Mug, Elec	B	170
Singing Birds Mug, Elec	P	200
Singing Birds Mug, Stippled	M	80
Singing Birds Mug, Stippled	M	80
Singing Birds Mug, Stippled	M	80
Singing Birds Mug, Stippled	M	80
Singing Birds Mug, Stippled	M	85
Singing Birds Mug, Stippled, Elec	B	850
Singing Birds Pitcher	G	450
Singing Birds Pitcher	G	450
Singing Birds Pitcher	G	525
Singing Birds Pitcher	M	375
Singing Birds Pitcher	M	375
Singing Birds Pitcher	P	325
Singing Birds Pitcher	P	325
Singing Birds Pitcher	P	350
Singing Birds Pitcher	P	475
Singing Birds Tumbler	G	27
Singing Birds Tumbler	G	60
Singing Birds Tumbler	G	65
Singing Birds Tumbler	G	85
Singing Birds Tumbler	M	20
Singing Birds Tumbler	M	70
Singing Birds Tumbler	TEAL	35
Singing Birds Tumblers X 4	P	40
Singing Birds Water Set, 7 Pc	G	700

DESCRIPTION	COLOR	BID
Singing Birds Water Set, 7 Pc	G	1000
Singing Birds Water Set, 7 Pc	G	1300
Singing Birds Water Set, 7 Pc	P	625
Single Flower Basket Whimsey	PO	250
Six Petals Compote	LIME G	450
Six Sided Candlesticks, Pr	M	400
Ski Star Bowl	PO	265
Ski Star Bowl, 3/1 Edge, Dome Ftd	PO	135
Strawberry Bowl Pc Edge Stippled	M	175
Strawberry Bowl, Pc Edge, Stippled	M	175
Strawberry Bowl, Plain Ext, Dark Mgold	M	675
Strawberry Bowl, Stippled	B	150
Strawberry Bowl, Stippled	B	375
Strawberry Bowl, Stippled	B	500
Strawberry Bowl, Stippled	B	600
Strawberry Bowl, Stippled	G	500
Strawberry Bowl, Stippled	LIME G	1600
Strawberry Bowl, Stippled	P	350
Strawberry Bowl, Stippled, Elec	B	600
Strawberry Bowl, Stippled, Glued Together	AO	1800
Strawberry Bowl, Very Rare Color For This Bowl	PO	2800
Strawberry Plate	G	135
Strawberry Plate	G	160
Strawberry Plate	M	125
Strawberry Plate	M	135
Strawberry Plate	M	140
Strawberry Plate	M	200
Strawberry Plate	M	210
Strawberry Plate, Bw Back	A	175
Strawberry Plate, Bw Back	A	220
Strawberry Plate, Bw Back Emr	G	400

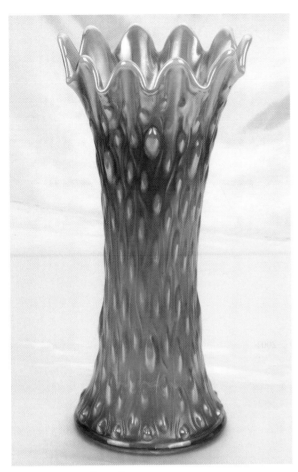

Tree Trunk, Northwood,
funeral vase, mid-size, aqua opal, $19,000.

Tree Trunk, Northwood, vases from left: squatty, ice blue, 7"; ice blue,
11", $400 each.

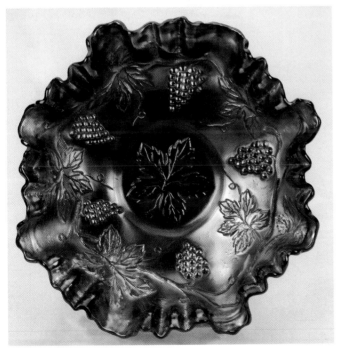

Vintage, Fenton, bowl, 8-1/2" 3-in-1, red, $2,000.

Vintage, Millersburg,
vase, 7-1/2", marigold, $1, 400.

DESCRIPTION	COLOR	BID
Strawberry Plate, Bw Back	M	150
Strawberry Plate, Bw Back	P	140
Strawberry Plate, Bw Back	P	155
Strawberry Plate, Bw Back	P	250
Strawberry Plate, Handgrip	M	105
Strawberry Plate, Handgrip	M	125
Strawberry Plate, Handgrip	P	250
Strawberry Plate, Opal On Tips	PO	425
Strawberry Plate, Smooth Back	M	95
Strawberry Plate, Stippled	G	850
Strawberry Plate, Stippled	G	1550
Strawberry Plate, Stippled	P	1400
Strawberry Plate. Stippled	G	1100
Strawberry Plate. Stippled	P	750
Strawberry Scroll Tumbler	M	125
Strawberry Scroll Tumbler, Silvery Finish	B	65
Strawberry Scroll Tumbler, Silvery Finish	M	70
Stretch 6 Sided Candlesticks, N, Pr	CUSTAR	300
Stretch Glass Perfume W/stopper	WISTER	575
Stretch Guest Set, Handled, 2 Pc	CELEST	375
Stretch Master Nut Bowl & 5 Cups	VAS AS	200
Stretch Nut Set, 6 Pc	VAS	175
Stretch Perfume Bottle, Fenton	WISTER	400
Stretch Tumble Up, Fenton	CELEST	115
Stretch Tumble Up, Fenton	IG	115
Sunflower & Diamond Vase, 7", Eda, Rare Color	P	3200
Sunflower Bowl, Ftd	A	100
Sunflower Bowl, Ftd	B	350
Sunflower Bowl, Ftd	B	375
Sunflower Bowl, Ftd	B	380

DESCRIPTION	COLOR	BID
Sunflower Bowl, Ftd	CLAM	100
Sunflower Bowl, Ftd	CLAM	200
Sunflower Bowl, Ftd	P	700
Sunflower Bowl, Ftd, Crack In Foot	IB	1350
Sunflower Bowl, Ftd, Elec	G	1450
Sunflower Bowl, Ftd, Elec	09-20	
Sunflower Pin Tray	A	600
Sunflower Pin Tray, Flake On Tip	G	250
Target Vase, 10"	B	140
Target Vase, 11"	G	425
Target Vase, 11"	PO	45
Target Vase, 6"	PO	105
Ten Mums Bowl	G	185
Ten Mums Bowl, 3/1 Edge	A	210
Ten Mums Bowl, 3/1 Edge	G	170
Ten Mums Bowl, 3/1 Edge	G	175
Ten Mums Bowl, Crimped Edge	A	120
Ten Mums Bowl, Ftd, 3/1 Edge	G	350
Ten Mums Bowl, Ftd, 3/1 Edge	G	800
Ten Mums Chop Plate, Only One Known	B	13000
Ten Mums Tankard	M	600
Ten Mums Tumbler	M	90
Ten Mums Tumbler	W	265
Ten Mums Water Set, 5 Pc	M	475
Thin Rib & Drape Vase, 4 1/2"	M	160
Thin Rib & Drape Vase, 5"	M	75
Thin Rib & Drape Vase, 5"	P	300
Thin Rib & Drape Vase, 5"	P	450
Thin Rib Candlesticks, Pr	CELEST	575
Thin Rib Vase, 10"	IG	160
Thin Rib Vase, 10"	TEAL	300
Thin Rib Vase, 10"	VAS	700
Thin Rib Vase, 11"	IB	270
Thin Rib Vase, 11"	IG	150
Thin Rib Vase, 11"	IG	235

DESCRIPTION	COLOR	BID
Thin Rib Vase, 12"	B	140
Thin Rib Vase, 7"	B	210
Thin Rib Vase, 7"	W	135
Thin Rib Vase, Gold Trim, 11"	SAPH B	525
Thin Rib Vase, Jester Cap	M	300
Thin Rib Vase, Mid Size	G	200
Thin Rib Vase, Mid Size	G	225
Thin Rib Vase, Mid Size	M	160
Thin Rib Vase, Mid Size	P	125
Thin Rib Vase, Mid Size	SAPH B	950
Thin Rib Vase, Mid Size	W	255
Thin Rib Vase, Small Size, 12"	VAS	700
Thin Rib Vase, Squatty, 7"	IB	500
Thin Rib Vase, Squatty, 7	IB	540
Thin Rib Vase, Squatty, 7"	IG	255
Thin Rib Vase, Squatty, 7"	P	210
Thin Rib Vase, Squatty, 7	P	225
Thistle Banana Bowl	A	275
Thistle Banana Bowl	A	275
Thistle Banana Bowl	G	250
Thistle Banana Bowl	M	150
Thistle Banana Bowl	M	350
Thistle Banana Bowl	P	175
Thistle Banana Bowl	P	350
Thistle Bowl	P	90
Thistle Bowl, Cr Edge	A	115
Thistle Bowl, Crimped Edge	G	80
Thistle Bowl, Crimped Edge	G	140
Thistle Bowl, Horlacker Adv On Base	G	135
Thistle Plate	A	2000
Thistle Plate	A	5500
Thistle Plate	G	4000
Thistle Plate	G	4400
Thistle Plate, Satin Finish	A	1650
Thistle Plate, Smoothed Spot	G	1800
Three Fruits Bowl, Bw Back	G	300
Three Fruits Bowl, Dome Ftd	IG	375

Water Lily, Fenton,
footed sauce, vaseline, scarce color, $55.

Windmill, Imperial, milk pitcher, electric purple, unbelievable color, $2,000. A front view of the pitcher is also shown, at left.

Windmill, Imperial,
pitcher and four tumblers, marigold, $65.

Windmill, Imperial, bowl, ice-cream shape, 7", teal/green, covered with beautiful blue iridescence, $175.

Windmill, Imperial, bowl, deep, round, marigold over milk glass, $500.

DESCRIPTION	COLOR	BID	DESCRIPTION	COLOR	BID	DESCRIPTION	COLOR	BID
Three Fruits Bowl, Dome Ftd	W	135	Three Fruits Bowl, Stippled	SAPH B	400	Three Fruits Plate, Stippled	A	185
Three Fruits Bowl, Ftd	AO	500	Three Fruits Bowl, Stippled	W	275	Three Fruits Plate, Stippled	A	275
Three Fruits Bowl, Ftd	AO	525	Three Fruits Bowl, Stippled, Ftd	AO	450	Three Fruits Plate, Stippled	A	325
Three Fruits Bowl, Ftd	AO	550	Three Fruits Bowl, Stippled, Ftd	AO	575	Three Fruits Plate, Stippled	A	340
Three Fruits Bowl, Ftd	AO	625	Three Fruits Bowl, Stippled, Ftd	AO	800	Three Fruits Plate, Stippled	A	375
Three Fruits Bowl, Ftd	AO	795	Three Fruits Bowl, Stippled, Ftd	B	350	Three Fruits Plate, Stippled	A	400
Three Fruits Bowl, Ftd	B	450	Three Fruits Bowl, Stippled, Ftd	IB	700	Three Fruits Plate, Stippled	A	950
Three Fruits Bowl, Ftd	B	500	Three Fruits Bowl, Stippled, Ftd	IB	1050	Three Fruits Plate, Stippled	A	1300
Three Fruits Bowl, Ftd	G	105	Three Fruits Bowl, Stippled, Ftd	LGO	2700	Three Fruits Plate, Stippled	AO	3100
Three Fruits Bowl, Ftd	IB	450	Three Fruits Bowl, Stippled, Ftd	M	150	Three Fruits Plate, Stippled	AO	4500
Three Fruits Bowl, Ftd	IG	525	Three Fruits Bowl, Stippled, Ftd	W	300	Three Fruits Plate, Stippled	B	375
Three Fruits Bowl, Ftd	IG	575	Three Fruits Bowl, Stippled, Ftd, Elec.	B	600	Three Fruits Plate, Stippled	B	400
Three Fruits Bowl, Ftd	M	160	Three Fruits Bowl, Stippled, Pastel	M	260	Three Fruits Plate, Stippled	B	400
Three Fruits Bowl, Ftd	P	97	Three Fruits Plate	A	135	Three Fruits Plate, Stippled	B	400
Three Fruits Bowl, Ftd	W	155	Three Fruits Plate	A	225	Three Fruits Plate, Stippled	B	450
Three Fruits Bowl, Pc Edge	B	525	Three Fruits Plate	G	165	Three Fruits Plate, Stippled	B	775
Three Fruits Bowl, Pc Edge	TEAL	550	Three Fruits Plate	G	165	Three Fruits Plate, Stippled	B	800
Three Fruits Bowl, Pc Edge, Stippled	M	175	Three Fruits Plate	G	210	Three Fruits Plate, Stippled	B	1300
Three Fruits Bowl, Pumpkin, Stippled, Pc Edge	M	395	Three Fruits Plate	P	165	Three Fruits Plate, Stippled	B	1600
			Three Fruits Plate	P	190	Three Fruits Plate, Stippled	HORE	1500
Three Fruits Bowl, Stippled	AO	800	Three Fruits Plate	SAPH B	2800	Three Fruits Plate, Stippled	LAV	300
Three Fruits Bowl, Stippled	AO	1025	Three Fruits Plate, Apple Green	G	650	Three Fruits Plate, Stippled	M	150 09-13
Three Fruits Bowl, Stippled	AO	1200	Three Fruits Plate, Bw Back	G	120	Three Fruits Plate, Stippled	M	275
Three Fruits Bowl, Stippled	B	175	Three Fruits Plate, Bw Back	P	135	Three Fruits Plate, Stippled	M	300
Three Fruits Bowl, Stippled	B	425	Three Fruits Plate, Bw Back	P	155	Three Fruits Plate, Stippled	M	350
Three Fruits Bowl, Stippled	B	525	Three Fruits Plate, Bw Back	P	205	Three Fruits Plate, Stippled	M	375
Three Fruits Bowl, Stippled	G	200	Three Fruits Plate, Bw Back, Pastel	M	100	Three Fruits Plate, Stippled	P	285
Three Fruits Bowl, Stippled	M	200	Three Fruits Plate, Fenton	A	140	Three Fruits Plate, Stippled	P	400
Three Fruits Bowl, Stippled	M	225	Three Fruits Plate, Fenton	G	105			
Three Fruits Bowl, Stippled	M	275	Three Fruits Plate, Fenton	G	105			
Three Fruits Bowl, Stippled	M	350	Three Fruits Plate, Fenton	M	100			
Three Fruits Bowl, Stippled	P	220						
Three Fruits Bowl, Stippled	P	300						
Three Fruits Bowl, Stippled	PEARL	425						

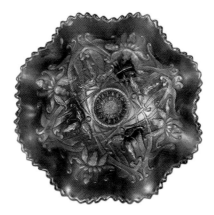

Wishbone, Northwood,
footed bowl with Ruffles and Rings exterior,
purple, very nice, **$125**.

Wishbone, Northwood,
footed bowl, green, **$80**.

Wishbone, Northwood, footed bowl, blue,
has electric highlights, **$300**.

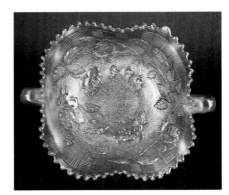

Wreath of Roses, Fenton,
bon bon, amethyst, **$50**.

Wishbone, Northwood, footed bowl, electric
purple, **$210**.

Wreath of Roses, Dugan, rose bowl,
marigold, **$10**.

Zipper Loop, Imperial,
lamp, large size, marigold, **$300**.

Zig-Zag, Millersburg, square bowl with
candy ribbon edge, amethyst, **$500**.

Zig-Zag, Millersburg, ruffled bowl, amethyst
radium, **$175**.

DESCRIPTION	COLOR	BID
Three Fruits Plate, Stippled	P	500
Three Fruits Plate, Stippled	P	500
Three Fruits Plate, Stippled	P	800
Three Fruits Plate, Stippled	P	825
Three Fruits Plate, Stippled	SAPH B	2600
Three Fruits Plate, Stippled	VIOLET	900
Three Fruits Plate, Stippled, Lt Wear	M	150
Three Fruits Plate, Stippled, Wear On Fruit	AO	850
Three Fruits Plate, Stippled, Wear On Fruit	AO	2400
Thumbprint & Ovals Vase	M	145
Thumbprint & Ovals Vase	M	300
Thumbprint & Ovals Vase	M	350
Thumbprint & Ovals Vase	P	850
Thumbprint & Ovals Vase	P	1000
Tiger Lily Pitcher	M	115
Tiger Lily Pitcher	TEAL	120
Tiger Lily Tumbler	P	85
Tiger Lily Tumbler	P	110
Tiger Lily Tumbler	TEAL	50
Tiger Lily Water Set, 5 Pc	HELIOS	275
Tiger Lily Water Set, 6 Pc	M	120
Tiger Lily Water Set, 6 Pc	M	225
Tiger Lily Water Set, 7 Pc	G	225
Tiger Lily Water Set, 7 Pc	M	210
Tiger Lily Water Set, 9 Pc	LIME G	115
Tomahawk, 7 1/4", Very Rare	P	4400
Tornado Vase, Green Tornados, Experimental	M	4750
Tornado Vase, Lg	G	525
Tornado Vase, Lg	G	650
Tornado Vase, Lg	P	475
Tornado Vase, Ribbed	B	3100

DESCRIPTION	COLOR	BID
Tornado Vase, Ribbed, Damaged Base	LAV	425
Tornado Vase, Ribbed, Small	B	3600
Tornado Vase, Ribbed, Small	P	925
Tornado Vase, Small	M	225
Tornado Vase, Small	P	400
Tornado Vase, Small	P	550
Tornado Vase, Small	P	650
Tornado Vase, Small, Base Ground	P	425
Tornado Vase, Small, Nicks On Base	P	215
Town Pump	P	425
Town Pump	P	675
Town Pump	P	875
Town Pump	P	875
Town Pump	P	950
Town Pump, Light	M	1600
Tracery Bon Bon	G	350
Tracery Bon Bon	G	525
Tracery Bon Bon	G	650
Tree Of Life Rosebowl, One Known, Mgold/custrd	CUSTAR	1300
Tree Trunk Funeral Vase, 17"	P	1300
Tree Trunk Funeral Vase, 18"	P	3000
Tree Trunk Funeral Vase, Elephant Foot, 13"	P	1500
Tree Trunk Funeral Vase, Peeling On Edge	B	2500
Tree Trunk Vase, 10"	B	185
Tree Trunk Vase, 10"	B	300
Tree Trunk Vase, 10"	IB	350
Tree Trunk Vase, 10"	SAPH B	400
Tree Trunk Vase, 10"	VIOLET	110
Tree Trunk Vase, 10", Elec	B	250
Tree Trunk Vase, 10", Elec.	B	395
Tree Trunk Vase, 11"	P	60
Tree Trunk Vase, 11"	W	125
Tree Trunk Vase, 9"	B	300
Tree Trunk Vase, 9"	G	45
Tree Trunk Vase, Mid Size	B	850
Tree Trunk Vase, Mid Size	G	285

DESCRIPTION	COLOR	BID
Tree Trunk Vase, Mid Size	G	350
Tree Trunk Vase, Mid Size	G	500
Tree Trunk Vase, Mid Size	M	165
Tree Trunk Vase, Mid Size	M	275
Tree Trunk Vase, Mid Size	P	115
Tree Trunk Vase, Mid Size	P	275
Tree Trunk Vase, Mid Size	P	300
Tree Trunk Vase, Mid Size, Elec.	B	825
Tree Trunk Vase, Mid Size, Plunger Base	P	475
Tree Trunk Vase, Squatty, 6 1/2"	IB	1500
Tree Trunk Vase, Squatty, 7"	B	1050
Tree Trunk Vase, Squatty, 7"	IG	3700
Triple Dolphin Flared Console Bowl, Fenton	IB	300
Trout & Fly Bowl	A	325
Trout & Fly Bowl	A	375
Trout & Fly Bowl	A	475
Trout & Fly Bowl	A	500
Trout & Fly Bowl	G	475
Trout & Fly Bowl	G	600
Trout & Fly Bowl	M	450
Trout & Fly Bowl, 3/1 Edge	A	235
Trout & Fly Bowl, 3/1 Edge	A	365
Trout & Fly Bowl, 3/1 Edge	A	400
Trout & Fly Bowl, 3/1 Edge	G	350
Trout & Fly Bowl, 3/1 Edge	G	400
Trout & Fly Bowl, 3/1 Edge	G	475
Trout & Fly Bowl, 3/1 Edge	M	235
Trout & Fly Bowl, 3/1 Edge	M	255
Trout & Fly Bowl, 3/1 Edge	M	275
Trout & Fly Bowl, 3/1 Edge	M	350
Trout & Fly Bowl, 3/1 Edge	M	425

A sampling of rare carnival glass items

Grape and Cable, Northwood,
bon bon, peach opal, one of only three known, $7,000.

Folding Fan, Dugan, ruffled compote, 7", purple, $300-$600 (rare).

Ripple, Imperial,
mid-size vase, 11-1/4" h, with a 3-7/8" base,
teal, $275-$500 (rare).

People's, Millersburg,
vase, ruffled edge, one of only 10 vases
known, amethyst, six known in this color,
$55,000.

Imperial Grape, Imperial,
deep round bowl, 7", blue, $1,200-$1,500 (rare).

DESCRIPTION	COLOR	BID
Trout & Fly Bowl, Ic	A	650
Trout & Fly Bowl, Ic	G	475
Trout & Fly Bowl, Ic	G	575
Trout & Fly Bowl, Ic	G	600
Trout & Fly Bowl, Ic	G	650
Trout & Fly Bowl, Ic	G	650
Trout & Fly Bowl, Ic	G	700
Trout & Fly Bowl, Ic	G	750
Trout & Fly Bowl, Ic	G	825
Trout & Fly Bowl, Ic	LAV	900
Trout & Fly Bowl, Ic	M	625
Trout & Fly Bowl, Ic	M	700
Trout & Fly Bowl, Square	A	525
Trout & Fly Bowl, Square	A	1050
Trout & Fly Bowl, Square	M	650
Trout & Fly Bowl, Square	M	750
Trout & Fly Bowl, Square	M	900
Trout & Fly Bowl, Square, Cracked	G	155
Trout & Fly Bowl, Square, Sharp Point	M	725
Trout & Fly Bowl, Square, Spotted	A	775
Tulip & Cane Cordial	M	250
Tulip & Cane Wine	M	105
Tulip Scroll Vase, 10"	M	300
Tulip Scroll Vase, 7"	A	575
Tulip Scroll Vase, 8"	M	375
Twigs Vase, Crimped Edge, 4"	P	425
Twigs Vase, Crimped Edge, 4"	P	475
Twigs Vase, Flared, 4"	P	375
Twigs Vase, Straight Sides, 4 1/2", Pastel	LAV	1600
Twins Bowl, 6 1/2", Light Blue	B	290
Two Flowers Bowl, 10"	AQUA	115
Two Flowers Bowl, 10"	M	75
Two Flowers Bowl, Lg	B	180
Two Flowers Bowl, Lg Ftd	P	135
Two Flowers Bowl, Lg Ic	POWD B	275
Two Flowers Plate, Ftd	M	425
Two Flowers Sauce, Ftd	A	45
Two Fruits Bon Bon	G	165
Venetian Giant Rosebowl	G	800
Victorian Bowl	P	140
Victorian Bowl	P	155
Victorian Bowl, Ic	P	1200
Vineyard Pitcher	M	55
Vineyard Pitcher	M	85
Vineyard Pitcher	M	105
Vineyard Water Set, 7 Pc	M	120
Vining Leaf Vase, 6"	M	95
Vining Twigs Vase, 9"	P	245
Vintage Banded Mug	M	11
Vintage Banded Mug	SMOKE	900
Vintage Banded Tumbler	M	100
Vintage Bowl Pers	B	410
Vintage Bowl Pers	B	700
Vintage Bowl, 3/1 Edge	RED	2100
Vintage Bowl, 6"	AMY O	900
Vintage Bowl, 6" Round, Fenton	AMY O	325
Vintage Bowl, 7", Fenton	VAS	125
Vintage Bowl, 8", 3/1 Edge	AO	1500
Vintage Bowl, 8", Fenton Pers	B	675
Vintage Bowl, Crimped, 8"	AO	950
Vintage Bowl, Hobnail Back, 10", Mbrg	M	1025
Vintage Bowl, Hobnail Back, Ic	G	2700
Vintage Bowl, Tri Corner, 6"	A	90
Vintage Compote	B	55
Vintage Compote	B	95
Vintage Compote	M	20
Vintage Epergne, Small Size	A	115
Vintage Epergne, Small Size	A	145
Vintage Epergne, Small Size	B	100
Vintage Epergne, Small Size	G	155
Vintage Epergne, Small Size	M	125
Vintage Epergne, Small Size	P	125
Vintage Fernery	B	30
Vintage Fernery	B	135
Vintage Fernery	B	150
Vintage Fernery	G	40
Vintage Fernery	M	25
Vintage Fernery	RED	225
Vintage Plate	A	3900
Vintage Plate, 6"	A	250
Vintage Plate, 6"	M	255
Vintage Plate, 7"	A	135
Vintage Plate, 7"	B	85
Vintage Plate, 7"	B	105
Vintage Punch Set, 8 Pc, Wreath Of Roses Ext	M	375
Vintage Punch Set, 8 Pc, Wreath Of Roses Ext.	M	250
Waffle Block Pitcher	CLAM	70
Waffle Block Punch Set, 8 Pc	M	145
Waffle Block Tumbler	CLAM	150
Waffle Block Tumbler	M	335
Waterlily & Cattails Tumbler	M	40
Waterlily Sauce, Ftd	AQUA	145
Waterlily Sauce, Ftd	G	135
Waterlily Sauce, Ftd	G	165
Waterlily Sauce, Ftd	IGO	725
Waterlily Sauce, Ftd	RAO	800
Waterlily Sauce, Ftd	RED	450
Waterlily Sauce, Ftd	RED	500
Waterlily Sauce, Ftd	RED	750
Waterlily Sauce, Ftd	RO	750
Waterlily Sauce, Ftd	VAS	105
Waterlily Sauce, Ftd, Rim Chip	RAO	600
Western Thistle Vase, Light	M	90
Whirling Leaves Bowl	A	110
Whirling Leaves Bowl	A	180
Whirling Leaves Bowl	A	180
Whirling Leaves Bowl	A	255
Whirling Leaves Bowl	G	105
Whirling Leaves Bowl	G	145
Whirling Leaves Bowl	G	175
Whirling Leaves Bowl	G	220
Whirling Leaves Bowl	P	125
Whirling Leaves Bowl	P	125
Whirling Leaves Bowl, 3/1 Edge	B	4750
Whirling Leaves Bowl, Crimped Edge	A	700

DESCRIPTION	COLOR	BID
Whirling Leaves Bowl, Crimped Edge	G	475
Whirling Leaves Bowl, Crimped Edge, Square	M	1200
Whirling Leaves Bowl, Square	G	750
Whirling Leaves Bowl, Tri Corner, Crimped	G	300
Whirling Leaves Bowl, Tri Corner, Crimped	G	325
Whiskey Decanter & Stopper	M	275
White Oak Tumbler	M	85
White Oak Tumbler	M	85
White Oak Tumbler	M	130
Wickerworks Bowl	M	180
Wide Panel Epergne	IG	7000
Wide Panel Epergne	M	525
Wide Panel Epergne	M	900
Wide Panel Epergne	M	950
Wide Panel Epergne	P	1000
Wide Panel Epergne	P	1250
Wide Panel Epergne, Chips At Insert	G	550
Wide Panel Epergne, Damage At Insert On Base	W	450
Wild Blackberry Bowl, 3/1 Edge	A	175
Wild Clover Tankard Enameled Very Rare	M	500
Wild Rose Candy Dish	B	135
Wild Rose Candy Dish	M	85
Wild Rose Candy Dish Tri-corner	LAV	65
Wild Rose Lamp, 8" H, 6" Base, Bubble Burst	G	900
Wild Rose Lamp 9 1/2" H, 5 1/2" Base	A	2000
Wild Rose Lamp, 9 1/2" H, 5 1/2" Base	M	2700
Wild Rose Lamp, Mid Size	A	1800
Wild Rose Lamp Mid Size Ladies Medallions	G	4000
Wild Rose Nut Bowl	B	150
Wild Strawberry Berry Set 6 Pc	A	190
Wild Strawberry Bowl, Lg	A	150
Wild Strawberry Bowls, Small, (6)	A	270
Wild Strawberry Plate, Handgrip, 6"	A	205

DESCRIPTION	COLOR	BID
Wild Strawberry Plate, Handgrip, 7"	G	155
Wild Strawberry Plate, Handgrip, 7"	M	350
Wild Strawberry Plate, Handgrip, 7", Bright	P	395
Wildflower Compote	M	1700
Windflower Plate	B	100
Windflower Plate	B	160
Windflower Plate	B	175
Windflower Plate	M	220
Windmill Berry Bowl, Small	LAV	120
Windmill Bowl	P	145
Windmill Bowl	P	150
Windmill Bowl	P	155
Windmill Bowl	P	160
Windmill Bowl, 7"	TEAL	175
Windmill Bowl, 7", Round	MOON	350
Windmill Bowl, Deep Round	MMG	425
Windmill Bowl, Electric	P	200
Windmill Bowl, Round	P	165
Windmill Dresser Tray	P	400
Windmill Milk Pitcer	P	2000
Windmill Milk Pitcher	LIME G	125
Windmill Milk Pitcher	M	70
Windmill Milk Pitcher	P	675
Windmill Milk Pitcher	SMOKE	295
Windmill Milk Pitcher, Electric	P	800
Windmill Pickle Dish	A	70
Windmill Pickle Dish	P	105
Windmill Pitcher	SMOKE	500
Windmill Tumbler	P	100
Windmill Tumbler	P	115
Wine & Roses Cider Set, 7 Pc	M	225
Wishbone & Spades Bowl	P	225
Wishbone & Spades Bowl, 10"	P	525
Wishbone & Spades Bowl, Ic	PO	110
Wishbone & Spades Chop Plate	P	900
Wishbone & Spades Chop Plate	P	1000
Wishbone & Spades Chop Plate	P	1150

DESCRIPTION	COLOR	BID
Wishbone & Spades Plate, 6"	P	295
Wishbone & Spades Plate, 6"	P	305
Wishbone & Spades Plate, 6"	P	350
Wishbone & Spades Plate, 6"	P	375
Wishbone & Spades Plate, 6"	P	500
Wishbone & Spades Plate, 6"	PO	295
Wishbone & Spades Plate, Bw Ext, 6"	P	100
Wishbone Bowl, Ftd	B	350
Wishbone Bowl, Ftd	B	350
Wishbone Bowl, Ftd	B	475
Wishbone Bowl, Ftd	B	500
Wishbone Bowl, Ftd	EMR G	475
Wishbone Bowl, Ftd	G	100
Wishbone Bowl, Ftd	G	105
Wishbone Bowl, Ftd	G	110
Wishbone Bowl, Ftd	G	130
Wishbone Bowl, Ftd	G	135
Wishbone Bowl, Ftd	G	150
Wishbone Bowl, Ftd	G	350
Wishbone Bowl, Ftd	IB	1700
Wishbone Bowl, Ftd	LIME G	750
Wishbone Bowl, Ftd	M	90
Wishbone Bowl, Ftd	M	100
Wishbone Bowl, Ftd	M	150
Wishbone Bowl, Ftd	M	175
Wishbone Bowl, Ftd	M	205
Wishbone Bowl, Ftd	P	95
Wishbone Bowl, Ftd	P	115
Wishbone Bowl, Ftd	P	125
Wishbone Bowl, Ftd	P	165
Wishbone Bowl, Ftd	W	450
Wishbone Bowl, Ftd, Dark	M	650
Wishbone Bowl, Lg	P	160
Wishbone Bowl, Pc Edge	G	150
Wishbone Bowl, Pc Edge	M	120
Wishbone Bowl, Pc Edge	M	125
Wishbone Bowl, Pc Edge	P	160
Wishbone Bowl, Pc Edge	P	575

DESCRIPTION	COLOR	BID
Wishbone Chop Plate, Bw Back	M	1400
Wishbone Pitcher	G	700
Wishbone Plate, Ftd	A	300
Wishbone Plate, Ftd	A	300
Wishbone Plate, Ftd	G	700
Wishbone Plate, Ftd	M	750
Wishbone Plate, Ftd	M	900
Wishbone Plate, Ftd	P	220
Wishbone Plate, Ftd	P	250
Wishbone Plate, Ftd	P	350
Wishbone Tumbler	G	135
Wishbone Tumbler	G	150
Wishbone Tumbler	M	55
Wishbone Tumbler	M	65
Wishbone Tumbler	P	75
Wisteria Tumbler	IB	500
Wisteria Tumbler	IB	650
Wisteria Tumbler	LIME G	600
Wisteria Tumbler	W	400
Witches Pot Novelty	M	135
Wreath Of Roses Bon Bon	P	35
Wreath Of Roses Compote	G	30 09-13
Wreath Of Roses Compote	G	135
Wreath Of Roses Compote	M	135
Wreath Of Roses Punch Bowl & Base, Plain Int	A	400
Wreath Of Roses Punch Bowl Top	G	250
Wreath Of Roses Punch Set, 4 Pc	B	575
Wreath Of Roses Punch Set, 8 Pc	G	850
Wreath Of Roses Punch Set, 8 Pc	M	375
Wreath Of Roses Punch Set, Pers Med Int, 8 Pc	G	675
Wreath Of Roses Punch Set, Vintage Int, 2 Pc	A	350
Wreathed Cherries Banana Bowl	BA	100
Wreathed Cherries Banana Bowl	W	145
Wreathed Cherries Berry Set, 7 Pc	P	300
Wreathed Cherries Tumbler	W	135
Zig Zag Bowl, 3/1 Edge	G	405

DESCRIPTION	COLOR	BID
Zig Zag Bowl, Ic	A	325
Zig Zag Bowl, Square, Crimped	A	425
Zig Zag Bowl, Square, Crimped	P	800
Zig Zag Bowl Tri Corner, Crimped Edge	A	525
Zig Zag Bowl Tri Corner Crimped Edge	G	550
Zipper Loop Finger Lamp Amid Size	M	325
Zipper Loop Finger Lamp, Mid Size	M	1100
Zipper Loop Finger Lamp Mid Size	M	1500
Zipper Loop Finger Lamp, Small Size	M	1200
Zipper Loop Finger Lamp, Small Size	M	1300
Zipper Loop Finger Lamp, Small Size	M	1600
Zipper Loop Finger Lamp, Small Size	SMOKE	2200
Zipper Loop Lamp, 10" H, 6" Base	SMOKE	1200
Zipper Loop Lamp, 11"	M	550
Zipper Loop Lamp, 6 1/2" H, 4" Base	M	750
Zipper Loop Lamp, 7 1/2" H, 4 1/2" Base	M	325
Zipper Loop Lamp, 7 1/2" H, 4 3/4" Base	M	550
Zipper Loop Lamp, 7 1/2" H, 5 1/2" Base	M	525
Zipper Loop Lamp, 7 1/2" H, 5 1/2" Base	M	600
Zipper Loop Lamp, 8"	M	380
Zipper Loop Lamp, 8" H, 4 3/4" Base	M	300
Zipper Loop Lamp, 8" H, 5" Base	SMOKE	750
Zipper Loop Lamp, Small Size	SMOKE	1050
Zipper Stitch Wine Set W/tray, 7 Pc	M	800
Zipper Stitch Wine Set W/tray, 7 Pc	M	800
Zipper Stitch Wine Set W/tray, 7 Pc	M	800

Carnival Glass Big Bucks, 2003

Description	COLOR	BID
Roses & Greek Key Plate, Only One In Smoke	SMOKE	17000

DESCRIPTION	COLOR	BID
Soldiers & Sailors Monument Plate, Indiana	B	15000
Grape & Cable Punch Set, Mid Size, 8 Pc	IB	15000
Peacock At Urn Bowl, Lg Ic, N, Out Of Round	AO	14000
Big Fish Bowl, Tri Corner Outstanding Irid.	G	13000
Ten Mums Chop Plate, Only One Known	B	13000
Orange Tree Plate, No Tree Trunk In Center	G	13000
Peacock At Urn Plate, Fenton, 1 Amethyst Known	A	12000
Dragon & Lotus Plate, Collar Base, One Known	G	10000
Coolleemee Plate, J.n. Ledford/ Heart & Vine	M	9000
Grape & Cable Pitcher, Table Size	IG	9000
Cleveland Memorial Ashtray, Bit Of Extra Glass	A	9000
Big Fish Rosebowl Whimsey, 1 In This Color	M	8500
Grape & Cable Punch Set, Master, 13 Pc	B	8000
Multi Fruits & Flowers Pitcher, Collar Base	A	8000
Grape & Cable Punch Set, Mid Size, 8 Pc	IG	8000
Grape & Cable Punch Set, Master, 8 Pc	B	7000
Daisy & Plume Rosebowl, Raspberry Int	AO	7000
Farmyard Bowl, 6 Ruffle, Electric	P	7000
Advertising, Greengard Furniture Plate, Hndgrp	A	7000
Wide Panel Epergne	IG	7000
Cleveland Memorial Ashtray	A	7000
Embroidered Mums Bowl	AO	6500
Aurora Pearls Bowl, 12"	B	6200
Peacock Tail Chop Plate, 1 Known	M	6000
Thistle Plate	A	5500
Perfection Pitcher	A	5500
Acorn Burrs Punch Set, 10 Pc	W	5500
Holly Bowl, Ic	CELEST	5250

DESCRIPTION	COLOR	BID
Fleur De Lis Bowl, Dome Ftd, Square	VAS	5000
Orange Tree Syrup Whimsey, From Small Mug	B	5000
Poppy Show Plate, Elec	B	4900
Butterfly & Berry Water Set, 7 Pc	A	4750
Christmas Compote	P	4750
Whirling Leaves Bowl, 3/1 Edge	B	4750
Tornado Vase, Green Tornados, Experimental	M	4750
Grape Leaves Bowl, Radium, Blue Irid, Rfld, Mbrg	G	4600
Farmyard Bowl, 3/1 Edge	P	4600
Three Fruits Plate, Stippled	AO	4500
Primrose Bowl, 3/1 Edge	B	4500
Peacocks Bowl, Pc Edge	AO	4500
Poppy Show Plate, Elec	G	4500
Blueberry Pitcher	W	4400
Thistle Plate	G	4400
Tomahawk, 7 1/4", Very Rare	P	4400
Poppy Show Vase	SMOKE	4400
Orange Tree Bowl, Ruffled	RED	4300
Poppy Show Plate	G	4200
Hobnail Jardiniere, Mbrg, Very Rare	A	4200
Little Flowers Bowl, 10", Ruffled	RED	4100
Poinsettia Milk Pitcher, Electric	P	4100
Chrysanthemum Bowl, Ruffled, Outstanding	RED	4100
Blackberry Block Tankard	W	4000
Raspberry Milk Pitcher	LIME G	4000
Farmyard Bowl Square Small Rub On Edge	P	4000
Courthouse Bowl Unlettered 3/1 Edge	A	4000
Thistle Plate	G	4000
Wild Rose Lamp Mid Size, Ladies Medallions	G	4000
Rustic Funeral Vase, 17"	G	4000
Peacock At Fountain Punch Set, 8 Pc, Round	W	4000
Vintage Plate	A	3900

DESCRIPTION	COLOR	BID
Kookaburra Bowl, Float Bowl, 11", Australian	P	3900
Blueberry Pitcher, Elec	B	3800
Corn Vase, Glued Back Together At Bottom	AO	3750
Persian Medallion Plate	G	3750
Courthouse Bowl, Unlettered, Ic	A	3700
Tree Trunk Vase, Squatty, 7"	IG	3700
Nesting Swan Bowl, Deep Round, Blue Irid.	M	3700
Hanging Cherries Chop Plate	G	3700
Embroidered Mums Bowl	AO	3600
Tornado Vase, Ribbed, Small	B	3600
Advertising, Roods Chocolates Plate	A	3600
Rustic Funeral Vase, 22", Plunger Base Emr	G	3600
Hattie Chop Plate	AMBER	3500
Seaweed Bowl, 10", Ic	B	3500
Peacock At Urn Bowl, Lg Ic, N, Stippled	SMOKE	3500
Hanging Cherries Plate, 6"	M	3400
Peacock Bowl, Lg Ic, Mbrg	M	3300
Nippon Bowl, Pc Edge	AQUA	3300
Sunflower & Diamond Vase, 7", Eda, Rare Color	P	3200
Peter Rabbit Plate, Chip On Back	G	3200
Grape & Cable Hatpin Holder, Emerald Emr	G	3100
Three Fruits Plate, Stippled	AO	3100
Tornado Vase, Ribbed	B	3100
Acorn Compote, Ruffled, Mbrg	G	3100
Peacock At Urn Giant Compote, Mbrg	G	3000
Christmas Compote	P	3000
Soldiers & Sailors Plate, Illinois	M	3000
Advertising, Brokers Flour Plate	A	3000
Tree Trunk Funeral Vase, 18"	P	3000
Rustic Funeral Vase, 23", Plunger Base, Elec.	B	3000

DESCRIPTION	COLOR	BID
Deep Grape Compote, Square, Heat Check	G	3000
Farmyard Bowl, 6 Ruffle	P	2900
Elegance Bowl, 7"	IB	2900
Strawberry Bowl, Very Rare Color For This Bowl	PO	2800
Elks Bowl, Detroit, 1910, 2 Eyed, Mbrg.	A	2800
Peacocks Plate	HORE	2800
Bernheimer Brothers Bowl, Many Stars	B	2800
Three Fruits Plate	SAPH B	2800
Grape & Cable Punch Set, Mid Size, 8 Pc	B	2800
Picture Frame, Old And Original	P	2800
Orange Tree Loving Cup, Electric	B	2750
Farmyard Bowl, 3/1 Edge, Lite Irid In Center	P	2750
Wild Rose Lamp, 9 1/2" H, 5 1/2" Base	M	2700
Good Luck Bowl, Variant With Smaller Pattern	M	2700
Vintage Bowl, Hobnail Back, Ic	G	2700
Farmyard Bowl, 6 Ruffle	P	2700
Holly Bowl	MMG	2700
Grape & Cable Punch Set, Master, 10 Pc	P	2700
Homestead Chop Plate	P	2700
Acorn Burrs Punch Set, 8 Pc, Dark	M	2700
Orange Tree Hatpin Holder, Irid Choc Glass Chol 2700	11-22	
Grape & Cable Punch Set, Master, 12 Pc	M	2700
Grape & Cable Plate, Stippled	SAPH B	2700
Rose Pinwheel Bowl, Maker Unknown	M	2700
Acorn Burrs Punch Set, 8 Pc	G	2700
Embroidered Mums Bowl, Pc Edge	SAPH B	2700
Peacock At Urn Bowl, Lg Ic, N, Large Cinder	G	2700
Three Fruits Bowl, Stippled, Ftd	LGO	2700
Morning Glory Tumbler	M	2700

Collectors' Clubs

Carnival glass collectors are able to join with other collectors to further their education, research, read and contribute to newsletters as they enjoy their collecting hobby. Information about these clubs follows. In this edition of *Warman's Carnival Glass*, we have strived to present accurate information, but often club members move, dues may change, etc.

Air Capital Carnival Glass Club
15201 E. 47th St.
Derby, KS 67037
Annual dues: $15

American Carnival Glass Association
5951 Fredericksburg Road
Wooster, OH 44691.
Web site: www.woodsland.com/acga
Annual dues: $19

Australian Carnival Enthusiasts Association (SA) Inc.
P.O. Box 1028
New Haven, SA, 5018
Annual dues: $12, $15 overseas.

Australian Carnival Enthusiasts Association (Victoria) Inc.
RSD Fryerstown
Victoria, Australia 3451
Annual dues: $15

Canadian Carnival Glass Association
12 Dalhouse Crescent
London, Ontario N6G 2H7 Canada
Annual dues: $20

Carnival Club of Western Australia
179 Edgewater Drive, Edgewater
Western Australia 6027

Carnival Glass Collectors Association of Australia, Inc.
4 Scarborough Chase
NARELLAN NSW 2567
Web site: www.austarmetro.com.au/~wdelahoy/cgcaa

Collectible Carnival Glass Association
2001 Fairway Drive
Joplin, MO 64804
Annual dues: $12

Gateway Carnival Glass Club
108 Riverwoods Cove
East Alton, IL 62024
Annual dues: $5

Great Lakes Carnival Glass Club
612 White Pine Blvd.
Lansing, MI 48917
Annual dues: $10

Heart of America Carnival Glass Association
4305 W. 78th St.
Prairie Village, KS 66208
Annual dues: $25

Hoosier Carnival Glass Club
944 W. Pine St.
Griffith, IN 46319
Annual dues: $10

International Carnival Glass Association
P.O. Box 306
Mentone, IN 46539
Web site: www.inernationalcarnivalglass.com
Annual dues: $20

Keystone Carnival Glass Club
719 W Brubaker Valley Road
Lititz, PA 17543
Annual dues: $10

L'Association du Verra Carnaval du Quebec
3250 rue Leon Brisbois
Ile Bizard, QC, H9C IT6 Canada
Annual dues: $20 (Canadian)

Lincoln-Land Carnival Glass Club
P.O. Box 320
Tremont, IL 61568
Web site: www.cgc.homestead.com
Annual dues: $20

National Cambridge Collectors, Inc.
P.O. Box 416
Cambridge, OH 43725
Web site: www.cambridgeglass.org.

National Duncan Glass Society
P.O. Box 965
Washington, PA 15301

National Imperial Glass Collectors
P.O. Box 534
Bellaire, OH 43906
Web site: www.imperialglass.com

New England Carnival Glass Club
P.O. Box 100
Limerick, ME 04048-0100
Web site: necga.com
Annual dues: $15

Northern California Carnival Glass Club
1205 Clifton Avenue
Modesto, CA 95355
Web site: home.pacbell.net/doris-qlevents.htm
Annual dues: $10

Pacific Northwest Carnival Glass Club
22424 94th Avenue South
Kent, WA 98031
Web site: carnival.ksnews.com/pacific/
Annual dues: $15

San Diego County Carnival Glass Club
9500 Harritt Road, #226
Lakeside, CA 92040-3544
Web site: aol.com/sdccgcc/sandiego.htm
Annual dues: $18

San Joaquin Carnival Glass Club
3906 E. Acacia Ave.
Fresno, CA 93726
Annual dues: $5

Southern California Carnival Glass Club
1430 Kendall Ave
Camarillo, CA 93010-3606
Web site: geocities.com/sccgcl.
Annual dues: $18

Sunshine State Carnival Glass Association
9087 Baywood Park Drive
Seminole, FL 33777
Web site: www.carnivalglass.net/sscga
Annual dues: $25

Tampa Bay Carnival Glass Club
5501 101st Ave. N
Pinellas Park, FL 34666
Annual dues: $7.50

Texas Carnival Glass Club
P.O. Box 7332
Round Rock, TX 78683-7332
Web site: www.texascarnivalglass.com
Annual dues: $20

The Carnival Glass Society (UK)
P.O. Box 14
Hayes, Middlesex, England UB3 3NU
Annual dues: 15 pounds

www.cga
210 W Market St
Hartford, NC 27844
Web site: www.cga.com
Annual dues: $18

Auctions

Much of the carnival glass collectors seek is sold through specialized carnival glass auctions. Some of these interesting auctions are held in conjunction with carnival glass collector club conventions, but are usually open to the general public as well. Do check often with local auctioneers for small carnival collections that they may offer from time to time.

Here is a list of auctioneers who have the largest specialized auctions. Those interested in learning more about carnival glass and the rainbow of colors that are so enchanting are encouraged to contact these auctioneers to obtain their catalogs or flyers, as well as visit their Web sites.

Ayers Auction Service
P.O. Box 320
Tremont, IL 61566-0520
309 925-3115
Web site: www.ayerauction.com

Burns Auction Service
P.O. Box 608
Bath, NY 14810
607 776-7932
Web site: www.tomburnsauction.com

Dotta Auction Company, Inc.
330 W Moorestown Rd.
Nazareth, PA 18064
610 759-7389
Web site: www.dottaauction.com

Kaufman Realty
233 Factory Street
Sugarcreek, OH 44681
330-852-4111
Web site: www.kaufmanrealty.com

Mickey Reichel Auction Company
18350 Hunters Ridge
Boonville, MO 65233
660-882-5292
Web site: www.awk-shn.com

Remmen Auctions & Appraisal Services
P.O. Box 301398
Portland, OH 97294
503 256-1226
Web site: www.remmenauction.com

Seeck Auctions
P.O. Box 377
Mason City, IA 50402
641-424-1116
Web site: www.seeckauction.com

Woody Auction Company
Douglas, KS 67039
316-747-2694
Web site: www.woodyauction.com

Jim Wroda Auction Services
5239 St. Rt 49 South
Greenville, OH 45351
937 548-2640
Web site: www.jimwrodaauction.com